Globalizing Civic Engagement

Civil Society and Transnational Action

Edited by

John D Clark

Earthscan Publications Ltd
London • Sterling, VA

First published in the UK and USA in 2003 by
Earthscan Publications Ltd

ISBN: 1-85383-989-2 (paperback)
        1-85383-988-4 (hardback)

Typesetting by Denis Dalinnik, Minsk, Belarus
Printed and bound by CPD (Wales), Ebbw Vale
Cover design by Danny Gillespie

For a full list of publications please contact:

Earthscan Publications Ltd
120 Pentonville Road
London, N1 9JN, UK
Tel: +44 (0)20 7278 0433
Fax: +44 (0)20 7278 1142
Email: earthinfo@earthscan.co.uk
Web: **www.earthscan.co.uk**

22883 Quicksilver Drive, Sterling, VA 20166–2012, USA

A catalogue record for this book is available from the British Library

Library of Congress Cataloging-in-Publication Data

Globalizing civic engagement : civil society and transnational action / edited by John D.
    Clark.- 1st ed.
        p. cm.
    Includes bibliographical references and index.
    ISBN 1-85383-989-2 (pbk. : alk. paper) - ISBN 1-85383-988-4 (cloth : alk. paper)
    1. Social movements-International cooperation. 2. Protest movements-International
    cooperation. I. Clark, John, 1950-

HM881.G559 2003
303.48'4-dc21

                                                        2003007492

Earthscan is an editorially independent subsidiary of Kogan Page Ltd and publishes in association with WWF-UK and the International Institute for Environment and Development

This book is printed on elemental chlorine-free paper

Contents

List of Tables, Figures and Boxes

TABLES

FIGURES

BOXES

Preface

Much has been written about how the era of globalization is impacting on the worlds of business, economics and politics. Many in civil society have sought to challenge or reform the management of global change, and a variety of social movements and campaigns has come together to form a global protest movement that is storming the institutions and principles of global governance. But little has been written about how the technological and political opportunities of globalization affect civil society itself – hence the motivation for this book.

It is clear that a wide array of civil society organizations – ranging from environmental pressure groups and development charities to trade unions and churches – are increasingly emphasizing international advocacy work and networking with others. The benefits and the opportunities are clear; but there are many obstacles, challenges and dilemmas along the path. In particular, there are issues of organizational structure and governance that crop up frequently, and challenges regarding the culture and focus of networks as their memberships diversify. Moreover, new communications technology is allowing new ways of working and new organizational forms to arise – in particular, the web-based campaigns (or 'dot causes'). Just as the 'network age' is transforming management theory in the private sector, so, too, it creates imperatives in civil society to work in different ways and with non-traditional partnerships.

This book surveys these issues. It is the result of a research project of the Centre for Civil Society at the London School of Economics and Political Science (LSE). The project started with a review of the issues through discussion with leaders of a wide range of civil society organizations and consultation of the literature (published and internal) on those organizations' strategic thinking. We next held an international seminar at LSE bringing together practitioners from different types of organization – North and South – and academics studying civil society. This provided new insights, as well as better ideas as to where knowledge gaps lie. Chapter 1 covers this preparatory stage. We then undertook a series of case studies, investigating the experience of a number of transnational civil society endeavours (Chapters 2 to 8). These studies used the same approach as the initial review and probed the issues that it had brought to the surface. The final chapter summarizes the projects' main findings and offers some conclusions that are intended to be of use to civil society practitioners, policy-makers and academics.

This project has been made possible by a generous grant from the Ford Foundation, to whom go our sincere thanks. We also thank Helmut Anheier, David Lewis, Lisa Carlson, Jane Schiemann and other staff at the Centre for

Civil Society for their help and valuable suggestions, and we thank LSE itself for being an accommodating host for this project. Thanks, also, go to many practitioners and scholars who have contributed their valuable ideas and experience, especially: Dave Brown, Ernst Ligteringen, Julie Fisher, John Foster, Petr Hlobil, Lisa Jordan, Richard Langhorne, Alan Leather, Jan Aart Scholte, Salil Shetty, David Stark, Rajesh Tandon, Sid Tarrow, Aurelio Vianna and Dennis Young. We would also like to thank the participants at the LSE seminar of June 2001 for their treasure chest of ideas, which we have ruthlessly plundered, and the many people who generously gave their time to be interviewed or to give advice.

Finally, we would like to thank Jonathan Sinclair Wilson and his colleagues at Earthscan – both for having faith in this project and for being flexible with slipping deadlines for delivery of the final manuscript.

John Clark (editor), on behalf of all the contributors
Visiting Fellow, London School of Economics
March 2003

List of Contributors

John Clark is currently Project Director for the High-Level Panel on United Nations–Civil Society Relations, established by the secretary-general and chaired by Fernando Henrique Cardoso (former president of Brazil). He worked for the World Bank from 1992 to 2000 as manager of the NGO and Civil Society Unit and lead social development specialist for East Asia. He then moved to the UK, where he has served on a task force advising the UK prime minister on Africa and wrote a book on globalization, *Worlds Apart: Civil Society and the Battle for Ethical Globalization* (Earthscan, UK, and Kumarian, US, 2003). He was also visiting fellow at the Centre for Civil Society, London School of Economics and Political Science (LSE), where he manages the research project on which this book is based. Prior to joining the World Bank he worked in non-governmental organizations (NGOs) for 18 years, mostly in Oxfam GB. He is the author of three other books, including *Democratizing Development: The Role of Voluntary Agencies* (Earthscan, UK, and Kumarian, US, 1991).

Paola Grenier is a Lord Dahrendorf scholar in the Centre for Civil Society, LSE, researching social entrepreneurship in the UK. Prior to that she worked in Hungary for two years on supporting the development of Roma communities, and organizing the first European-wide conference on homelessness. Her background in the UK voluntary sector is within the fields of homelessness, social housing and regeneration, where she has been involved in management, fund raising, research and policy development. Her research interests include leadership in voluntary organizations and NGOs, organizational development, social entrepreneurship and social capital.

Tasneem Mowjee has worked for WomenAid International, a small UK NGO specializing in humanitarian assistance to the former Yugoslavia and the Caucasus. This led to a PhD on NGO–Donor Funding Relationships: UK Government and European Community Funding for the Humanitarian Aid Activities of UK NGOs from 1990–1997 at the Centre for Civil Society, LSE. Since completing the PhD, she has been working as a freelance researcher, mainly on humanitarian-aid funding issues and the European Commission's humanitarian policy.

Diego Muro is currently editor of the journal *Studies in Ethnicity and Nationalism* and is a doctoral student in the Department of Government, LSE. His research focuses on civil society, nationalism and political violence.

Günther Schönleitner is a PhD student and Lord Dahrendorf scholar at the Centre for Civil Society, LSE, researching civil society participation and local governance in Brazil. He holds a first degree in law from the University of Salzburg (Austria) and an MSc in development studies from the LSE. Prior to his doctoral studies, he worked for eight years with an Austrian development NGO, first as a project officer in Brazil and later as a country programme manager based in Vienna.

Nuno Themudo is part-time lecturer at the Centre for Civil Society, LSE, where he teaches on the Masters course NGO Management, Policy and Administration. He is completing his PhD thesis titled Managing the Paradox: NGOs, Resource Dependence and Political Independence. His research interests include NGO and non-profit management, information and communications technology and civil society, and sustainable development.

List of Acronyms and Abbreviations

ABONG	Brazilian Association of Non-Governmental Organizations
ACTSA	Action for Southern Africa (UK)
AGM	annual general meeting
AI	Amnesty International
AIDS	acquired immune deficiency syndrome
ALOP	Latin American Association of Popular Organizations
ALP	AIDS Law Project (South Africa)
ANC	African National Congress
ARV	antiretroviral (treatment for HIV/AIDS)
ASEAN	Association of South-East Asian Nations
ATTAC (-I)	Association for the Taxation of Financial Transactions for the Aid of Citizens (-International)
BC	Brazilian Council (World Social Forum)
CA	Consumers Association (UK)
CAP	Consumers Association of Penang
CBJP	Brazilian Commission for Justice and Peace
CEE	Central and Eastern Europe
CEO	chief executive officer
CETIM	Centre Europe–Tiers Monde
CI	Consumers' International
CIVES	Brazilian Association of Entrepreneurs for Citizenship
CIVICUS	World Alliance for Citizen Participation
CJG	Centre for Global Justice (Brazil)
CNBB	National Conference of the Bishops of Brazil
CODE-NGO	Caucus of Development NGOs (The Philippines)
COICA	Coordinating Body of Indigenous Organizations of the Amazon Basin
COSATU	Congress of South African Trade Unions
CPT	Consumer Project on Technology (US)
CS	civil society
CSO	civil society organization
CSR	corporate social responsibility
CU	Consumers Union (US)
CUT	Central Única dos Trabalhadores (Brazilian Union Federation)
CUTS	Consumer Unity and Trust Society (India)
DCN	Debt Crisis Network

DISHA	Development Initiative for Social and Humanitarian Action
EC	Executive Committee (World Social Forum)
EMH	efficient markets hypothesis
EPZ	export processing zone
ETA	Basque separatist movement
ETUC	European Trade Union Confederation
EU	European Union
EURODAD	European Network on Debt and Development
EZLN	Ejercito Zapatista de Liberación Nacional (Zapatistas National Liberation Army, Mexico)
FARC	Fuerzas Armadas Revolucionárias de Colombia
FOE, FOE-I	Friends of the Earth, FOE-International
FPA	Fundação Perseu Abramo
FSM	Fórum Social Mundial (World Social Forum)
FTAA	Free Trade Area of the Americas
G7, G8	the group of the seven largest economies (G8 = plus Russia)
GATT	General Agreement on Tariffs and Trade
GDP	gross domestic product
GMO	genetically modified organism
GSK	GlaxoSmithKline
GUF	Global Union Federation
HAI	Health Action International
HIPC	Heavily Indebted Poorer Countries Initiative (IMF/World Bank debt-relief programme for poor countries)
HIV	human immunodeficiency virus
HRW	Human Rights Watch
IBASE	Brazilian Institute of Social and Economic Analysis
IBFAN	International Baby Foods Action Network
IC	International Council (World Social Forum)
ICBL	International Campaign to Ban Landmines
ICEM	International Federation of Chemical, Energy, Mine and General Workers' Unions
ICFTU	International Confederation of Free Trade Unions
ICM	International Council Meeting
ICRC	International Committee of the Red Cross
ICRT	International Consumer Research and Testing
ICT	information and communications technology
IFBWW	International Federation of Building and Wood Workers
IFI	international financial institution
IFRC	International Federation of Red Cross and Red Crescent Societies
ILO	International Labour Organization
IMF	International Monetary Fund
INGO	international NGO
IOCU	International Organization of Consumers Unions (precursor of CI)
IP	intellectual property

IRA	Irish Republican Army
ISO	International Standards Organization
ISTR	International Society for Third Sector Research
ITS	International Trade Secretariat (precursor of GUF)
JDC	Jubilee Debt Campaign
JMI	Jubilee Movement International
LSE	London School of Economics and Political Science
MC	Mobilization Committee (World Social Forum)
MCC	Medicines Control Programme (South Africa)
MEP	Member of the European Parliament
MG	Minas Gerais (Brazil)
MR	Millennium Review (ICFTU)
MSF	Médecins Sans Frontières
MST	Brazilian Landless Peasants Movement
NAFTA	North American Free Trade Association
NGO	non-governmental organization
NOP-FPA	Núcleo de Opinião Pública – Fundação Perseu Abramo (Brazil)
OC	Organizing Committee (World Social Forum)
OECD	Organization for Economic Cooperation and Development
OI	Oxfam International
PAIC	programme of support for community initiatives
PGA	People's Global Action
PMA	Pharmaceutical Manufacturers' Association (South Africa)
PRIA	Society for Participatory Research in Asia
PRSP	Poverty Reduction Strategy Paper
PSI	Public Service International
PT	Partido dos Trabalhadores (Brazilian Workers' Party)
R&D	research and development
ROAP	Regional Office for Asia and the Pacific (CI)
SAP	structural adjustment programme
SM	social movement
TAC	Treatment Action Campaign (South Africa)
TCSN	transnational civil society network
TNAN	transnational advocacy network
TNC	transnational corporation
TRIPS	Trade-Related Aspects of Intellectual Property Rights agreement
TSM	transnational social movement
TU	trade union
TUAC	Trade Union Advisory Committee (OECD)
TWN	Third World Network
UERJ	University of the State of Rio de Janeiro
UFMG	Federal University of Minas Gerais (Brazil)
UFRGS	Universidade Federal do Rio Grande do Sul (Federal University of Rio Grande do Sul, Brazil)
UMWA	United Mine Workers of America

UN	United Nations
UNAIDS	Joint United Nations Programme on HIV/AIDS
UNCHR	United Nations Commission on Human Rights
UNCTAD	United Nations Conference on Trade and Development
UN-GA	United Nations General Assembly
UNHCHR	United Nations High Commissioner for Human Rights
UNI	Union Network International
USP	University of São Paulo
USTR	US Trade Representative
VSO	Voluntary Service Overseas
WCC	World Council of Churches
WCL	World Confederation of Labour
WDM	World Development Movement (UK)
WEF	World Economic Forum
WFTU	World Federation of Trade Unions
WHO	World Health Organization
WSF	World Social Forum
WTO	World Trade Organization
WWF	World Wide Fund for Nature

Chapter 1

Introduction: Civil Society and Transnational Action

John Clark

Recent years have seen a strong and accelerating trend towards working more actively across national frontiers within many segments of civil society. This shift is particularly evident amongst civil society organizations (CSOs), who seek to influence policies and practices of governments and international organizations.

The trend is due partly to need and partly to opportunity. Policies are increasingly forged at supranational levels, either within inter-governmental bodies – such as the World Trade Organization (WTO), the International Monetary Fund (IMF) or the World Bank – or in regional blocs, such as the North American Free Trade Association (NAFTA), the European Union (EU) or the Association of South-East Asian Nations (ASEAN). Moreover, transnational corporations (TNCs) have become increasingly able to dictate policy and shape our world. Hence the pre-eminence of the nation state as the locus of policy-making has lessened. To influence policy it is now necessary, rather than merely prudent, to act at those international levels and coordinate advocacy across relevant countries. Modern information and communications technology (ICT), cheap telecommunications and air travel and the increased prominence of English as the lingua franca of international communications provide the opportunities for transnational civil society action.

Policy-influencing CSOs comprise development and human rights non-governmental organizations (NGOs), environment and other pressure groups, trade unions, consumers' organizations, faith-based and inter-faith groups and certain professional associations. As with the private sector, each segment has seen the emergence of 'market leaders', and these are generally CSOs that are either better placed for, or have more energetically pursued, transnational networking. These CSOs not only achieve greater credibility amongst policy-makers, but also apparently gain advantage over their competitors amongst potential supporters. If we view civil society as a market-place of interests, ideas and ideologies, then it is a fast-globalizing market and – as with other markets – transnational pioneers reap the rewards.

Though there is evidence of decreasing associational activity amongst the US public (Putnam, 2000), much of the world has witnessed an 'associational revolution' over the past 20 years (Salamon, 1994), and a vibrant civil society has emerged in many developing and transition countries where local political realities previously denied this. Although still highly heterogeneous, there is now more global uniformity in the distribution and composition of CSOs, though not yet in their membership, resources and impact. This also drives the move towards international networking.

This shift beyond a national focus to a transnational focus necessitates major changes in the structure and governance of CSOs and is influencing both their mandates and cultures. This chapter provides a review of these issues as they affect a range of transnational civil society actors. It is based on interviews with key stakeholders in major and illustrative CSOs and networks,[1] a review of their internal literature, conclusions of the London School of Economics and Political Science (LSE) seminar and the case studies in following chapters. It looks, firstly, at the various organizational arrangements that are used for transnational networking; secondly, it summarizes the key governance challenges – issues of representation, legitimacy, accountability, leadership, decision-making and use of name; thirdly, it surveys changes in focus, mandate and culture as CSOs increasingly work transnationally; fourthly, it asks how this trend impacts questions of membership and partnership, including the more regular tensions surfacing in North–South partnerships. Finally, it offers some general conclusions, which were also highlighted by the LSE seminar.

Various commentators have described how wide arrays of policy-oriented CSOs are increasingly seeking to operate in transnational alliances with counterparts or like-minded civic groups in other countries (Keck and Sikkink, 1998; Florini, 2000; Clark, 1999). This entails major challenges for CSOs. Amongst diverse CSO networks,[2] a remarkably similar spectrum of problems is encountered and a new literature is beginning to address such issues (see Lindenberg and Bryant, 2001, on development NGOs).

There are interesting parallels with the private sector. Many CSOs (such as consumers' associations or development NGOs) are evolving from hierarchic or unitary structures, where the identity of the CSO at national level is paramount, towards network modes in which topic specialists from different countries collaborate in opportunistic alliances with counterparts in other countries. The literature on civil society and conventional organizational theory regarding NGO management and behaviour offers little insight into these matters, though this is starting to change (Anheier et al, 2001; Anheier and Themudo, 2002).[3]

The internet has enabled citizens to network with one another internationally without the need for CSO intermediaries (at least those who can afford the technology). As a result, a variety of web-mediated advocacy and protest cells ('virtual CSOs') have arisen – we nickname these 'dot causes' – ranging from the Nobel prize-winning International Campaign to Ban Landmines (ICBL) to a smorgasbord of protest groups (see Chapter 6).

Another feature of CSO dynamics in today's fast-changing world is the growing tendency to work with non-traditional partners in other segments of civil society. NGOs, trade unions, faith groups, professional associations, think tanks and social movements increasingly cooperate with one another. Oxfam International (2000), for example, is committed to working with others and learning from the achievements of other movements to foster the notion of 'global citizenship' and global economic and social justice. Similarly, trade unions (TUs) increasingly collaborate with human rights, environment and other NGOs in campaigns targeting multinational companies or global industry umbrellas. Until recently, they had tended to disdain NGO partnerships. And religious organizations increasingly seek collaboration with those of other faiths.

Unions comprise the CSO category for which working transnationally is most need-driven, since globalization is radically changing their environment (see Chapter 3). The Millennium Review of the International Confederation of Free Trade Unions (ICFTU), underway at present, seeks to modernize and internationalize the union movement – in particular, by overhauling the international architecture of trade union networks and federations. Due to be completed by 2004, it seeks to identify TU priorities, structures and strategies to 'increase the strength of the trade union movement as an international campaigning and negotiating force', and to influence the structures and policies of inter-governmental organizations (ICFTU, 2000 and 2001).

A relatively new and increasingly powerful force is that of transnational networks led by Southern or transition-country organizations such as Social Watch, Third World Network and the recent campaign (led by the Treatment Action Campaign (TAC) of South Africa) to press for cheaper generic drugs for poor countries (Chapter 4).[4] Some Southern or transition-country organization leaders, however, are frustrated that progress is slow because Northern CSOs are reluctant to hand over the reins (Chiriboga, 2001).

ORGANIZATIONAL FORMS

Transnational networking necessitates structures that facilitate CSOs in different countries working together; there are many organizational forms that can be chosen for this. They are influenced by the legal traditions of the country where the CSO or network is registered and by national laws applying to members or branches. The spread of 'civil law' practices (such as US models for non-profit organizations across Central and Eastern Europe) and the promotion by donors of more enabling laws governing civil society is, however, leading to greater uniformity. Three broad forms define the spectrum, each of which can be subdivided:

- *International CSOs:* single, coherent organizations; major decisions are reached globally by international boards; policies are implemented by global secretariats or head offices; there is a global hierarchy of staff accountability. Within this form there is considerable variation, depending upon the degree of autonomy vested in the national branches or sections. It includes:

    - Unitary structures: the equivalent of TNCs, these are CSOs with global decision-making processes (albeit with some devolution). Examples include the Catholic Church, Human Rights Watch (HRW) and Plan International.
    - Centralized associations: these provide greater national autonomy; but major decisions are made by global headquarters, which also control the use of name and standards. Examples include Greenpeace and CARE.
    - Federations: global boards (representing the member CSOs) make global decisions in a framework of subsidiarity (considerable autonomy at the national level). They are serviced by strong global secretariats, accountable to the boards. Examples include Amnesty International (AI), CIVICUS (World Alliance for Citizen Participation) and Consumers International (CI).

- *CSO networks:* these are collaborative arrangements formed for broad partnership amongst like-minded organizations or cooperation on specific activities. They may have international boards and secretariats; but most power and implementation capacity remains with the CSO members. They comprise:

    - Confederations: network members are fully independent but agree a set of common ground rules and work together on specific activities where there is mutual advantage. Examples include the World Council of Churches, the ICFTU, Oxfam International (OI), Friends of the Earth International (FOE-I) and international inter-faith networks (such as the United Religions Initiative).
    - Informal networks: CSOs come together around a common cause to seek cooperation but with little agreed governance arrangements, leadership or membership requirements. Examples include the ICBL and the Jubilee 2000 movement for developing-world debt relief.

- *Social movements:* these comprise amorphous and fluid groupings of activists, CSOs and supporters in which the bonds are common grievances or convictions, and shared goals for societal and policy change (rather than structure). They connect people with causes through developing communities of interest around shared conditions and include:

    - Rooted movements: these are webs of citizens formed at the national level to attack mutually experienced grievances. International exchange and networking with counterparts in other countries can be powerful for sharing ideas and boosting morale; but mobilization and analysis is primarily at the national level. Examples include feminist, agrarian reform, gay rights and civil rights movements.

- Transnational movements: where the policy changes sought are largely determined by international governmental or corporate actors, movements become more transnational in character, although the boundary of this is not clear cut. Working internationally is not just for sharing ideas and building solidarity but also for forging collective energy and a globally coherent strategy around shared social change goals. Examples include the human rights movement, the climate change movement and the modern protest movement relating to globalization.

Each form has different ways of making decisions, handling leadership, communicating internally, responding to governance challenges, and developing external partnerships. These are summarized in Table 1.1. This chapter mostly deals with the first two forms, which involve conscious efforts to work transnationally. Social movements may exist in multiple countries, but they don't use defined governance procedures or structures to promote their aims (these are discussed more in Chapters 5, 6 and 7). Two key variables influencing transnational citizen action are the degree of decentralization, exemplified by the above organizational forms, and the degree to which decision-making lies with volunteers and CSO members (via elected committees of representatives) or with professional staff in international secretariats. Do CSOs help citizens to achieve a voice for themselves or do they speak for citizens? The former are more evidently representative and democratic; the latter usually have swifter, clearer decision-making and may appear more professional. There are other variables (such as whether a network is truly global or just operates in a few countries; or whether the transnational activities represent a large or small part of their members' activities); but these are less relevant to our topic.

Table 1.1 *Characteristics of different transnational civil society forms*

	International CSO (unitary)	International CSO Network	Social Movement
Modes of decision-making; structures	Defined vertical/ hierarchical	Defined but negotiated; horizontal	Not defined; organic; can be leader oriented or supporter driven; depends on nature of movement.
	Clear institutional structure	Cooperative; may be structured or unstructured	
			Different elements of movement may make different decisions
Leadership style or features	Single functional leadership in hierarchical structure	Multiple leadership by small groups of core activists; delegation by defined network membership; network plays centralized coordination function	Leadership likely to be political rather than managerial; shifts as different factions and cliques gain ascendancy

Table 1.1 *Characteristics of different transnational civil society forms (Continued)*

	International CSO (unitary)	International CSO Network	Social Movement
Communications, information – dissemination	Vertical; institutionalized along hierarchical and functional lines; instrumental for core objectives of the CSO	Horizontal, perhaps informal, spontaneous, issue specific; intense information exchange is core activity	Ad hoc; sharing of views/analysis of movement thinkers; partly to inform, partly to build shared culture/language
Governance:			
a Accountability	Clearly defined – to board or managers; also to funders; moral accountability to members, beneficiaries etc, but this is vague	Self-accountability, not externally; the network apportions tasks amongst members; reciprocity based on shared principles; reputation and trust	No defined accountability; subject to the 'market test' (ie leaders need to retain support through enthusing rather than elections)
b Transparency	Varies; most resist external sharing of critical evaluations or details of sensitive management or board debates	Often rather opaque; information is shared with members only, little to public	Highly transparent; since membership is usually informal and self-selected, all information is open to everyone
c Representivity	Membership; CSOs may represent their members, but vary in efforts to seek views; may speak for clients or beneficiaries	Varies; some require a consensus, others a majority, others allow joint action by sub-group of network	Of members/supporters, but likely to be informal; spokespeople *reflect* rather than *represent* a mass public mood
Motivations for participation	Identify with CSO; share professional objectives; self-interest (eg career)	To help the members of the network; shared discourse, values, causes	Shared grievances and convictions in context of perceived opportunities
Nature of outside partnerships	Strategic; well defined; on pragmatic basis; usually not dense; emphasis on CSO's own work	Horizontal clusters of networks based on shared goals; voluntary cooperation rather than leverage; can be dense webs	Social movement (SM) members may identify with other SMs, hence interaction; but a SM itself is not sufficiently defined institutionally to have partners
Fixity/clarity of strategy	Clearly defined and institutionally approved strategies; but multiple accountabilities can create internal problems of coherence	Focus on single core issue; membership likely to be like-minded; this helps it to form clear, powerful messages and well-targeted strategy	Strategies likely to be negotiated between leadership, internal factions and external allies

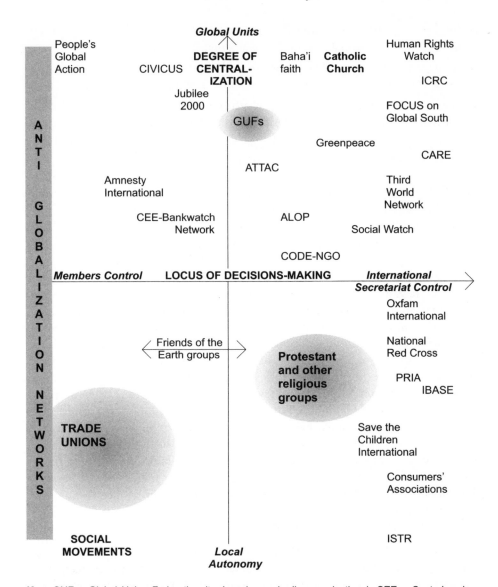

Key: GUF = Global Union Federation (trade union umbrella organizations); CEE = Central and Eastern Europe; ISTR = International Society for Third Sector Research; ICRC = International Committee of the Red Cross; ATTAC = Association for the Taxation of Financial Transactions for the Aid of Citizens (pressure group for a Tobin tax); PRIA = Society for Participatory Research in Asia; CARE = large US-based development NGO; IBASE, CODE-NGO and ALOP = NGO networks in Brazil, the Philippines and Latin America, respectively.

Figure 1.1 *The organizational forms of selected CSOs and CSO networks*

Figure 1.1 (borrowed from a framework suggested by Amnesty International, 2000) uses these two principal variables to present a taxonomy of transnational civil society in four quadrants:

1   strongly member-controlled; decisions taken largely locally (such as trade unions or international peasants' movements) (bottom left);

2   strongly member-controlled, but major decisions largely reached internationally (such as Amnesty International or some of the new protest groups) (top left);

3   secretariat-driven (volunteers less powerful); decisions largely reached globally (such as Greenpeace or Third World Network) (top right); and

4   secretariat-driven; decisions taken largely at local levels (such as most faith-based organizations and consumers' associations) (bottom right).

The figure is schematic and approximate, and is intended to illustrate a useful CSO taxonomy rather than comment on the work of any organization.

Though all CSOs face the same organizational choices as they work in more transnational and network modes, some general patterns emerge. Policy-oriented NGOs have generally been fastest to adapt to these new approaches. They have expanded the clout, resources and professionalism of their international secretariats (although these may be decentralized) to become more effective global negotiators, researchers and campaigners. Such NGOs operate in the issues, and the public are urged to support them in this task. Trade union networks tend to emphasize the provision of professional support to member unions at the national level, including information exchange and basic coordination between their members; ultimately, therefore, they see their role as supporting their rank and file members, not the other way around. Faith-based networks can be very strong when uniting a religion globally (the Catholic Church is an obvious example), but multi-faith networks are generally weak. Faiths tend to be naturally hierarchical (at least at the national level) and more competitive with respect to rivals than other types of CSO. Hence, although there are clear issues uniting faiths, they tend to find it easier to collaborate with secular CSOs than with other faiths. We now explore these organizational choices by looking at specific examples.

NGOs working transnationally

Policy-oriented NGOs can be thought of as *products* of advanced democracy that are generally not *hampered* by democracy. The majority do not have mass memberships who take major decisions. Many (such as Oxfam) depend heavily on public subscription; but the public are supporters, not members. Some, such as Greenpeace and Consumers' Association (UK) have 'members' but delegate few powers to them regarding policies, programmes or selection of chief executives. Other NGOs may be influential but have little or no public base (such as the New Economics Foundation, numerous think tanks and Focus on the Global South). Only a few, such as Amnesty International, are membership organizations in the sense that members control the NGO.

There is, therefore, a paradox. NGOs have recently emerged within well-established democracies (North and South; East and West) as influential voices in their special fields, and they are increasingly seen as plugging the deficiencies in orthodox democracy created by globalization (Clark, 2003). They contribute to democracy, but most influential NGOs are not, in themselves, democratic. This is not to say that they don't enjoy the enthusiastic support of their subscribers and the wider public; however, they feel no obligation to sound out those publics regarding the policies they advocate or to be accountable to them for their campaign efforts. Hence, they can swiftly adapt their messages and activities to accord with new realities or to seize new opportunities. They also exercise great flexibility in forming alliances and refining their positions. They greatly influence democratic processes, therefore, but are not themselves hampered by cumbersome democratic deliberations.

Perhaps due to their subject matter, environmental groups have often been fastest to change to the opportunities of working transnationally. Friends of the Earth (FOE) provides a good example of a global network. FOE International (FOE-I) started 30 years ago as a network of four Northern FOEs (from the US, the UK, France and Sweden). FOE groups then started to form elsewhere, and, more particularly, other environmental groups applied for FOE-I membership. In the early 1990s, FOE-I decided to accelerate this trend (particularly in Southern or transition countries), and by 2001 the membership had expanded to 68, with more than half being from these regions. Membership requirements include being a truly national organization (ie working throughout the country); maintaining grassroots as well as nationwide activities; independence from the state, political parties, religions and ethnic organizations; working on a full range of environmental issues; and adopting open and democratic structures, free of sexism and discrimination. Only one FOE member is admitted per country. FOE-I also has affiliates, which may be single-issue campaigns, research organizations or international groups.

Combined, FOE's network has over 1 million members, 5000 local groups and a US$200 million budget. The international secretariat expanded from 1.5 in 1992 to 23 in 2001 (of which 15 are seconded by, and work within, national FOE offices). The major international campaigns are shaped by FOE-I, serviced by secretariat staff, and supervised by an FOE-I sub-committee comprising senior staff from national FOEs. Usually there are two lead agencies – one Northern, one Southern or transition country. There is, however, considerable variation within the network. The majority of FOE-UK campaigns, for example, now have a strong international dimension, while FOE Germany remains focused largely on domestic issues.

Other leading environmental NGOs are more centralized. Greenpeace and the World Wide Fund for Nature (WWF), for example, are, in effect, international CSOs. Greenpeace is a centralized association headquartered in The Netherlands with national and regional offices in about 40 (mostly Northern) countries. Greenpeace International licenses the use of the name and coordinates global programmes (Anheier, 2000). The international secretariat accounts for a quarter of the global Greenpeace budget. WWF is a federation of semi-independent national conservation organizations in Northern countries and some larger developing countries. Members are serviced by a large Swiss secretariat (WWF-International). To diversify and expand the Southern and transition country voices, since the mid 1990s they have included programme offices in the deliberating processes; although, in practice, these have less weight, and the three big offices (International, US and The Netherlands) dominate decision-making.

Environment and human rights NGOs deal with discrete issues and make an interesting comparison. An array of environmental groups evolved and grew during the 1970s and 1980s as public concern about environmental issues emerged and coalesced into the environment movement. These groups both fed this growing concern and benefited from it. Hence, the diversity of the sector reflects differing styles and differing success rates in getting messages across. The human rights movement, however, is largely the product of one NGO, Amnesty International (AI), which grew in prominence as it demonstrated its expertise in international law and mobilized public opinion (mostly in Northern countries) about human rights abuses. It is only more recently that other large human rights NGOs have formed and AI has faced tough competition. As a result, the environment NGOs traditionally have a mixed attitude towards each other. On the one hand, they are accustomed to cooperating, since they share an interest in building the movement; on the other hand, they are highly competitive – constantly striving to be seen as 'leading the pack', either by being first on a topic or by being most radical. The traditional challenge for AI, conversely, has been to demonstrate credibility to diplomats and politicians. It has worried less about competition. Hence, it has been anxious to demonstrate that it has a strong and growing base of thoughtful supporters, that it speaks for a growing constituency and that it is scrupulously accurate. It has competed more with political apathy and exigencies of diplomacy than with rival NGOs.

AI was established in 1961 and has always been a centralized federation of national members (or sections), now numbering about 50. Its large international secretariat in London services the sections and implements campaigns and policies agreed by the membership. During the last few years there has been a strong growth of Southern or transition country members, who now comprise about half the sections. AI's main rival is Human Rights Watch (HRW), whose structure and history is very different. HRW is relatively new. Although its precursor, Helsinki Watch, preceded it by many years as a specialist watchdog, HRW was only established in 1988 as a global NGO. It is, in essence, a highly centralized, US NGO with specialist sections (Americas Watch, Asia Watch, Africa Watch, among others) and global outreach.

International development and humanitarian NGOs are virtually all driven by their secretariats rather than their supporters. Their popular appeal has traditionally been that they are able to provide help in situations of desperate need. For Northern publics, they are vehicles for compassion, rather than self-interest or politics. Supporters want their preferred NGO to do more as a result of their support, but don't traditionally expect it to campaign on political issues, still less to speak on their behalf. Hence, the NGOs' structures generally evolve to maximize efficiency as conduits of aid – improving aid targeting and publicizing their success in fighting poverty. Most NGOs are international in that they have well-resourced offices in their programme countries; but these report to the international headquarters where major decisions are taken. Increasingly, NGOs have become dependent on official funding (Clark, 1991) and, consequently, have come under pressure to coordinate their programmes more assiduously to avoid duplication. Some have also given increasing attention to research and advocacy activities. As a result, there has been a strong tendency in recent years to build international networks of like-minded NGOs.

Oxfam International (OI), for example, is a confederation comprising 12 national organizations in Northern (fund raising) countries. Their collective budget was US$504 million in 1999, most of which goes to support the activities of 3000 partner NGOs in the South. The total budget of OI's secretariat in Oxford is about US$1.5 million, including a professional advocacy team in Washington, DC, Brussels and Geneva and a Development Investment Fund. OI has three main goals: programme harmonization, particularly in countries where confusion may arise from various Oxfams running different programmes; joint advocacy on agreed topics; and promoting a more unified public perception of what Oxfam does and stands for, or 'branding' (OI website: www.oxfam-international.org).

Other NGO networks, such as CARE, Save the Children International, World Vision, Plan International and Médecins Sans Frontières (MSF), are somewhat similar. They are networks of donor agencies in Northern countries in which there are varying degrees of centralization and programme harmonization. The International Federation of Red Cross and Red Crescent Societies (IFRC) is rather different. It is an umbrella organization of 178 national Red Cross or Red Crescent societies who are bound by a set of global principles (the most controversial ones of which are 'neutrality' and acting under the approval of the government in question). The national members are autonomous (including in the South), though most funding for Southern or transition-country activities comes from international appeals. The IFRC secretariat in Geneva coordinates the international appeals and other aspects of the network, represents national societies at the international level, and works with national societies to plan and direct major relief efforts. It has about 250 employees and mobilized US$230 million in 2001.

Trade union networks

Most unions (especially in industrialized countries) are facing enormous challenges in terms of declining membership, technology reducing the demand for manual workers, greater mobility of capital and production, neo-liberal economic policies, and increasingly 'flexible' labour markets throughout most of the world (see Chapter 3). Employment policies (especially within TNCs) are increasingly determined internationally. To be effective in protecting their members' interests, unions need to work internationally, and need to influence policies relating to labour markets. These are difficult challenges, however, at a time when union membership in much of the world is declining and workers, especially young people, tend to find unions unexciting and old-fashioned. These problems are particularly acute in Western Europe, but may be easing in the US where, for many years, the major unions have shifted tactics from traditional member-service activities to campaigning.

Responding to these trends, there is currently a major regrouping of unions underway internationally. While the powerful shift during much of the 20th century was towards forging strong national-level unions out of workplace and local unions, today's pattern is towards stronger global alliances of national unions by sector. Most teachers' unions outside of communist countries, for example, have federated into Education International, and 560 national-level unions representing public-sector workers have formed Public Service International (PSI). Such Global Union Federations (GUFs) have existed for more than a century; but their roles and influence have significantly changed of late (see Chapter 3). They now emphasize international campaigning and negotiation with both governmental agencies and multinational employers.

What distinguishes unions from other civil society sectors is that they take their representative function much more seriously. They exist not just to serve their members and speak for them, but to give them voice. Hence, the secretariats at both national and international levels are loath to make policy statements unless debated and ratified by their rank and file. This means that their participation in policy debate is more cumbersome – a result of dry resolutions, rather than pithy statements – and they usually don't respond rapidly. However, when they speak out they do so with the considerable authority of their huge memberships. They tend to resent the more flexible NGOs, who – they feel – often command greater attention of the media and policy-makers because of their ability to respond swiftly and clearly, but who only speak for themselves.

The GUFs are decentralized to varying degrees. Hence, for example, PSI – which used to be highly centralized – has opened a whole new set of offices in the last six years. It is now the most decentralized GUF, with 4 regional and 20 subregional offices. All GUFs engage in macro-economic and other international policy discussions and urge their member unions to realize the imperative to work internationally in order to remain relevant. This includes working with NGOs, academics and other non-traditional partners (see Chapter 3).

Transnational and inter-faith networks

Like trade unions, many religions have experienced declining membership and mounting questions of relevance. In response, they increasingly engage in issues of morality and society beyond narrow questions of faith. As a result, three trends have emerged. Firstly, transnational, intra-faith networking has accelerated; most religions now invest more in international coordination, exchange of ideas and general cooperation. Secondly, religious leaders are increasingly willing to join networks with secular organizations – for example, joining with environment, development or human rights groups to press for debt relief, action on climate change or the abolition of the death penalty. Thirdly, but least evident until recent years, are efforts of inter-faith cooperation. As noted above, the tradition of inter-faith competition has tended to deter partnerships between religions; but certain ramifications of global change – including heightened concern about the role of religious divides in many of the world's most serious conflicts (not least since 11 September) – have catalysed new efforts to form partnerships between faiths.

Most religions (excepting the Catholic Church, the Baha'i, etc) are locally focused, are not based on global hierarchies and, hence, are not well suited to international work. Furthermore, Cold War political constraints have made it difficult, until recently, to discuss religious issues within the United Nations (UN) and other international forums. New technology, cheaper travel, the end of the Cold War and other globalization-related opportunities have, however, expanded international cooperation within most religions, enhancing their international vision and their concern about global policy issues. This has convinced many faiths that the reforms they seek will not be forthcoming without cooperation, in particular with other faiths. This is not universally accepted, however, and at least one – the Catholic Church – is cautioning its members to be wary of religious pluralism.

Until recent years, most inter-faith cooperation focused on matters that affect groups directly, such as protecting the right to worship and specific 'safe' areas, such as education. Now, however, there are many initiatives promoting inter-faith, international cooperation in wider subject areas. Although there was an unsuccessful bid to form a 'world parliament of religions' as early as 1893, and other efforts to promote better inter-faith understanding since, it was not until 1970 that an international joint-faith venture was established to promote the role of religions in peace-building (the World Congress of Religion and Peace). Furthermore, it was not until the 1990s that inter-faith cooperation started to take off. The two recent notable initiatives were the birth of the United Religions Initiative in 1996 (launched at a major conference in San Francisco) and the establishment of the World Faiths Dialogue on Development in 1998 (whose driving forces are the leaders of the Church of England, the Ismaili faith and the World Bank). Inter-faith activities today tend to concentrate on issues of peace, sustainability, human rights, poverty, education and – more recently – economic globalization.

The World Council of Churches (WCC) is an early, but narrow, example of inter-faith networking – embracing, as it does, just Christian organizations. It is a membership body comprising two-thirds of the Protestant churches by congregation (or one third of the Christian faith). The Catholic Church is not a formal member; but it cooperates actively with it. Though it is unlikely that many churches consider themselves to be represented by the WCC, it is influential; in particular, it has effectively challenged its members to address questions of economic justice.

There also appears to be weak coordination between the inter-faith bodies and the faith-based development organizations, such as Caritas, the Association of Protestant Development NGOs and the Lutheran World Federation.

Box 1.1 *Chronology of major inter-faith initiatives*

1893   First Parliament of World Religion, Chicago (150,000 participants)
1900   International Association for Religious Freedom (formed in Oxford)
1936   World Congress of Faith
1948   World Council of Churches formed (now comprises 300 churches in 120 countries)
1950   World Fellowship of Religions, India
1960   Temple of Understanding established
1970   World Congress of Religion and Peace (conservative, but truly inter-faith)
1988   Council for Parliament of World Religion established
1993   Centennial meeting of the 1893 Parliament
1993   International Inter-faith Centre established in Oxford
1996   United Religions Initiative, launched by Bishop Swing of San Francisco; this has been a radical, high-profile, grassroots-oriented and fast-growing initiative
1997   Inter-faith centre set up in New York
1998   World Faiths Dialogue on Development
1999   Cape Town meeting of the Council for the Parliament for World Religion (decided to stay as a council, rather than pursue the parliament concept)
2000   Millennium World Peace Summit, comprising 1000 senior religious leaders (little consensus or agreed action, but showed growing interest in inter-faith networking)

Source: adapted from Boehle, 2001

Southern-led CSO networks

Though most international CSO networks are led by Northern groups, a number of strong Southern-based and Southern-led networks have emerged during
recent years. For example, Social Watch came together during preparations for
the World Summit on Social Development in Copenhagen in 1995. It is a Uru-
guay-based alliance of largely Southern and transition-country development,
human rights, labour and women's groups that raises macro-economic concerns
within international forums and acts as a citizens' watchdog over social development policies. It monitors the implementation of major commitments made by
governments and international agencies at UN summits, reports on this progress
(in particular, by publishing an annual Social Watch report) and provides a global forum for NGO advocacy. Its global and country-level reports are highly
praised and it comprises very effective regional and national coalitions. Social
Watch seeks to bridge the South–North gap. A coordinating committee (comprising seven men and seven women – ten from Southern or transition countries
and four from the North) sets its policies while each national group is responsible for its own fund raising, although global funds are provided by Novib and
other Northern sources.

   Groups such as Social Watch and Third World Network (a Penang-based
transnational network of radical intellectuals, activists and journalists that challenges globalization and related issues) seek to redefine the division of labour
between Northern and Southern or transition-country advocacy. Northern NGOs
tend to talk easily about 'partnerships'; in reality, there is not the basis of equality
or even trust that such a term implies. 'Development alliance' might be a better

term, says Social Watch. Northern NGOs need to be discouraged from speaking 'on behalf of' Southern or transition-country people or NGOs, and should be urged to form relationships based on cooperation rather than competition.

The Amazon Coalition provides another interesting illustration of a success-ful Southern-led NGO network. The Coordinating Body of Indigenous Organi-zations of the Amazon Basin (COICA) was set up in 1991 by Brazilian NGOs (especially those representing indigenous people) to counter the neglect of social issues in international NGO campaigning regarding the Amazon. It was largely a reaction to US environmental groups having an influential voice on Amazon affairs in the world at large, but portraying these purely in terms of rainforest and species conservation, with little mention of the people who depend on Amazon resources. COICA has managed to persuade many (but not all) Northern NGOs to broaden their advocacy and has established its own lobbying office in Washington, DC (Selverston-Scher, 2000).

There is similar transnational networking emerging in the former Eastern bloc (Hlobil, 2001; Stark, 2001). The very rapid growth of civil society activity, including transnational networking, in Central and Eastern Europe owes much to the influx of new ICT, as well as to the dramatic rise of NGOs. Before 1989 there were very few, and these only had access to the most basic technology – not even photocopiers. Today, there are tens of thousands of NGOs in each country of the region and these have full access to advanced ICT. While in the US e-business was at the forefront of internet use, in this region NGOs have led the way.

Southern or transition country-based transnational networking tends to emphasize regional, rather than global, collaboration due to common historical links and shared needs. For example, the struggles for democracy in Latin America or for reconstruction after civil war in Central America have led to the establish-ment of regional networks. Whereas ten years ago these emphasized sharing best practice and solidarity networks, they have recently become more policy-oriented.

However, few Southern or transition-country CSO networks are fully inde-pendent of influence from their Northern counterparts. They mostly depend on Northern funding, which sometimes presents dilemmas and creates pressure to prioritize matters of Northern concern. For example, groups concerned about trade issues in Latin America feel pressure to concentrate on the free trade area of the Americas or the World Trade Organization (WTO), although what seems more immediately relevant to them is the Colombia Plan. Southern or transi-tion-country networks often experience confusion and mixed signals in relations with their Northern partners. For example, on the one hand, they relate to pol-icy and campaigning staff in policy advocacy; on the other hand, they relate to project departments when it comes to funding. Frequently, departments within the same NGO demonstrate poor communication and have different concerns. Southern or transition-country networks also often experience internal tension between their locally born and locally educated members, their locally born and Western educated members, and between their local and ex-patriot staff.[5]

Roles and financing of the international secretariat

As civil society networks focus more on transnational action, they generally expand their international secretariats. Some (such as Oxfam, Amnesty International and Public Service International) have opened offices in cities that are strategically important to their advocacy roles. Secretariat roles and responsibilities vary significantly, however. Some represent their networks, advocating on their behalf, while others simply facilitate the participation of their members in policy discussions. There are various ways of financing secretariats. Some networks have a standard membership contribution (typically, a percentage of the members' income); some encourage in-kind contributions (staff seconded to work on projects for the international network); and some seek funding from foundations, governments or elsewhere.

Oxfam International has a burden-sharing approach in which the largest members (UK and The Netherlands) bear most of the costs. CARE and Save the Children members all pay 0.25 per cent of their incomes to the international secretariats. Médecins Sans Frontières (MSF) members pay a negotiated sum (ranging from 0.22 to 0.4 per cent of their income) to MSF-I. Friends of the Earth-International (FOE-I) members pay 1 per cent of their 'unrestricted income', plus 0.1 per cent of all other income to FOE-I (though up to half of this fee can be in-kind contributions for Southern and transition-country members). In the case of trade union networks, the member unions pay contributions towards core costs, but sympathetic Northern governments often finance special activities. And most inter-faith activities are financed through short-term grants from foundations, wealthy individuals and some specialist church organizations (such as the Unitarians). In North–South CSO networks, the Northern members generally mobilize the funding for international campaigns. Southern and transition-country members frequently complain that their Northern partners jealously guard these funds (Jordan and van Tuijl, 2000).

GOVERNANCE ISSUES

Interviews with senior staff of major transnational civil society networks (TCSN)[6] have revealed a similar range of governance questions confronted across all categories of CSOs. These issues are summarized below.

Issues of legitimacy and representivity

Though CSO leaders often give much attention to these issues, government and corporate officials often level the most serious charge – questioning legitimacy – when TCSNs rub up against powerful interests who think they wield disproportionate influence. The related charge is that they are not 'representative' in ways that they purport to be. There is a growing literature on these issues (Edwards, 1996 and 2000; Clark, 1999 and 2003).

Mass membership can confer legitimacy; for example, the GUFs all represent millions of workers (25 million teachers in the case of Education International).

The unions are proud of this, and often challenge NGOs with whom they disagree to demonstrate their representivity. NGOs may have millions of members (for instance, Greenpeace), as do other CSO networks (such as consumers associations). In practice, those members may be casual donors or subscribers with no active involvement; they don't recognize the CSO as speaking for them. Religions have large memberships (even excluding passive members), but rarely seek to represent their congregations on anything other than theological issues.

CSOs have other avenues in which to claim legitimacy (these issues are discussed more fully in Clark, 2003). Some, with virtually no grassroots base, are widely seen as world authorities in their field. Some claim bona fides through their participatory styles of work, their acknowledged experience or impact, their local knowledge or their web of partners (for example, close Southern or transition-country associates). Some also weight decision-making according to their local membership. For example, Amnesty International apportions voting shares in its international council according to the number of local groups in each national section. Many CSO networks gain credibility because of internal discipline, enforcing high standards of governance and ethics on their members. AI and FOE, for example, have both suspended or expelled errant members.

Jordan and Van Tuijl (2000) argue that 'political responsibility' is a better lens than legitimacy and representation. They describe four levels of political responsibility in transnational NGO relationships:

- cooperative (joint management);
- concurrent;
- disassociated; and
- competitive (no sharing of information and no recognition of risks).

Accountability

This topic is also widely discussed in the literature on NGO management (see, for example, Edwards and Hulme, 1995; Fowler, 1997). In looking at transnational civil society networks (TCSNs), two specific questions arise. Does working in a TCSN entail greater discipline and, therefore, enhance a CSO's accountability (in other words, do the networks incorporate a self-regulation discipline)? There is considerable evidence that national networks of NGOs and other CSOs often encourage higher standards of ethics and governance (for example, The Philippines, Bangladesh and Palestinian NGO networks), and there is some evidence that more formal transnational networks do the same, but the evidence is sketchy. Secondly, does network membership strengthen or reduce emphasis on accountability to rank-and-file members? It appears that TCSN membership introduces stronger accountability to peers in other countries, perhaps (but not necessarily) at the cost of grassroots accountability; but this can also insulate Southern and transition-country CSOs from Northern donor pressures.

Box 1.2 *The Philippines code of NGO ethics*

The Philippines has thousands of development and social-sector non-governmental organizations (NGOs). Their influence expanded in the mid 1990s after the government devolved power to the local level, promoted community development and decreed NGO involvement in all local councils, school boards and other local government activities. NGO–government partnerships have generally been successful, as has network development. The largest NGO network (the Caucus of Development NGOs, or CODE-NGO) represents 3000 organizations; other CSOs have formed similar networks, and these networks cooperate amongst themselves.

In 1995 the NGO networks came together to agree a code of ethics for NGOs. This was designed, in particular, to clarify the relationship between government, businesses and NGOs and to 'police' NGO activities. Besides helping to identify which NGOs are doing quality work (used to qualify NGOs for government tax concessions), this self-regulation has checked a tendency of many NGOs to act as if they were 'shadow governments' or to claim to be 'better than government'.

The development of the NGOs' Code of Ethics – which recognized the roles, responsibilities and obligations of the non-profit sector and donor relationships – has enriched NGO contributions through fostering a culture of sharing and responsibility, increasing NGO visibility, strengthening the donor base and fostering a shift of work to a more global mode.

National CSOs are generally accountable to boards that comprise active supporters, whereas TCSNs' accountability may be oriented towards CEOs and senior specialists of the member CSOs. TCSNs, therefore, are more removed from the grassroots level. Some countries have CSO watchdogs and, occasionally, parliamentary and press scrutiny of leading CSOs; but these rarely look at the activities of TCSNs. Institutional funders (such as foundations and liberal governments) are major supporters of many TCSNs and have structured approaches to monitoring and evaluation. However, again this is a form of upward, not downward, accountability. Many NGO networks admit, internally, that their accountability mechanisms are weak. 'In practice, lines of accountability and implementation reports are poorly monitored and rarely challenged, and there are limited tools for accountability', says an internal report of one prominent NGO network.

Few TCSNs have developed accountability mechanisms that emphasize their Southern or transition-country members. Oxfam International now solicits input from their Southern and transition-country staff in their monitoring and evaluation activities, and is considering extending this to strategic Southern and transition-country partners. Many practitioners are concerned that, while professionalization of TCSNs can enhance advocacy effectiveness, this may be at the expense of widening gaps between national- and local-level activists, and between activists at national and international levels.

Leadership and decision-making

For sustainability and harmony, CSOs must feel in control of the networks to which they belong. In order to be effective in influencing policy, they need clear and strong leadership ensuring concerted advocacy. These needs can be contradictory. Strong leadership is often resented by member CSOs, who may feel eclipsed. The latter may prefer their networks to share information and coordinate activities, but not to *direct* anything. To what extent should networks *serve* or *drive* their membership? Some members have criticized the leadership of both UK-based Jubilee 2000 and French-based ATTAC (campaign for Tobin taxes) for being too directive; but both have made remarkable achievements. It may be that successful networks tend to have leaders who are more skilled in mobilizing and in formulating mass-action strategies than in consensus building and coordination.

Strong network leadership must be balanced by decision-making procedures that are endorsed by the members and are equitable. Amnesty International (2000) declares seven principles of decision-making that most CSO networks would subscribe to (empowerment; participation/inclusion; transparency; accountability; cohesion; effectiveness; and direction/prioritization). However, in practice, the dictates of the first five often work against the punchiness and speed required by the last two. Voting patterns vary widely. Some formal TCSNs arrive at consensus decisions; some take votes; some give greater voting power to their larger members than to their smaller ones. This is often a vexed issue, particularly when smaller members feel marginalized. In general, the networks agree major decisions at international board meetings (larger networks, such as unions, may have regional as well as global meetings), where executive committees are also appointed for interim decisions. Some networks (for example, Oxfam International) have found that their structure becomes more cumbersome as their membership grows. Others (such as FOE-I) use a 'sign-up' approach in which actions are agreed as options that members can adopt or not as they please (reflecting a 'voice-and-exit' approach). Few long-established networks appear to use the internet or video-conferencing extensively for decision-making (seeing these more as media for exchange of information).

No network demonstrates the dilemmas of decision-making more clearly than Amnesty International. Many within it, and friends outside, say that it is in crisis because its decision-making, though democratic, is too slow and hidebound in procedure. Much hinges on the international council meeting (ICM) of all sections, held every two years. This has become overtaken by long and technical debates about mandate changes (see below) that are inaccessible to most new or smaller members, especially if they aren't fluent in the major languages. AI also has an executive committee that meets several times per year and an annual meeting of section directors – but major decisions are not delegated to these forums. Though ICMs allow for majority voting (and each section has between three and eight votes, depending upon the number of local groups it has), in practice, major splits are avoided. As a result, issues are often deferred if consensus decisions cannot be reached. This has led to AI being bogged down in long and unclear debates about whether gay rights or landmines are suitable topics for AI action (and, if so, whether these topics are conducive to full campaigns or just educational exercises). AI leaders recognize that its decision-making has become too slow for the modern age and too technical to maintain popular appeal. The problem is in agreeing on the changes. This is currently a topic of hot internal debate (AI, 2000).

AI's major competitor, Human Rights Watch (HRW), has no such decision-making bottlenecks. While AI is bound by its mandate (a charter of agreed human rights interpretations that delineate what the organization can and cannot do), HRW has no such restriction. It can adopt any human rights cause (whether concerning a political, civil, economic or social right). HRW is also a centralized organization, governed by a primarily US board. It is weak on participation and empowerment, but has attained a reputation as one of the world's most effective human rights NGOs.

Jubilee 2000, in contrast, had a very informal decision-making structure. It was, in reality, a UK network with a British board; but its appeal led to Jubilee groups being set up throughout the world, most of whom elected to adopt the same campaign targets and strategies. Throughout 1998–2000, Jubilee 2000 held informal consultations in the margins of its international meetings, which were also the occasions for South–South caucusing, and these resulted in mounting internal tension and the emergence of different platforms (see Chapter 5).

Use of name and branding

Some networks (such, as Amnesty International and Greenpeace) require their members to use their brand name, logo and a common house style. Some, such as Oxfam International (OI), ask all members to set a timetable for incorporating the name 'Oxfam' within their national name (for example, Novib: the Oxfam of The Netherlands). Other networks, such as Friends of the Earth-International (FOE-I), are happy for their members to use completely different names (for instance, WALHI in Indonesia). Conversely, the Jubilee 2000 name is used in many countries but without a global agreement on what this entails. Jubilee South (a network of Southern intellectuals with little grassroots base) declared a more radical platform than Jubilee 2000 and asserted that it had a better right to represent the Southern voice. The lack of name licensing had benefits as well as problems – it helped to publicize the campaign name internationally. Some networks (for example, OI and Save the Children) have taken legal actions against those using their name without authorization.

FOCUS, MANDATE AND CULTURE

CSOs in transnational networks experience three pressures that lead to organizational tensions regarding focus and mandate: supranational forces pull CSOs toward standardization and uniformity; sub-national forces pull toward decentralization; and horizontal forces emphasize linking and coordination across geographic and sectoral frontiers.

Box 1.3 *Amnesty International and its mandate dilemma*

At its birth in 1961 Amnesty International's (AI's) mandate was clear: the release of prisoners of conscience (defined on religious or political grounds). During its first 30 years, there were very few mandate changes to such issues as the death penalty, extra-judicial killings, torture, cruel treatment and disappearances. However, there has been a mandate explosion since 1990 (in particular as Southern and transition-country AI groups have proliferated), and dozens of new clauses have been adopted, covering topics such as homosexuality, female genital mutilation, armed opposition groups, laws on wars, human rights promotion and education, forcible exile, fair trial, international criminal court and landmines. This now means that the mandate, far from being a succinct mission statement reminding supporters what the organization stands for, has become a legalistic tome that few in AI have a good grasp of, and that is increasingly seen as a millstone, preventing AI from responding flexibly to world events as they arise.

The 'mission creep' has far from ended. As more development interests have arisen and as diverse specialist groups and networks have formed, new mandate changes are constantly being proposed, particularly regarding social and economic rights. Proponents argue that globalization has diminished the strength of sovereign nation states. Other actors – such as international financial institutions – are gaining power; and armed opposition groups often have de facto control over territories and their populations. Hence, they argue, it is no longer sufficient for AI to focus on violations perpetrated by governments. Abuses arising from extreme poverty and social exclusion increasingly occupy the human rights agenda.

Furthermore, as AI works more closely with others (such as development non-governmental organizations and unions), it is pressured into lending reciprocal support to their campaigns. While the mandate determines its mainstay 'oppositional work' (campaigns on specific human rights abuse), AI is greatly expanding its more general 'promotional work' (education and campaigning in support of broad human rights). The growth of Southern sections has also challenged AI's founding principle against 'working on own-country' issues (designed to ensure impartiality and avoid becoming embroiled in partisan politics). Southern members find this anachronistic. For them, participation in AI only makes sense if they can work on issues in their countries, and define human rights as the broad human rights movement in what their country does.

Expanding transnational activities (especially by expanding Southern or transition-country membership) can precipitate a change in the focus and mandate of established networks as new actors bring in new priorities that challenge the network's traditional style and culture. These challenges may lead to difficult choices, and perhaps to shifts in the traditional support base. This, in turn, may lead to significant changes in the organizational culture of both the network and constituent CSOs. Amnesty International illustrates this most dramatically (see Box 1.3).

Southern FOEs, to give another example, have challenged their Northern counterparts to halt their dialogue with oil companies – urging investment in alternative energy generation – since they regard these companies as violators of human rights, particularly regarding indigenous people. This has been a difficult discussion, resulting in a compromise permitting continued dialogue but subject to careful ground rules designed to avoid implying any endorsement of the company.

Trade union networks have also been influenced by the growing weight of their Southern and transition-country membership. Traditional union concerns of collective bargaining within the formal sector, while still important, have been supplemented by concerns about 'flexibilization' of labour contracts, part-time workers, the informal sector and even macro-economic issues, such as structural adjustment that impacts upon employment in the South.

Questions of culture and style

Changes in network membership and new working modes (made possible by ICT) can trigger rapid cultural change in well-established networks. The Southern and transition-country members have influenced FOE, for example, in repositioning itself as a sustainable development movement rather than as an environmental movement. And Amnesty International now has many international special-interest groups, as well as local groups. These 'networks within the network' represent population groups (such as doctors, lawyers, teachers and youth), specific causes (for example, concerning the death penalty or homosexual rights) or country interest. They act as pressure groups within AI, account for some of its most effective campaigning, and are changing how AI operates. However, they are not yet recognized in AI's governance structure (currently only local groups are counted, even though this mode of mobilization is becoming outdated). Other TCSNs, such as FOE and Greenpeace, reveal a similar pattern of internet-connected special-interest groups.

Network cultures also change as they become more dependent upon professional staff, rather than upon voluntarism. Increased transnational networking, the serious (though sometimes hostile) response of institutions attacked by CSO advocacy, and increased sources of funding all heighten TCSN professionalism, leading more young people to consider careers in CSOs. Grassroots supporters are reinforced by seeing 'their' CSO field as an effective lobbying team at international forums, but may find themselves relegated to raising funds and signing petitions rather than being lobbyists themselves.

MEMBERSHIP AND PARTNERSHIP ISSUES

Though the sector is becoming more influential, many CSOs are experiencing declining membership and a reduction in activists' time. Working internationally and developing non-traditional partnerships offer ways of increasing a CSO's clout, though tensions may arise due to the different cultures of the new partners. In particular, as Southern and transition-country CSOs become more confident, North–South tensions within TCSNs are becoming more evident. Some networks seek to increase their influence or credibility by creating new members in strategic 'gap' countries or by admitting associates or affiliates.

The whole discussion of membership within CSOs and their networks is fraught with terminological difficulties. What is a member to some CSOs is a supporter, or even a customer, to others. One can be a member of an interest group in the same way as one can be a member of American Express because you want a service the CSO provides. This is very different from, say, being a member of the Catholic Church. Similarly, membership in a network can entail full commitment (as in federations) or a single, perhaps peripheral, overlapping interest.

Non-traditional partnerships

Though partnership between like organizations is not new, a recent phenomenon has been collaboration between organizations in different sectors. For example, trade union networks increasingly work with NGOs; human rights groups work with religious organizations; and CSOs work with academia, business groups and even governments.

Such collaboration has been controversial for some trade unionists, who regard unions as having a special status, representing mass memberships. They think that this could be compromised by working with advocacy NGOs (see Chapter 3). This is compounded by differences in style; most pressure groups largely focus on opposing things, while unions traditionally have an eye to the negotiating table and to brokering agreements. Conversely, some NGOs (particularly in the South) criticize unions for allowing labour and environment standards to be used as protectionist trade barriers.

Most faith-based organizations have little tradition of networking with others, though this is now changing. Some, however, are alarmed at the trend towards inter-faith activities. A September 2000 statement from Cardinal Ratzinger (responsible for the Vatican's Doctrine of the Faith) expressed considerable unease about religious pluralism; this was construed as a warning following the Millennium Faiths Summit.

Amnesty International has also not found it easy to network with others. It was, at first, suspicious and territorial when other human rights NGOs started to form (such as Human Rights Watch), seeing them as competitors. It gradually came to appreciate the value of partnership because it has helped to engender a human rights movement that has elevated their issues in the political agenda. AI now, often, has joint missions, statements and publications with others. Today, AI frequently works with trade unions, religious groups, development NGOs and others (for example, in the campaign for an international criminal court and the coalition to stop child soldiers). Within the broader human rights movement, however, AI is often seen as conservative – partly due to the mandate style and partly because it does little on economic and social rights.

Collaboration can be problematic even within networks. For example, Oxfam GB has traditionally determined its own campaign agenda and sometimes finds it difficult to follow the discipline of collaborating within Oxfam International. And some close partners criticize OI for being a rather aloof system that expects them to support its campaigns without reciprocating. Friends of the Earth-International is more inclined to promote collaboration with others, but leaves this up to national members and the lead agencies for specific campaigns (generally, one Northern and one Southern or transition-country member share the leadership of a campaign).

The World Wide Fund for Nature (WWF) has emphasized partnership building (the subject of its 2001 annual meeting), in particular with the private sector and large development agencies (including the World Bank, UN agencies and CARE).

Membership and support base

All membership CSOs have stratified support; only a fraction of their membership will be active. Hence, FOE-UK has about 100,000 members who provide the NGO's income. Of these, approximately 15,000 are members of the 200 local groups; but of those, only about 2000 are real activists. As CSOs move into campaigning or international alliances, they must think about the likely impact that this will have on different categories of members, recognizing that the basis for their legitimacy in the eyes of policy-makers is their overall membership, while their ability to achieve change depends more upon their paid lobbyists and activists.

Some networks find that the characteristics of their members vary greatly from country to country. For example, government staff belonging to Public Service International (PSI) unions may be amongst the lowest paid in Organization for Economic Cooperation and Development (OECD) countries, but relatively elite in developing countries. Oxfam International, however, has found that the differences in the profile of supporters at its launch in 1994 have narrowed, largely because the 12 members increasingly use common marketing ideas and consciously seek to become a universally recognized 'brand'.

North–South issues

Though policy-oriented CSOs in Southern and transition countries increasingly look beyond their national frontiers – and therefore welcome opportunities to join TCSNs – they often feel second-class citizens amongst their Northern partners. They feel welcomed as sources of information and legitimization, but not as equals. Vianna (2000) suggests that international campaigns (for instance, on debt, the World Trade Organization, World Bank reform, tropical rainforests and corruption) have established the importance of TCSNs, but the North–South imbalance leads Northern NGOs to emerge as mediators between the global and local levels due to their privileged knowledge of inter-governmental processes. This makes 'the civil society of the rich countries – especially the US – more important politically than that of the poor countries', potentially undermining Southern democratic processes. This is compounded by many NGOs (such as Greenpeace, WWF and Transparency International) setting up Southern or transition-country branches, but retaining decision-making in their headquarters rather than decentralizing. Vianna (2000) calls for better standards of transnational networking, with equality, reciprocity and exchange. This would help Southern CSOs in 'democratizing and strengthening national states'.

Jordan and van Tuijl (2000) develop a similar theme from their perspectives in sympathetic Northern NGOs. They also flag North–South tensions in the control of funding sources, in the failure to address communication and language barriers, and in inadequate grassroots connections. WWF finds that North–South splits occur over issues such as ivory or timber trade. Northern members tend to emphasize species conservation and animal rights, while Southern members emphasize sustainable use and social issues. The Northern partners are generally the grant makers on which Southern CSOs depend, hence easily influence what is discussed and where.

In Brazil, for example, the campaign to reform the World Bank-funded Planafloro project was initially driven by international NGOs with a few national-level Brazilian NGOs. It therefore largely ignored the interests of the indigenous people living in Rondonia. In 1991, local groups formed the Forum of Rondonia's NGOs and Social Movements, which came to play a leadership role in the campaign – shifting it from a largely conservationist focus to a broader thrust, incorporating social needs and promoting a programme of support for community initiatives (PAIC). Some international NGOs resisted this diversion from a Green agenda and dropped out of the international campaign; but most recognize the importance of PAIC's productive projects. Initiatives like this are transforming how CSOs around the world view 'environmentally sustainable development' (Rodrigues, 2000).

In Mexico, Greenpeace, mindful of its internal North–South balance, sided with its Latin American branches in asserting that Mexico's tuna fishing technology no longer posed a threat to dolphins. Southern NGOs welcomed this as a mature stance against 'eco-imperialism', but Greenpeace experienced a backlash in the US when Earth Island Institute (a purely US NGO and Greenpeace competitor) denounced its rival as 'anti-dolphin'. Internal wrangles followed within Greenpeace, the support for Mexican partners was dropped, and Greenpeace USA lost members (Fox, 2000).

North–South imbalances are not all one way, however. The growth of Southern and transition-country memberships can contribute to an elite drift. For example, some African or former Soviet country environmental groups are more academic and capital city-oriented than their Northern counterparts, and have few grassroots supporters. Their voice in TCSN decisions outweighs what would be warranted by dint of membership or scale of activities. For example, about 95 per cent of Amnesty International supporters are from OECD countries; but almost half of the international council delegates are from elsewhere. Northern and Southern or transition-country groups may also have campaigning styles that clash or sit uneasily together. Southern and transition-country NGOs tend to be more radical than their Northern counterparts, and more oriented towards mass protests rather than letter writing or high-level lobbying. This can be complementary, but it can also be a source of tension. Southern and transition-country trade unions have also brought new styles and priorities into international union networks.

An increasing concern amongst Southern and transition-country CSO leaders is the impact that participation in transnational networks has on their sector. Some argue that it provides a global platform for their advocacy and, hence, strengthens their local work. Others worry that it distracts activists from local to (arguably more glamorous) international activities. Self-evidently, many Southern and transition-country CSO leaders spend an increasing proportion of their time at international meetings, and their organizations may shift from a local and practical to an international advocacy focus. Some Southern and transition-country regional and national networks are better known in the North than at home, and may be criticized by local peers as being out of touch. But, without a doubt, participation in transnational networks can greatly strengthen local efforts. For example the work of the Development Initiative for Social and Humanitarian Action (DISHA) in India, analysing government budgets and advocating pro-poor reforms in public expenditure, has been greatly strengthened by its participation in the International Budget Project. Similarly, the Uganda Debt Network has been strengthened through participating in Jubilee 2000. In both cases, the TCSN has provided a global platform, international recognition (thereby elevating their status at home), information (which may be difficult to access locally) and methodological ideas. The benefit is two way: these NGOs have also greatly strengthened the TCSNs.

North–South differences can be macro-political, due to very different analysis of these issues, or micro-political, concerning the governance, culture, and leadership of the network. They can also be meso-political, concerning the structure of civil society. In the North, CSOs tend to be categorized as environmental, human rights, labour or development groups, whereas in most developing countries these distinctions are unclear, and civil society tends to be divided into the categories of membership organizations, social movements and NGOs.

CONCLUSIONS

Working transnationally and entering networks with non-traditional allies are important disciplines for all major CSO categories in order to maximize effectiveness in influencing policy, shaping public opinion and providing imaginative programmes and services. But these are difficult challenges for CSOs. The most pressing policy issues with which they wrestle are horizontal in nature – they spill over national frontiers and demand global remedies. Yet, like governments, their structures are generally vertical and are based on national-level organization and influence. To shift to transnational and horizontal modes of working poses major challenges to established CSOs. Of these, six challenges are of great importance:

- *Adopting the right structure:* there are different models, ranging from the global, unitary organization to the loosest, informal network. Which model is most appropriate depends upon the context and relies upon critical balances between formalizing a global network and retaining flexibility; between global coherence and decentralization; between professionalism and voluntarism; and between forging a permanent alliance and temporary alliances for specific purposes.

- *Adopting bold policies and implementing them:* this requires transnational decision-making that is inclusive (especially of newer, weaker elements) and effective;

leadership that is visionary but alert to all voices in the network; and balancing democracy within the network by ensuring succinct, swift decisions.

- *Ensuring North–South harmony:* true transnational networking demands high standards of ethics and respect, or 'political responsibility'. The division of labour between Northern and Southern or transition-country CSOs needs to be mutually agreed; the former must accept a diminishing role as Southern and transition-country CSOs become more powerful. Northern CSOs must reflect hard on whether what they offer is what Southern or transition-country colleagues want. Drawing them into global activities may divert them from their domestic and regional priorities, and establishing offices in Southern or transition countries can undermine indigenous CSOs.

- *Defeating the barriers of geography:* network leaders must use new technology creatively to help ensure that far-flung voices are effectively engaged in deliberations; they must help to ensure that all CSOs in the network have access to this technology; and they must strive to overcome language barriers. Northern CSOs are often well placed to assist South–South and South–East exchanges.

- *Networking should promote internal as well as external reforms:* as CSOs become more powerful internationally, their own governance deficiencies become Achilles heels. Effective transnational networks should encourage frank debates about standards of ethics and should exist as forums for peer review and self-regulation.

- *Contributing to international democracy:* TCSNs are achieving prominence today because they enable citizens to have a voice in the transnational decisions of governments and corporations. They also strengthen the accountability of inter-governmental organizations and processes. Some argue that they only offer an interim solution – until new institutions of democracy are built for the globalized age. Whether temporary or long term, TCSNs are, in effect, vehicles of democracy and need a greater discipline in order to demonstrate their own democratic credentials and transnational support base. This is easier for networks that contain unions and other mass-membership CSOs when they can demonstrate that they have consulted their members responsibly in developing their advocacy positions.

The following chapters illustrate how these issues are perceived, addressed or ignored within a range of important transnational civil society networks.

NOTES

1   Particularly, Oxfam International (OI); Amnesty International (AI); Friends of the Earth (FOE); the World Wide Fund for Nature (WWF); the Lutheran World Federation; the International Council of Voluntary Agencies; Jubilee 2000; Participatory Research in Asia (PRIA, India); the Latin American Association of Popular Organizations (ALOP, based in Ecuador); the Caucus of Development NGOs (CODE-NGO, The Philippines); the International Confederation of Free Trade Unions (ICFTU); Public Service International (PSI); Education International; Union

Network International; the United Religions Initiative; and the World Council of Churches (WCC); as well as participants in an international seminar on Transnational Civic Society: Issues of Governance and Organization, London School of Economics, June 2001.

2   We use the term 'network' broadly to include federated organizations such as Amnesty International, formal networks such as Friends of the Earth International, informal networks such as Jubilee 2000 and even looser CSO groupings that are the mobilizing agents within common social movements.

3   Some aspects of network analysis and new approaches in organizational population ecology are clearly relevant.

4   'Southern' refers to developing countries; 'transition' to the countries of the former Eastern bloc.

5   Manuel Chiriboga's presentation to the international seminar on Transnational Civil Society: Issues of Governance and Organization, London School of Economics, June 2001.

6   See endnote 1.

Chapter 2

Consumers Unite Internationally

Tasneem Mowjee

This chapter focuses on the international consumer movement – in particular, Consumers International (CI), founded in 1960 as the International Organization of Consumers Unions (IOCU).[1] CI is an independent non-profit organization that isn't aligned with, or supported by, any political party or industry. It supports, links and represents consumer groups and agencies, and is funded by fees from member organizations and grants from foundations, governments and multilateral agencies. In autumn 2000, CI had a membership of 263 consumer organizations in 119 countries.

This chapter starts with a brief history of consumer groups until the IOCU's establishment, and then describes CI's main objectives, as well as its structure and governance, including a discussion of membership issues, such as North–South tensions, and legitimacy questions. It then examines the impact of globalization and information and communications technology (ICT) on CI and its external relationships, particularly with businesses, and concludes with some thoughts on CI's future developments.

HISTORY[2]

Although the IOCU was established in 1960, the consumer movement dates back to the formation of the US Consumers Union (CU) by Colston Warne in 1936 to test products and provide consumers with sound and unbiased information in order to inform their choice. It produced *Consumer Reports*, a magazine that promoted the concept of independent testing and provided consumers with information. By 1957, its circulation had grown to 800,000.

As the magazine found its way overseas, people became interested in setting up similar consumer groups elsewhere. The Consumers Association (CA – first known as the Association for Consumer Research) was established in the UK in 1956 with the active involvement of Lord Young. Its magazine *Which?* was first published in October 1957. By 1959 there were three other consumer groups in Europe – in The Netherlands, Belgium and France. The Australian Consumers Association was started the following year.

Sim (1991) attributes this growth in Western consumer organizations to two factors. Firstly, by the 1950s, mass production and greater affluence had created a consumer society that urgently wanted objective and useful product information. A CA interviewee agreed that while businesses were the first to spot global opportunities in the post-war years, the consumer movement was not far behind. Secondly was the 'near missionary zeal of the early pioneers of the consumer movement' (Sim, 1991: 3). Although the groups had little or no capital (depending upon donations or loans from well-wishers), and were vulnerable to attacks from manufacturers over their product ratings, they persisted and even provided support to new consumer organizations in other countries. In 1952, CU established a grants programme focusing mainly on consumer protection efforts in the US, but also helped small groups abroad.

In early 1958, Elizabeth Schadee, member and then chair of the board of the Dutch consumer organization, met with Caspar Brook, the first president of the UK Consumers Association, to discuss joint product testing and how this would save the organizations money and enable them to present a united front in the face of potential corporate attacks. They realized that other consumer groups might want to cooperate and formulated the idea of an international association. The first step was a conference, in 1960, on product testing for consumers that was attended by 34 people from 17 organizations in 14 countries. The conference established an international technical exchange committee to supervise joint testing of products, such as small cars and watches, and founded the IOCU, with a secretariat in The Hague, whose functions were to:

- undertake comparative testing of consumer products;
- act as a clearing house for information on test programmes and results;
- regulate the use of ratings and reprint materials of member organizations;
- organize international meetings to promote consumer testing; and
- improve communication between member groups, especially via the *IOCU Bulletin.*

The IOCU's name was formally changed to Consumers International in 1994 (although the old name continued to be used for about three years in order to maintain continuity). There were two main reasons for this change. Firstly, many considered IOCU a somewhat old-fashioned and cumbersome name and thought a better one was needed for the 1990s. Secondly, as its membership grew, members increasingly felt that the name associated it with trade unions – an inaccurate representation of its work.

OBJECTIVES

Today, CI's stated goal is to promote a fairer society by defending the rights of all consumers, including poor, marginalized and disadvantaged people, by:

- supporting and strengthening member organizations and the consumer movement in general; and
- campaigning at the international level for policies that respect consumer concerns.

This section provides an overview of the development of these two objectives.

Supporting the development of consumer organizations

The early IOCU members attached great importance to supporting the development of consumer organizations. At its third congress in Oslo in 1964, prompted by a CA representative, delegates became concerned about Southern consumers. The congress's 'Statement of General Aims' called upon consumer groups in developed countries not to overlook the needs of consumers in developing countries. The congress also adopted various resolutions that led to the establishment of a working group and fund in order to promote and support Southern consumer organizations.[3]

Support for Southern consumer organizations was strengthened when Anwar Fazal, director of the IOCU's first Regional Office for Asia and the Pacific (ROAP), became IOCU's president. He is credited with transforming the IOCU from a self-help collective to an outward-looking organization concerned with promoting the consumer movement. Hence, for example, although sharing research on product testing was one of the IOCU's main functions when it was set up, it has not conducted any work on this for 25 years.[4]

Currently, one reason for CI's promotion of Southern consumer groups is its belief that strong national groups and effective international advocacy go together. In other words, the organization sees its two objectives as closely linked: CI needs strong national organizations to inform global policy and advocacy. In the case of a recent study on trade issues, it drew on various national studies of the impact on consumers of World Trade Organization (WTO) agreements on agriculture and services. CI also acknowledges that many decisions affecting all countries are not taken by national governments individually but internationally. It tries, therefore, to influence international decisions affecting consumers by promoting national consumer organizations, which can lobby their governments when they are participating in international decision-making. Furthermore, the power of strong national consumer organizations, apart from promoting the rights and interests of domestic consumers, is being able to participate directly in international negotiations.

The support for Southern consumer groups provided by the IOCU's original members is still continuing. According to CI's director-general, the larger and wealthier Northern consumer organizations do not join CI to buy value-for-money services but to express commitment to the global consumer movement. For example, the UK CA's underlying philosophy is that proceeds from its magazine should be spent on supporting the consumer interest, generally, in the UK or on its general advocacy. Therefore, its membership of CI is part of its wider support for the consumer movement. Other members have expressed their support for Southern consumer groups more directly. CU in the US and Consumentenbond in Holland have set up trust funds to support Southern consumer groups directly. However, during the last decade there has been a shift away from replicating Western-style consumer groups who chiefly undertake publishing work – now not seen as a Southern priority – and towards greater support for community-based work.

International protection and representation[5]

CI has, thus, been committed to the protection of Southern consumer interests from its earliest days. In 1968, it amended its constitution (see below) and revised its objectives with a key aim of representing consumer interests at the international level, primarily at the United Nations (UN). This undoubtedly resulted from the IOCU having received consultative status with the UN Economic and Social Council in 1963. One early reason for seeking UN links was that the IOCU thought that Southern consumer groups weren't strong enough to undertake effective representation on their own. The UN's development objectives broadly coincided with the IOCU's objectives, and the IOCU believed that the UN had the resources, influence and global reach to promote consumer interests widely. The IOCU's first representative at the UN, Persia Campbell, was an eminent economist as well as a consumer advocate. She put forward the consumer position on a wide range of issues, from free trade and the problems caused by multinational corporations to product standards. One early success of the IOCU's advocacy work was the inclusion of consumer concerns in the UN's *Declaration on Social Progress and Development*.

During the early 1980s, following a global lobbying effort by CI members, the UN General Assembly (UN-GA) mandated the creation of a UN List of Products Banned, Withdrawn or Severely Restricted by Governments. At the time, it was extremely difficult to find out what pesticides, pharmaceuticals and products were banned in Northern countries for safety reasons. Multinational corporations took advantage of this by 'dumping' such products in developing country markets. The UN list was then used by consumer groups to remove hazardous products from sale in countries such as Korea, Ecuador, Brazil and Mexico. In a number of countries, it also helped to create systems for regulating hazardous products.[6] In April 1985, following ten years of persistent interventions by IOCU representatives, the UN-GA adopted the most significant UN document on consumer protection, the *UN Guidelines on Consumer Protection*. This was despite fierce opposition from international corporations and even some industrialized countries, such as the US.

With the UN guidelines as a starting point, CI has developed Model Consumer Protection Laws in Latin America, the South Pacific and Africa. The need for consumer laws is now recognized globally. Promoted by national consumer groups and CI's regional offices, these model laws have been used as the basis for national legislation in many countries. Most recently, several countries in Africa and Latin America have introduced legislation following stakeholder meetings promoted by CI.[7]

CI's current director-general noted that it would be impossible to get the UN to adopt statements like the UN guidelines now, but that these documents established the foundation for CI's campaigning during the 1990s.

In addition to the UN guidelines, CI's work is guided by the Bill of Consumers' Rights. This emerged due to the political lobbying of US President Kennedy. The president then made a historic speech to the US Congress on 15 March 1962. He argued that consumer rights were not distinct from human rights and listed four basic rights. Subsequently, the consumer movement, after internal debate, added four more. Together, these are the rights to:

- satisfaction of basic needs;
- safety and protection against hazardous products and processes;
- be informed and make informed choices;
- choose between a variety of products and services;
- be heard in the making and execution of policies;
- fair settlement of just claims;
- consumer education in order to acquire skills and knowledge to become an informed and responsible consumer; and
- live in a healthy and sustainable environment.

In particular, the first and last of these emerged from Southern concerns and reflected a widening of the consumer agenda. The Bill of Consumer Rights is different from the UN guidelines in that it has not been validated externally – it is not something to which governments have agreed. However, it acts as an implicit backdrop to the guidelines, addressing what governments need to do to ensure that consumers enjoy these rights.

Although CI's two main objectives have not changed significantly in recent years, there have been changes in the specific issues that it addresses and in its policy positions, largely due to changes in trade rules. For example, CI's stance on trade negotiations emphasized trade liberalization during the 1960s and 1970s, when it was heavily dominated by a small number of US and European organizations. But CI is now far more cautious about liberalization and it seeks to ensure that it is in the consumer's interest. This shift has been difficult for some members whose national consumers perceive it as a restraint on the open market.

STRUCTURE AND GOVERNANCE

Most CI members are independent non-governmental organizations (NGOs). About a quarter are from government agencies, standards bodies and other public interest groups involved in consumer affairs. CI has three types of members: full, affiliate and government affiliate. Both full and affiliate members must act exclusively on behalf of the interests of the consumer and be unconcerned with commercial activities. A full member, however, must meet additional criteria. It must not:

- be connected in any way with commercial or trading ventures;
- advance party political causes;
- accept advertisements in its publications;
- be profit-making; and
- be influenced or restricted by any subsidies that it receives.

A government affiliate is a government department, regulatory authority or anti-trust agency, which is part of a government's machinery. It must support and complement independent CI members, be active on behalf of consumer interests and be unconcerned with the advancement of commercial activities.

CI has a democratic structure in that full members have voting rights. These rights are exercised for two principal purposes. One is to endorse, amend or add issues to CI's strategic policy statement. This statement, covering a wide range of issues, is made at the World Congress, a three-yearly meeting of all CI members. The other purpose is to elect the council, CI's governing body, also during the World Congress. The council was, at the outset, the IOCU's sole governing body and not elected by the general membership; but in 1968 the constitution was changed. Although the council remained the governing body and IOCU founding members retained the right to be represented on it, the majority of its members would now be elected by a general assembly, comprising IOCU's voting members. Thus, the balance of authority shifted from the council to the voting members. The general assembly also elects the president during the congress and adopts resolutions. The council meets once a year and, in turn, appoints an eight-member executive committee, which meets every six months. The executive plays a very direct role in policy development, selecting external partners and strategic planning. The secretariat submits work plans to each executive meeting. CI's president also plays an active role in supervising and directing the organization.

Once the executive has set the strategic direction, CI's staff worldwide are responsible for implementing programmes. But the membership is also directly and actively involved. Most CI delegations to international meetings comprise members, either partly or entirely. So, both staff and members undertake its advocacy work. Members are also engaged in campaigns and advocacy work with their own governments. Finally, externally funded CI programmes all involve some member participation.

As highlighted in Table 2.1, CI has established regional offices for Asia/Pacific (ROAP), Latin America and Africa, and an office for developed and transition economy countries. From its inception, ROAP has undertaken a wide range of innovative activities and coordinated global campaigns on the export of hazardous products and pharmaceuticals. Sim (1991) attributes its success to two main factors:

Table 2.1 *Key dates in the development of IOCU/Consumers International*

1960	International Organization of Consumer Unions founded; secretariat in The Hague
1974	Regional Office for Asia and the Pacific (ROAP) established in Singapore; later moved to Penang
1986	Regional Office for Latin America established in Montevideo
1989	Head Office and Regional Office for Europe/North America established in The Hague
1992	Regional Office for Latin America relocated to Santiago
1993	Head Office and Regional Office for Europe/North America relocated in London
1994	Name change from IOCU to CI formally approved Regional Office for Africa established in Harare, and Programme for West and Central Africa in Dakar
1999	Creation of Office for Developed and Transition Economies in London
2000	ROAP relocated to Kuala Lumpur

Source: adapted from CI's website: www.consumersinternational.org

- support (in the form of human resources, as well as testing) from several IOCU members; and
- significant income from development aid.

A CA interviewee also attributed its success to the vision and activities of its first regional director, Anwar Fazal.

All regions are represented on both the council and executive committee. CI has about 75 staff members around the world reporting to the council and executive through the director-general. The bulk of CI's staff are based in the regional offices, since these are pivotal to the various CI priorities and enable CI to stay in touch with its members. For example, each office has a team who works on the trade agenda. At a practical level, the team is better equipped to deal with members in local languages and enables CI to adjust to the cultural, economic and philosophical differences in approaches in different parts of the world. CI has a directors' team, comprising the regional directors, who must collectively agree on CI's strategy.

Income

When the IOCU was founded in 1960, it had a budget of UK£5000, with CU providing UK£2000 and the other four members of the original council each contributing 1 per cent of their budgets. Other members paid UK£50 each. Today, CI has an annual turnover of approximately UK£3 million. About one third of this comes from fees, as members contribute a percentage of their income. The rest comprises grants from governments, multilateral agencies, NGOs, trusts and foundations. This represents a considerable change in income sources. About six years ago, the proportions were the reverse, with two-thirds of income from members. According to the director-general, this is merely a reflection of 'the reality that the growth in the consumer movement has come from new and small organizations' so that CI has needed to find other sources of funding.

MEMBERSHIP: NORTH–SOUTH RELATIONS

CI has seen an explosive growth in its membership during the last 15 years, from about 110–115 to around 260 members. As mentioned, CI's work is very much driven by members – based on building consensus on policy issues across a wide spectrum of views from different countries. CI sees itself as operating differently from most international NGOs because of this. It believes that this is positive and adds to CI's authority. However, it also means that the organization is 'much less light on its feet'. One member, the UK CA, acknowledges that it is not easy for CI to operate by consensus. Many new members are small and lack resources, although they are perceived as highly relevant. While CI is clearly keen on providing forums for members to provide input, it is difficult for it to respond to the many diverse issues that members raise. Furthermore, there is sometimes a tension between the need to 'do deals' in international negotiations and to stay within the mandate from members. This is not difficult in areas such as standard making. Here there is an established cycle of meetings, it is clear what will be discussed, and papers can be circulated in advance. But in other situations, issues surface on the agenda more quickly and, in the middle of negotiations, CI representatives may have to come back and check the position with the president. There is a trade-off between being more responsive and speaking with the force of CI membership. This generates tension between members who want CI to be 'out there, making statements' and those who want the secretariat to check all positions with them. Therefore, when the US president announced the imposition of high tariffs on imported steel early in 2002, although the matter was fairly straightforward, CI had to be very careful not to make a strong statement without referring back to its members because it did not have an existing policy on the issue.

The difficulty of this balancing act has led the CI secretariat to be criticized for excessive emphasis on consensus building. The head of one CI member argued that, like a good conductor, CI should be able to bring forward divergent, heterogeneous viewpoints, but also be bold enough to refrain from taking a position on an issue where there is no consensus. He maintained that CI's inability to provide leadership and convey the diversity of members' views with clarity and cogency had weakened members' ability to come together on the WTO issue. However, this may also be because the WTO and international issues are not a priority for all members. Certainly, the Consumers Association of Penang (CAP) claimed that it was not active in CI since its focus was on national issues, not the international matters on which CI works. But trade is a small part of the agenda of even some large members such as the CA.

North–South relations

The substantial increase in CI's membership has largely comprised small groups from developing and transition countries, leading to some changes in the nature of the network. According to CI's director-general, the parallel availability of technology has allowed for a policy-making process that includes the views of Southern members on global issues such as trade, with the result that CI's position is not dominated by Northern members and that some policy positions have been changed. Furthermore, CI has deliberately adopted a strategy of bringing Northern and Southern members together to influence global institutions, increasing its authority and leading to a cultural shift in the consumer movement's representation.

CI members, like the UK's CA, believe that larger members do not have a disproportionate influence. They argue that, for example, the general statement made at CI's last World Congress in South Africa in 2000 was genuinely democratically discussed and 'embodies some good values'. However, others acknowledge a tension in the relationship between members from developed, developing and transition countries. One reason for this is that the IOCU's original constitution provided for permanent seats for the five founding members on the executive committee (rather like the UN's Security Council). Although these members have relinquished this privilege, Southern members believe that they will always, in practice, dominate the executive committee. This contributes to a sense of inferiority amongst Southern members, while also potentially reducing the level of fresh blood and ideas within the committee.

Also, as CI's director-general pointed out, using the example of the bill of eight consumer rights, while Organization for Economic Cooperation and Development (OECD) countries pursue the 'choice' agenda, in developing countries 'the emphasis is very, very strongly on access to basic needs'. Many of these organizations deliberately choose not to work on the issues that affect the mass consumer. So, there is a clear difference in the focus of these groups, both economically and socially. Even when groups from both sets of countries work on the same issue, there may be different emphases. For example, while food has always been on CI's agenda, in many developing countries, food security and access is more important than safety. The head of the Consumer Unity and Trust Society (CUTS), a Southern member of CI, supported this, arguing that the main task of Northern groups, particularly in the US, is to promote consumption – hence, 4 million copies of *Consumer Reports* are sold every year. Until recently, Northern members were largely unaware of the issues of importance to the South.

Another problem is the different access to resources and ICT in the North and South. One interviewee argued that, realistically, Southern members can contribute little in fees. While Northern groups get their revenue from the sale of magazines, Southern groups obtain their income mainly from donations (with little coming from members). Since CI members are not allowed to take advertising from businesses in their magazines, to avoid compromising their independent position, income sources for Southern consumer groups are further restricted (although some – for example, in India – survive on advertising from public-owned companies). Nevertheless, as discussed below, CI gains its credibility as a global federation because of widespread Southern membership.

Despite these obvious differences, CI members from the North and South have maintained that, on trade issues at least, the main division in CI is between reformist and radical organizations, rather than between groups from North and South. Hence, at least two Southern members, CAP and CUTS, take very different approaches on trade globalization. This is discussed further in the section on the impact of globalization.

LEGITIMACY

All interviewees agreed that CI's legitimacy and authority to speak on consumer issues came, first and foremost, from the diversity of its membership. A CA staff member noted that CI is connected to 'a huge number of grassroots organizations'. It can play an important role in representing these groups internationally because 'governments are craving grassroots participation', although they then make this difficult by holding international meetings in places such as Rome and Geneva, which are difficult for small groups to access. Despite the large numbers, though, CI has maintained strict governance rules for member organizations (regarding sources of income, for example). Members such as CA believe that this further strengthens CI's reputation as a legitimate organization.

Furthermore, the CI secretariat believes that the extensive participation of members in its policy-formulation, advocacy and decision-making gives it a stronger claim to legitimacy than many other NGOs. In addition, CI's ability to convene groups with a common agenda, cutting across geography, economics and social development – through its consensus approach – means that it is able to project a coherent message, ensuring that the voices of consumers are heard.

CI is also the only international body representing consumer interests. As the head of CUTS pointed out, while there are a number of global bodies such as the World Wide Fund for Nature (WWF) and Friends of the Earth (FOE) in the environment movement, there are no challengers of CI in the global consumer movement.

THE IMPACT OF GLOBALIZATION AND ICT

> *The 1980s are...a period during which the movement has become really global, being able to give an effective multinational response to multinational issues (speech by Anwar Fazal, president of the IOCU, at the 29th Annual Conference of the American Council of Consumer Interests, Kansas City, 16–19 March 1983; cited in Sim, 1991).*

Although interviewees did not believe that globalization was a new phenomenon, they acknowledged that the development of the WTO during the 1990s had raised new issues for the consumer movement. CI's director-general argued that the trade agenda 'spills over into everything', including traditional CI issues such as food safety standards. Therefore, CI has to re-examine these 'because the [WTO] rules now impinge on any kind of regulation that national governments introduce. So, an overarching theme has emerged which, ten years ago, wasn't there in the same way, affecting practical things like international standards.' Some of the new issues emerging include e-commerce and genetically modified organisms (GMOs).

It is also interesting that some of the tension between members described earlier stems from the difference in viewpoints regarding the WTO. As the head of one CI member pointed out, there is no debate or controversy about promoting the basic needs of consumers or their right to be represented at international levels. However, it is different with economic issues. As noted above, two CI Southern members have very different perceptions of the implications of trade liberalization. The head of CUTS maintains that globalization itself is not new but something that is inevitable, so 'we need to make the best of it' rather than adopting a 'futile' anti-globalization stance. Therefore, CUTS has worked to better inform other organizations about the issue and advocate government responsibility for domestic policies. For example, it has produced a booklet on the *Myths and Realities of Globalisation* and provided seminars and training to other consumer organizations, NGOs, the media and academia. CAP, on the other hand, believes that trade liberalization has proved to be nothing but problematic in Malaysia. According to a senior staff member, it has resulted in the promotion of excessive consumption and a credit culture through advertising and the development of shopping malls. CAP perceives the growing dependence on credit as a serious problem that is imbedding itself within Malaysian culture.

Although interviewees did not see globalization as a new phenomenon, as reflected in Anwar Fazal's speech, CI feels that the consumer movement itself has become global. A staff member argued that 'because of the word "consumer"', the movement is perceived as Northern. However, CI has always believed that it is important that the consumer voice is heard in countries where citizen voice is problematic; hence, it promotes measures to improve democracy through participation. CI's structure of regional offices also reflects the global nature of the movement. For example, the Latin American consumer movement initiated the development of CI's Latin America office, without intervention by the North. Another example of how consumer issues have become global is the current development of consumer protection legislation in several African countries where such legislation never previously existed. This has emerged partly due to CI's work on the issue and partly because the governments concerned recognize that it is an important part of the legal framework for market economies and for development. Thus, the need to protect consumer rights has become accepted far beyond Northern consumers' rights to exercise personal choice.

In addition to geographical growth, there has been a change in the nature of consumer organizations. Some, particularly in the North, are increasingly concerned with ethical issues, leading to a change in emphasis, and some are now more activist in their approach, partly because of the influence of Southern members. Unlike Northern consumer groups, these were not set up as information providers and sellers of consumer services but grew out of community action, with a focus on basic rights and opportunities. As a result, they tend to be activist.

However, some Northern members have also become more activist in their market interventions. The UK CA is a good example. In the past, it relied largely on influencing the market-place by providing information to consumers in order to inform their individual choices (although it also worked with the government on regulation). Recently, though, it has undertaken more direct action on car prices, introduced its own credit card and become a very successful internet service provider. Similarly, Belgian consumer groups have launched their own home insurance services, resulting from a research project that concluded that consumers don't have adequate policies available to them. They then wrote a set of criteria for what a policy should cover and wrote to insurance companies to ask if they were prepared to offer such a policy at a good price. They now actively promote these policies. Such actions are a way of using the power of membership to launch a market-leading product that will influence the way in which the market operates. According to a CA staff member, this is a necessary shift in its mode of operation, not only to ensure that the organization remains relevant to members, but because the previous tools for influencing the market no longer work. In addition, the organization has realized that it was punching below its weight in bringing about changes that are beneficial to consumers. The success of its campaign on car prices showed that it is more powerful than it thought.

Despite such successes, there is a sense, within CA at least, that NGOs are not always influential on international trade issues. According to one interviewee, they may have been emboldened by the perception of their success at the WTO ministerial negotiations in Seattle, however this is an illusion and Seattle was not the watershed that people assume.

Another change affecting the way in which CI works has been the advent ICT. Most interviewees believed that cheaper communication made networking easier. A CA staff member felt that consumer groups would be genuinely empowered as the cost of global communication fell sharply. The CI director-general stated that he would 'subscribe to the view that technology has transformed the way that NGOs operate [and] engage in advocacy', and influence international decision-making. As noted above, CI has a consensus-building approach to decision-making. Therefore, it has found the use of discussion listservs, the first of which was started at the end of 2001, very helpful because they speed up the process and make it more transparent, since everyone can see what has been said. It is also more efficient to distribute documents electronically because the method is quicker and more reliable than the post.

However, there have been some difficulties with new technology. Firstly, there are barriers to access. Initially, there was a danger that only some Northern members would be able to use the technology; but CI has been very careful to ensure that all members have access before making extensive use of it (this includes a programme in Africa to equip all member organizations with ICT). Still, it is extremely expensive to access the internet in Africa, and there are places where the electricity supply frequently breaks down. Secondly, language is a difficult problem to overcome, particularly when dealing with lengthy documents. Thirdly, it is difficult to cope with the volume of information. CI staff accepted that information overload in international advocacy is not a new problem, especially in areas such as food standards where there has traditionally been much consultation. However, the amount of correspondence generated through the use of ICT is greater as people tend to contribute more than before. Finally, ICT makes it possible for people with strong views to disrupt the process of consultation and discussion with aggressive and often 'rather futile interventions' that 'put other people off' and allow them to dominate the debate. Despite these difficulties, most CI members have strongly supported the use of ICT. Therefore, CI is considering increasing its use of ICT and providing a members-only area on the website.

Not all CI members are equally enthusiastic about ICT, however. For example, although CAP has a website, it is not very active. It uses the internet largely to download publications and information from other websites. CAP believes that 'there is too much hype about ICT. There is an illusion that change and transformation can be brought about through ICT and without mobilizing human beings.' While ICT has made it is easier to contact people around Malaysia in order to give initial information and for national campaigns, CAP has found that personal visits and discussions are crucial for mobilization.

NETWORKING AND PARTNERSHIP

CI has built partnerships with organizations outside of its structure 'on a pragmatic and flexible basis' when it believes that there is a common agenda, that will further the cause, and especially if it feels 'comfortable' with the organizations. Often, these partnerships or alliances are built on an ad-hoc basis – for example, at WTO ministerial meetings when groups tend to devise propositions and events that are designed to get press attention. CI often has to decide whether to join or not, and whether this would be consistent with its policy. Such alliances are, by their nature, short term and temporary. On a longer-term basis, CI works with groups such as the UK Trade Network, comprising highly influential NGOs, in order to keep up to date on various issues. Another example where CI has tried to build a coalition with other NGOs, business and academics is the World Economic Forum's agricultural task force.

CI builds alliances and coalitions because, individually, civil society organizations (CSOs) are limited in their effectiveness at the international level. Like other CSOs, it constantly thinks about how to use alliances more effectively and to which alliances it should formally commit itself, recognizing, from experience, that wide-ranging NGO caucuses are difficult to maintain. As the director-general jokingly pointed out, it is sometimes difficult enough to build consensus within CI's own membership! Therefore, CI has generally felt more comfortable in associations where there are specific objectives, such as Jubilee 2000. CI's overall strategy is to make selective agreements with organizations whom it knows and who have sufficient authority and resources to have an impact.

In addition to joining alliances and coalitions, the organization has fostered the development of specialist networks that are now well-known international organizations in their own right. These are:

- the International Baby Foods Action Network (IBFAN), established in October 1979 in Geneva in response to concerns about the promotion of infant formula in developing countries;
- Health Action International (HAI), formed in May 1981 in Geneva to campaign for safe, affordable medicines following the IOCU's early work on the drug clioquinol, which was found to have serious side effects; and
- the Pesticides Action Network, set up in June 1982 in Penang 'to halt the worldwide proliferation of hazardous chemical pesticides' (Sim 1991: 116).

Hosting what one interviewee described as 'a whole wave of citizens' movements' was a critical aspect of the IOCU's work at the time. This is because they enabled IOCU to move away from being an inward-looking organization, concerned with meeting members' needs, to one linking consumer interests to a far larger agenda for creating a better world. As the interviewee pointed out, there was a quantum leap in the concept of a consumer from that of 'user' to 'maker' – one who shapes the world through the things they buy or use or, perhaps more importantly, through the things they don't buy or use. With the accompanying widening of the concept of consumer protection to encompass a struggle for human rights and development justice, the IOCU accepted a leadership role on a whole range of issues, including environment and health. While many other NGOs were single-issue organizations, the IOCU had a more holistic agenda and, through these networks, could convene a wide range of groups. However, as the networks grew and the IOCU chose to focus more on its own growing agenda, it encouraged them to become independent. Recently, these networks have represented CI in some campaigns, where the organizations involved work very specifically on a particular issue. For example, HAI has been active in the campaign for reducing the price of HIV/AIDS drugs in developing countries, and HAI and IBFAN have represented CI at the World Health Organization (WHO).

Apart from other CSOs, CI has various dealings with business organizations since they have a strong voice on all of the issues on which CI works. Occasionally, it debates policy issues with businesses, particularly in international forums such as the World Business Council for Sustainable Development, which sends representatives to the same international meetings as CI. Sometimes, on issues such as agreements on the regulatory framework for electronic commerce, CI may agree with the business community on what is appropriate. In some cases, CI operates in parallel with the business world. For example, it has a secretariat for the Trans-Atlantic Consumer Dialogue, set up to parallel the Trans-Atlantic Business Dialogue that puts policy propositions to the US and the European Union (EU).

The Consumer Dialogue ensures that the consumer viewpoint is also conveyed on trade and regulatory issues and in the discussions in which businesses are engaging. But CI is also wary of business organizations, seeing them as predominantly self-interested, not interested in the public welfare and usually approaching issues from an opposite perspective. CI is very cautious about financial associations, in particular, as it is conscious of a history of CSOs being variously coopted by the business community.

CI members also have a range of relationships with the business community. For example, CUTS has engaged with chambers of commerce – such as the Federation of Indian Chambers of Commerce and the International Chamber of Commerce in Paris – on policy issues. It also has a seat on the National Advisory Committee on International Trade at the Indian Ministry of Commerce. Here, CUTS often has common positions with business organizations, particularly regarding the WTO. While the Indian government is often opposed to new WTO-related proposals, CUTS and the business community have a different view. Despite such common positions, relations with the business community can be frustrating for CUTS because it has more radical ideas and is prepared to annoy the ministry of commerce (which business federations avoid).

Other Southern consumer groups have had a far more antagonistic relationship with companies. Two CA interviewees highlighted the fact that these groups operate in a far more difficult and dangerous environment than Northern groups. Not only can they face intimidation and the threat of imprisonment due to their activities, but those exposing the illegal or dangerous activities of companies also risk their lives. They gave the example of Thai consumer activists who were machine-gunned when they uncovered the sale of unregulated pharmaceuticals in Phuket. It is not surprising, therefore, if such groups are far more suspicious of, and hostile to, business.

CA itself has a broader range of relationships with commercial organizations. On the one hand, it has worked with them to provide special deals and specific e-commerce services – while many CI members regarded such commercial activities with horror, some have adopted them. On the other hand, CA has been active to prevent anti-competitive behaviour. In this, some businesses have shared its position on the restrictions of business activities. Although these two sets of activities make CA appear schizophrenic regarding business organizations, one staff member argued that it has to both engage with and criticize them. He maintained that CA's focus is on the outcome that it can achieve through a particular relationship rather than on adopting a particular posture.

CONCLUSION: FUTURE DEVELOPMENTS

With its widespread membership and its active representation of the consumer voice at an international level, CI is an influential organization. According to one CA staff member who was a council member a few years ago, CI has been the most influential neutral NGO on a range of issues, such as the marketing of baby milk, UN Conference on Trade and Development (UNCTAD) rules of restrictive business practices and the UN's Codex Alimentarius. Its regional structure enables it to be responsive to local situations, while forming the basis for international advocacy. Interviewees from CI member organizations felt that the World Congresses provide a valuable opportunity for the consumer movement to come together and debate critical issues. Although its consensus-building approach has been criticized and it is clearly difficult for the secretariat to balance the opposing views of members on controversial issues such as the WTO, the secretariat is committed to this approach because of the authority it lends CI when it does make statements.

According to CI's director-general, the organization is likely to see two main developments in the future. One will be a bolder stance in international campaigning. This will involve making more substantial use of national members since CI has already done the necessary capacity-building work with these organizations. The second will be to seek a higher profile in the way that it campaigns – in particular, by building new but carefully selected alliances on important issues. Although some members believe that CI can play a decisive role because of its uniqueness, the secretariat believes that, acting alone, its influence on the world is marginal. Finally, CI will also be exploring how to make greater use of technology to promote its campaigning.

NOTES

1   The name change from IOCU to Consumers International was formally approved in 1994. Therefore, when referring specifically to the work of the organization prior to 1994, this chapter refers to it as the IOCU.
2   This section is based on Sim (1991).
3   Based on Sim (1991).
4   According to a CA interviewee, the IOCU undertook testing because this was what all its founding members did, and this was assumed to be the appropriate model for an international consumer organization. However, it was recognized quite early on that markets are very different, particularly in developing countries; so, it is neither cost-effective nor useful for a worldwide federation of consumer groups to undertake testing. Instead, there was agreement amongst members that the IOCU's unique selling point was its ability to focus on overarching issues and to support forums that bring members together. Therefore, testing work is now carried out by a separate organization, International Consumer Research and Testing (ICRT), based in London. Although many of CI's members belong to this as well, according to CI's director-general, this is for 'hard-nosed' commercial reasons. They pay a membership fee to ICRT and participate in it in order to save money through the sharing of test results amongst a lot of countries.
5   The historical description of the IOCU's relationship with the UN is drawn from Sim (1991).
6   Based on information on CI's website: www.consumersinternational.org.
7   Described on CI's website: www.consumersinternational.org.

Chapter 3

Trade Unions in a Changing World: Challenges and Opportunities of Transnationalization

Diego Muro and Nuno Themudo

The world's trade union movement is now in the greatest fight of its life. We are in a struggle against a globalization that has no place for the principles, values and standards we have fought for and established over the last 200 years... Our job is to become...more effective players in globalization. We must challenge its ideology, fight for democratic governance of the global economy and curb the power and greed of multinationals (Bill Jordan, ICFTU general secretary, 2000).

Trade unions live in contradictory times. Alongside other movements, trade unions have been effective in raising awareness about 'unfair globalization' (Tarrow, 2002). At the same time, the World Bank and other international institutions are opening up to lobbying by unions since they are important civil society actors representing the interests of a large membership (O'Brien et al, 2000). Yet, this increased international prominence coincides with declining membership in most industrialized countries. Aware of this downward trend, many leaders in the trade union movement have urged restructuring it in order to consolidate its current political clout and reverse membership decline. This chapter explores current challenges facing the union movement, with an emphasis on challenges brought about by accelerating globalization. Partly as a consequence of 'globalization', unions are increasingly experiencing a need to transnationalize the movement, which in turn brings about challenges and opportunities. In particular, this chapter focuses on the Millennium Review, managed by the International Confederation of Free Trade Unions (ICFTU), as a strategic effort to deal with those challenges and, therefore, to become a stronger player in an emerging system of global governance.

A CHANGING WORLD AND
THE TRANSNATIONALIZATION CHALLENGE

Trade union membership has been in decline for approximately 30 years. A recent study of the International Labour Organization (ILO) points out that during these years union membership has suffered a decline of 35.9 per cent in Central and Eastern Europe, 19.4 per cent in Oceania, 19.0 per cent in Central America and 15.6 per cent in Western Europe (Gordon and Turner, 2000: 5). The decline is particularly acute in Organization for Economic Cooperation and Development (OECD) countries, who have experienced the sharpest fall. In four G7 countries (US, UK, Japan and Germany) union membership has fallen 30 per cent since 1980 (ICFTU, 2001). Figure 3.1 plots the recent decline in the UK. Similarly, strike action has been falling in the same period, as shown in Figure 3.2.

The situation is dramatic compared to unions' 'golden age' in the aftermath of World War II. In the post-war settlement, unions were key players in the compromise between labour and capital that drove economic growth and social improvement. By the 1950s and 1960s, the unions of Europe, North America and the Pacific region represented between one third and two-thirds of all workers (Western, 1997: 143).

However, since the 1970s various factors have weakened unionism, which has often translated into worsening conditions for workers worldwide. US research, for example, shows that de-unionization means lower wages (Rifkin, 1995: 168).

The causes for weakening unionization include at least five factors. Firstly, increased competition worldwide forced OECD countries to reorganize production from manufacturing (with strong unionism) to services (with weak unionism). Privatization also contributed to a decline in membership (Western, 1997). In the UK, for example, 60 per cent of public-sector workers are unionized, but just 19 per cent in the private sector.

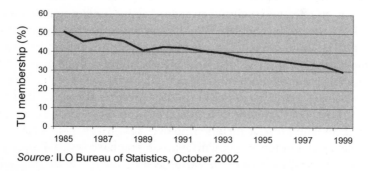

Source: ILO Bureau of Statistics, October 2002

Figure 3.1 *UK trade union membership as a percentage of total work force (1985–1999)*

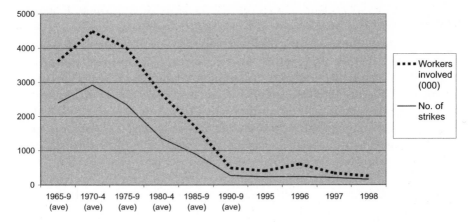

Source: Labour Market Trends, Office for National Statistics, June 1999

Figure 3.2 *Strike action in the UK (1965–1999)*

Secondly, with the growth of post-industrialism, unions' traditional constituencies have declined. They have traditionally represented full-time, formal-sector workers with open-ended contracts for which they bargained to provide optimal working conditions. The changing economy has increasingly incorporated women, youth and immigrants into the workplace, often on a temporary or part-time basis. Unions have not been well placed to represent the interests of these constituencies, especially informal sector workers (Castells, 1996).

Thirdly, unions lost some major battles during the 1980s when governments hostile to unions were in power. In the UK, Thatcher's Conservative government put in place a legal framework that reduced the ability of unions to coordinate. The UK union umbrella – the Trades Union Congress – now represents just 7.8 million workers (around 30 per cent of the work force), 5 million less than in 1980 (Brook, 2002).

Fourthly, unions, like political parties, suffer from the weakening of mainstream political processes. New forms of political participation, such as non-governmental organizations (NGOs) and social movements, have attracted new recruits who, traditionally, may have joined unions. The decline is particularly pronounced among young workers. In 1983, in the UK, 44 per cent of 18- to 29-year-old workers were union members and 57 per cent in the 40-plus age group, but the comparable figures fell to 18 and 33 per cent respectively by 1998.

Fifthly, capital is increasingly global while most labour remains stubbornly national or regional (Moody, 1997). As a result, bargaining with employers has become tougher. At the first sign of collective struggle by workers, employers can shift production elsewhere where unions are weaker, wages lower and working conditions are worse. Unions have, therefore, lost leverage, are keener to forge 'partnership' agreements with employers and are more reluctant to press their demands aggressively for fear of job losses.

The media and academics often portray these trends as features of 'globalization'. But unions are affected by 'new' as well as 'old' problems – such as the global nature of capital. Describing the decline of unionism as the result of globalization masks the fact that the picture is far from uniform. Many countries undergoing strong 'globalization' have not experienced union decline. In Europe, for example, the membership has remained stable in countries where unions were integrated as social partners within state administration, particularly Belgium and the Scandinavian countries. In South Africa, the rise of the national liberation movement and the demise of the apartheid regime has triggered membership affiliation, which rose from 39.3 per cent in 1988 to 58.4 per cent in 1993 (ILO, 2002). Brazil, China, India and Malaysia have also seen union growth. There is a need, therefore, to unpack the various processes loosely described as globalization or global change in order to understand their influence upon the union sector and the challenges that they create. They have brought threats but also new opportunities, including cheapness of travel, e-mail, the internet, the establishment of English as a lingua franca and the erosion of boundaries in general (see Chapter 1). The development of international institutions and international rules and norms have also facilitated the formation of transnational social movements (Tarrow, undated), and the end of the Cold War has facilitated a rapprochement between formerly antagonistic groups of nations.

A changing trade union movement: the transnationalization challenge

In historical terms, trade unionism is entering a new era. During the 19th century, workers joined together in local factories to confront the power of industrialists. As capital expanded to new boundaries, so did unions. In recent decades, capitalism has finally expanded at a global level and has brought with it a new series of outcomes that transcend national borders.

Unions now operate in a more international arena. As the power of states diminishes, and as transnational corporations (TNCs) and international institutions become more powerful shapers of working conditions and labour-market policy, unions must engage with these actors. To influence TNCs, unions must ensure collaboration across countries where the employer works. This implies not only enhanced communications between national unions, but also decision-making structures capable of signing global agreements and organizing coordinated protests and strikes. In dealing with international institutions, especially the World Bank, the International Monetary Fund (IMF) and the World Trade Organization (WTO), the unions use advocacy to shape labour-market policies at the international level.

In addressing wider social issues, unions are increasingly finding common cause with advocacy NGOs and other social movements. They are shifting from a 'partnership with management' to 'partnership with the poor' (Moody, 1997). In cooperating with NGOs, unions have incorporated new issues in their agenda, such as development and human rights – for example, in campaigns against child labour in which unions simultaneously protect children and their members who face possible job loss to child workers.

Box 3.1 *The international union movement*

The pioneers of international cooperation were the International Trade Secretariats (ITSs) – world confederations of unions, uniting workers based on industry, craft or occupation. The first was founded in 1889, and by 1914 33 ITSs had been established. In ensuing years many of these confederations sought to enhance their power and reduce transaction costs through merges. By 2002 there were just ten ITSs, and at this point they decided to call themselves Global Union Federations (GUFs). Together with the International Confederation of Free Trade Unions (ICFTU) they founded the Global Unions platform, which aims to create a central point for the international union movement.

The ICFTU is the largest international umbrella of unions. Based in Brussels, it now represents 157 million members from 148 countries, and has three regional organizations: Asia/Pacific, Africa and the Americas. Since the fall of the Berlin Wall the ICFTU has become the largest and most powerful group of unions in the world. During the last decade it has managed to attract unions from Central and Eastern Europe (CEE) and developing countries; hence, its membership is now double its 1982 level. The ICFTU also has very close links with the European Trade Union Confederation (ETUC) and the Trade Union Advisory Committee (TUAC) to the Organization for Economic Cooperation and Development (OECD).

Most CEE unions who joined the ICFTU formerly belonged to the World Federation of Trade Unions (WFTU). During the Cold War, the union community was divided along ideological lines – a Soviet-dominated WFTU and a Western-dominated ICFTU. Today, the WFTU has withered to a marginal organization based in Prague. It retains active affiliates in India, Vietnam, North Korea, Cuba and various other countries, and has good relations with a number of smaller Asian and South American federations.

A third umbrella of unions is the World Confederation of Labour (WCL), representing over 26 million members, mainly from developing world countries, but also Western Europe – particularly where Christian or humanist traditions are strong. Its membership remains quite stable.

Finally, the Commonwealth Trade Union Congress links union national centres, representing over 30 million union members. Its London headquarters lobbies Commonwealth institutions.

To adjust to a changing world, the union movement must make organizational changes in order to remain relevant and effective. In an increasingly interdependent world, the union movement must coordinate its members at international level in order to defend their interests. As a union activist points out:

> *The challenge we face is that of bringing our policies and principles together into a coherent whole, based on justice for the workers and the poor. We face the challenge of articulating and proclaiming a powerful alternative to the so-called Washington consensus. Globalization requires global unionism (Madisha, 2000).*

Current global economic trends force unions to search for a 'cohesive global voice'. To deal with increasingly transnational capital, labour must also act transnationally. Cooperation between diverse unions is difficult due to structure, ideology,

---

Box 3.2 *First International: workers of the world unite!*

The first initiative to create a 'global voice' came from Karl Marx himself. At the end of the 19th century, Marx organized the First International with the goal of organizing labour at the European and American level. According to Marx, capitalism needed a 'constantly expanding market' and effectively created a global economy understood as a single entity. In the global economy, the interests of the working class were the same regardless of the country to which they belonged. Hence, the transnational struggle of the working class had to be based on solidarity and internationalism. The First International was followed by other initiatives whose hallmark was international organization – demonstrating that the transnational challenge has been evident since the birth of the union movement.

---

culture and differing levels of economic development, but can generate increased collective power and a coherent voice worldwide. Unions, therefore, are trying to make the most of the new opportunities offered by globalization while responding to its threats. Will unions be able to meet this challenge? How can they adjust in order to remain relevant?

Paths to transnationalization

In grappling with global change issues, the union movement increasingly strives to act transnationally, such as by participating in the anti-globalization movement, to which unions make an important contribution. For example, unions mobilized about two-thirds of those taking part in the WTO demonstrations in 1999 (Tarrow, 2002). A second path has been the formation of transnational networks of unions for specific actions (Kidder, 2002). One example is the powerful dockers' network, which managed to coordinate transnational action in Spain, the UK and Canada against shipping companies in support of the Liverpool dockers (Munck, 2000).

A third path – the main concern of this chapter – involves strengthening formal international umbrella organizations in order to coordinate transnational action. With the end of the Cold War, it has become possible to create an all-encompassing labour movement (Ashwin, 2000: 102). The ICFTU has become the largest and most recognized platform for representing workers at global level, having an unparalleled track record for lobbying international institutions. The rest of this chapter focuses on the efforts of the ICFTU to become a truly global organization, representing the union movement, according to its secretary general (Ryder, 2002a). A central ingredient of this bid is the Millennium Review.

THE MILLENNIUM REVIEW

The Millennium Review (MR) was launched at the ICFTU's 17th World Congress in 2000 as an exercise to re-examine international trade unions' work and structures. The initiative was enthusiastically presented by the then general secretary, Bill Jordan, as the 'most radical review of the international trade union movement since unionism was born' (ICFTU, 2000b). The review seeks responses to current processes of globalization, as Jordan pointed out:

Our movement does not yet have the ability to deliver the mobile global solidarity need to match the flexible power of the TNC giants. So, congress launched the Millennium Review…it involved 145 trade union centres on all five continents. Its objective is to mobilize the resources of the world trade union movement to respond to that phenomenon of globalization (Jordan, 2000).

The ICFTU does not oppose globalization per se, but insists that it must be guided in order to protect workers' interests. It does not see globalization as inevitable or immutable, though it has made TNCs and the international financial institutions more powerful. Globalization has also opened new ways of organizing and fighting for workers' rights in the global economy. Information technologies, for example, give activists the opportunity to learn about campaigns or the problems of workers around the world and allow them to organize and promote action. The MR epitomizes this 'reforming view' of globalization.

It involves extensive consultation internally and externally, and at national, international, regional and sector levels. It also seeks dialogue with other organizations sharing similar goals, such as the World Confederation of Labour (WCL). The work has been carried out under the guidance of a group of senior union leaders, including representatives from the ICFTU, affiliates, the regional organizations, the Global Union Federations (GUFs) and the Trade Union Advisory Committee (TUAC).

The MR is an ongoing process with many faces, and the findings and recommendations are expected to be presented to the ICFTU's 18th World Congress in 2004. Hence, at the time of writing, a conclusive picture of this process could not be given. However, by consulting internal discussion papers, we can analyse the challenges that the ICFTU perceives as facing the trade union movement.

The most concrete change triggered by the MR so far is the setting up of Global Unions (see Box 3.1). Although this is in its initial stages, its creation responds to a perceived need for a common identity. As Guy Ryder pointed out:

Global Unions is an important vehicle today for giving our movement greater visibility. It is a way of getting across to trade unionists and to the wider public who we are and what we are doing in a more attractive and understandable way. It is also a platform for cooperation and for joint actions of the type, which I think we need if we are actually going to pack a harder punch in the world (Ryder, 2002a).

It is still unclear how much harder the 'punch' will be. So far, the Global Unions project has involved the creation of a network (with closer GUF–ICFTU collaboration), the establishment of a day of action (9 November) and a website for communication with trade union bodies and the public, though no new structures are envisaged. Although the intention is representation at international meetings, at the time of writing union officials had only used the Global Unions title when attending the 2002 World Economic Forum in New York and the 2001 WTO

Ministerial Conference in Doha.[1] It remains to be seen how much concerted action will be possible under Global Unions, especially since the goals and tactics of the different components may sometimes be incompatible.

The flexibility of Global Unions as a network, rather than as a formal organization, might, however, permit the participation of other international confederations of unions. As Tim Noonan has pointed out, the Global Unions are 'more of an evolutionary step than a major structural change', and the main goal is to 'increase communication between international trade union organizations'.[2] New opportunities have therefore emerged for greater cooperation with the WCL and the World Federation of Trade Unions (WFTU). The ICFTU views this as positive because these organizations share similar principles and interests (Ryder, 2002b).

The success of the Global Unions project as well as the broader MR will depend upon their ability to produce viable responses to current threats to the trade union movement. The ICFTU's most pressing need is to strengthen linkages between national, sector, regional and international union activities, and to organize internationally around issues of the global economy (ICFTU, 2001). The MR also seeks answers to other challenges: restoring membership; attracting young workers; supporting informal and unprotected workers; electing women into leadership positions; establishing strategic alliances with NGOs; and coaxing TNCs into global negotiations. Officially, MR objectives are divided under five main headings:

- tackling the power of TNCs;
- the global economy and development;
- campaigning and communications;
- strengthening national union organizations, trade union democracy and unity; and
- regional and constitutional issues.

These objectives fall into two inter-related themes: providing guidance for forming new relationships with other actors (the external agenda) and the re-structuring of the ICFTU (the internal agenda) (ICFTU, 2000a). We will start by discussing the former.

CHALLENGES OF CHANGING RELATIONS

One key MR concern is to re-orientate the relationship between unions and other actors in their environment – notably, international institutions, TNCs, and NGOs – whose power has risen greatly during the past two decades. At the same time, the state has retreated from traditional duties (for example, pensions and service delivery). To address the challenges facing the movement, unions must re-examine their relationships and their 'partnerships' with all power-holders of relevance to labour.

Influencing TNCs

As employers become transnational, so must the bargaining of workers. Although they continue to be largely constrained by territory and the laws of the host country, TNCs continue to show how flexible and mobile investments can be, in clear contrast to labour. Thus, while the TNCs are happy to comply with national or local legislation, the unions are increasingly pushing for global agreements that apply to all workers. From the union perspective, influencing TNCs is the unions' contribution to controlling a group of powerful and unelected agents of the global economy – many of whom have a larger turnover than the gross domestic product (GDP) of many countries.

Most TNCs treat workers differently in different countries. As a result, there are clear incentives to increase the linkages between workers from different countries in the same company to try and improve the working conditions of all. Unions have responded by organizing the collection and exchange of information, through solidarity campaigns such as boycotts or simultaneous strikes, and through political lobbying (Ramsay, 2000: 26). Workers facing worse conditions can learn from the bargaining strategies of the better-off. At the same time, the latter want to ensure that employers do not move their jobs to countries with worse conditions. One such case has been the formation of an 'action network' at the mining giant Rio Tinto. Organized by a GUF, the International Federation of Chemical, Energy, Mine and General Workers' Unions (ICEM), the network aims at linking all workers and keeping them informed of the TNC's activities. In the absence of any international institution regulating TNCs, unions are seeking to make them accountable for their actions, even threatening industrial action when considered necessary.

When on strike, unions seek to galvanize the support of their members and gain momentum even at the transnational level. One of the most interesting cases is the coal strike organized in 1993 by the United Mine Workers of America (UMWA) against Peabody Holding Co. Originally a dispute over secure jobs for union members, the strike also reflected how TNCs and unions behaved in a globalized economy (Zinn, 2000: 223). The UMWA took industrial action against Peabody in the US in order to secure good conditions for their affiliates, but realized that Peabody was a subsidiary of the TNC, Hanson plc, and that transnational action was needed. Hence, the action broadened from US to Australia, Colombia, South Africa and the UK, where the coal company had its headquarters. In addition to this 'action network', the campaign attracted the support of two International Trade Secretariats (since merged as ICEM) and the British Trades Union Congress. The strike was supported by 18,000 workers, lasted seven months and cost the company almost US$200 million. The dispute ended in a favourable five-year agreement for the workers, which also strengthened the position of the UMWA (Zinn, 2000: 236).

Although industrial action can be effective, it is a last resort against TNCs. Strikes and boycotts are resource-consuming events, and unions prefer to seek cooperation and negotiation where possible. One forum for cooperation has been the United Nation's (UN's) Global Compact, a neutral and voluntary forum to discuss issues of business ethics. Launched in 1999, this is a values-based platform designed to promote corporate social responsibility (CSR). Businesses are called upon to support nine basic principles related to human rights (based on the Universal Declaration of Human Rights and the UN covenants), labour standards (based on the ILO Declaration of Fundamental Principles and Rights at Work) and the environment (based on the Rio Earth Summit principles). In general, the GUFs support the compact because companies that subscribe to the principles, standards and agreements of the UN are easier to scrutinize. However, the lack of procedures for implementing and enforcing the principles, together with the obstacles to monitoring the conditions of workers, are weaknesses. Therefore, unions are sceptical of the Global Compact as companies could use it to improve their image without changing their actions. Because the compact is voluntary, there is still a need to build collective bargaining capacity at the transnational level.

Another example of collaboration between unions and TNCs is the mechanism of the global (or framework) agreements. Promoted by GUFs, these press a particular TNC to higher standards. They can involve governments and international institutions, are often based on ILO standards, and can be applied to both industrialized and developing countries. They help boost a sense of solidarity among workers – a prerequisite for industrial action at the international level. One such agreement was signed on 13 September 2002 in Johannesburg between the mining company AngloGold, ICEM and the National Union of Mineworkers of South Africa. This was the first such agreement in the mining industry and committed AngloGold to promote a socially and environmentally sustainable industry. The breakthrough was important as the media often characterizes this industry as exploitative. The agreement also commits AngloGold and ICEM to work in partnership for harmonious working relationships throughout the world. Another GUF that has actively pursued global agreements is the International Federation of Building and Wood Workers (IFBWW), who has reached similar agreements with IKEA, Faber-Castell, Hochtief and Skanska (IFBWW website: www.ifbww.org).

Transnational structures of the union movement have facilitated exchanges between unionists in different countries with a common TNC employer. Some employers, such as Vivendi, have agreed to enter global negotiations over their employment policies (there were 12 such framework agreements as of 2001). The food giant Danone has reached an agreement with the GUF representing workers in the food and allied industries to develop cooperation in five areas, including training, access to company information and promoting gender equality. Although the 1991 agreement is global, the implementation is carried out unevenly at a national or local level.

Whether by negotiating agreements, monitoring voluntary standards or sustaining transnational strike actions, unions face critical challenges in trying to influence TNCs. Often, however, a preferred strategy is to influence international rule makers.

Influencing international institutions

National governments and individual TNCs are not the sole determinants of many of the issues that the ICFTU faces. In an interconnected world, international institutions increasingly promote norms in all aspects of labour and social security policy in ways that lead towards harmonized policy. The unions, therefore, perceive a strong need to be involved in their deliberations. By doing so, they remain relevant and present themselves as a progressive force for the protection of workers at the international level. This includes working with the UN, through the Global Compact, to produce a joint statement between the UN, trade unions and TNCs that stresses the need for rules for the global economy and the important role of international social dialogue between unions and employers. It also involves taking part in the ILO's recently formed expert panel on the social impact of globalization.

The MR is encouraging unions to increase their lobbying of international organizations. For example, a wide network of unions throughout Asia has formed the Asia Labour Network on international financial institutions (IFIs) to monitor the IFIs, educate workers about their significance, organize campaigns to criticize them and engage them in dialogue. Union–IFI relations are typically problematic, though most GUFs have dealings with the World Bank and keep some sort of contact with other IFIs. Such is its interest in international institutions that some within the ICFTU want to move its headquarters (at the moment, in Brussels) to Geneva, where the ILO is headquartered, or Washington, DC, home of the major IFIs (see ICFTU, 2001).

Some argue that this focus on the global economy has helped unions to renew a movement that, according to Manuel Castells, was 'historically superseded' (1996). Although unions have realized this threat, they will continue to face their traditional challenges. Declining membership remains a problem and international solidarity is sometimes illusive. The international campaigns of Global Unions only work 'when they are backed up by the action of unions in the relevant countries' (Ashwin, 2000: 115). This is the case when implementing international agreements. A weakness in lobbying international institutions is that most international agreements are only voluntary and have weak enforcing mechanisms. For example, during the late 1990s, India's signature of ILO conventions made the approval of progressive legislation desirable; but a fragmented union movement is not capable of ensuring that these laws are enforced. Moreover, many countries opt out of international agreements and employers can thus move to areas where worker protection standards are lower. To increase their leverage, unions are therefore seeking new alliances with other civil society actors.

Working with NGOs

Unions are increasingly conscious of other civil society organizations (CSOs). During the Cold War, unions were suspicious of working with NGOs and other CSOs, often accusing them of being 'politically naïve idealists' (Ashwin, 2000: 113). Caught up in the East–West divide, international unionism often failed to recognize the importance of issues such as the informal sector, gender and development. All of this is now changing, and the ICFTU is keen to establish a dialogue with these organizations. The MR highlighted the importance of developing such strategic alliances when common goals are shared:

> *One modern development that trade unions should not ignore is the rise of NGOs to become powerful lobbyists nationally and internationally. The ICFTU should be ready to build relationships and alliances with those NGOs whose principles and practice do not conflict with trade unionism (ICFTU, cited in Ashwin, 2000: 114).*

NGOs provide the unions with a useful model. Amnesty International, Greenpeace and Oxfam International have demonstrated how much international advocacy can achieve with very limited resources. NGOs often have higher profiles than unions and are more successful communicators. As a result, we are now seeing a range of joint union–NGO campaigns, targeting issues such as child labour and export processing zones (EPZs).

This collaboration, however, also presents a challenge. NGOs often see unions as preserving formal-sector jobs and wages in the North at the expense of others who are more vulnerable. The fiercest differences have been with Southern advocacy groups concerning the incorporation of labour standards within WTO rules. Most unions want this (though they agree that sanctions aren't appropriate for enforcing social clauses). However, groups such as Third World Network and Southern consumers' groups are concerned that this would become a back-door way of protecting Northern markets and that such clauses would hurt the very workers about whom their proponents claim to be concerned. Unions reject such criticism and accuse those promoting them of being elitist and lacking a mass base.

These major differences clearly make for an uneasy alliance, as does the underlying conviction of many unionists that most advocacy NGOs don't really represent anyone other than themselves. Of course, this makes them more manoeuvrable (such NGOs can make decisions at the top level while unions must refer them back to their members), and so they have a powerful role in fast-moving campaigns. However, union leaders feel the need to keep a wary distance. This has been magnified by political and tactical differences since the 11 September terrorist attack, particularly in the US. US unionists have strongly supported their government's war against terrorism, while the more radical NGOs, who have been allies on issues concerning globalization, are seeking to direct the energy of the protest movement into a peace movement against the US military response. These differences have caused some analysts within the movement to ask whether such cooperation has been shelved permanently or just temporarily (Davis, 2002).

As a result, cooperation with NGOs is dealt with on a case-by-case basis, and is increasingly likely in the fields of human rights, development and gender. In the past, campaigns on human rights have seen strong NGO–union cooperation, while those in other areas have proved to be less harmonious. Other problems might arise when re-examining issues of legitimacy and accountability.

Child labour campaigning is a good example of how the union movement cooperates with CSOs, such as human rights and development NGOs. By working with the Global March Against Child Labour, for example, unions have elevated pressure against child labour and contributed to the new ILO Convention on the Worst Forms of Child Labour and to the huge growth in public awareness of the problem – thanks, also, to the strong media focus, coupled with outreach to the broader community (Ryder, 2002a).

Widening mandate

Campaigning against child labour in South-East Asia entails changing the nature of unions' relationships with TNCs, international institutions and NGOs. But it also signals a changing relationship with members. Unions are moving away from the simple representation of existing members to addressing wider social issues, such as development, gender and human rights. In fighting for social justice objectives, they are forging new relations with 'the poor' and those who defend their interests.

Addressing wide social issues of the 'global economy and development' is a major focus of the MR, reflecting:

> ...*our genuine commitment to fighting poverty and promoting development. We have done extensive work on development issues for many years, campaigning for debt relief and sustainable development, fighting to put the interests of all people at the centre of globalization (Ryder, 2002a).*

In an ever-integrated global economy, it is impossible to isolate the protection of national trade union members from wider social issues, both at the national (for example, migration) and international level (for instance, development).

Activism is no longer simply about conflict and negotiation with employers. In a global market, unions' roles are much wider – but these present important new challenges. For example, while the rights of, and accountability to, members is clear, what characterizes unions' links with non-members? Can they claim to represent 'the poor'? The MR apparently recognizes the need to widen the mandate of international union bodies and to form new relationships with external constituencies; but it does not offer answers to these issues of accountability and legitimacy – a potential weakness of the process.

Nonetheless, there is a belief underlying the MR that to be effective unions need to combine representing member interests with wider social issues. They need to integrate collective bargaining and member representation with advocacy. The change in strategies toward greater international advocacy and cooperation with other CSOs requires a change in structure, as well. How can nationally based unions who are used to collective bargaining undertake effective international advocacy? The change of tactics forces a change of structure: but what structure is adequate for the task at hand?

CHALLENGES OF CHANGING UNIONISM

Transnationalization also poses various challenges of internal organization, as recognized by the MR. Much of the union movement remains locally or nationally based, with few transnational links. But the need to increasingly work at the transnational level forces it to change the way in which it is organized – from nationally based and disintegrated into an internationally integrated movement.

Strengthening transnational union solidarity

Such a transition requires strengthening transnational union solidarity despite strong nationalist sentiments and a vast divide between 'the West and the rest', or between North and South (Ryder, 2002a). Since Marx proposed international solidarity as a guiding principle for 'the workers of the world', trade unionism has long strived to be an internationalist movement. However, nationalism is a difficult doctrine to beat. From World War I to the Cold War, unions have been driven by nationalist motivations. Nationalism continues to feed on the sense of community and shared culture that other forms of identity cannot provide, and the nation state continues to be the most relevant territorial entity. Industrial action continues to be organized largely at the national level – even workers take strongly nationalistic positions in opposing globalization. Both in the US and Western Europe, unions have often opted to push for protectionist policies, with little concern about the potential negative consequences for workers in the South. Textiles, steel and farming are examples.

In contrast, most transnational union bodies adopt an internationalist perspective: 'Sisters and Brothers, our challenge is to forge unbreakable links in the trade union's chain of global solidarity' (Jordan, 2000). Initiatives such as the MR or the formation of Global Unions demonstrate that unions are making a conscious effort to transnationalize and move beyond national boundaries, seeking to reform globalization rather than oppose it.

However, they will not be able to fully erase nationalistic sentiments. The MR needs to convince rank-and-file members that globalization should be reformed, not opposed, and that increased transnationalization of the union movement is crucial. Hence, international union bodies are at odds with those who actively oppose globalization. The image of the French farmer José Bové wrecking a McDonald's branch while defending French agricultural products appeals to many union members because of the clear and emotional logic of nationalism and the excitement of direct action.

Even when transnational solidarity is strong, there are major differences in culture, key challenges and organizing traditions between unions in different parts of the world. Unions in the South may be more concerned with state repression or informal sector working conditions, while Northern unions may be more concerned with health and safety or formal social safety nets. There are, similarly, important cultural differences that render much of the work of Northern-based international union bodies of doubtful value to the South.[3]

These differences are aggravated by the emergence of different union tradi-tions in different parts of the world, particularly between North and South. US and UK unions have traditionally organized around crafts and industries. French, Italian and Spanish unions have organized around political parties. The Japanese organize around specific companies. In the South, countries such as Brazil or South Africa have organized unions around a 'social movement unionism' (Moody, 1997), which refers to the emergence of a social movement linking trade unions, civil society and other sympathetic actors in a fight against poverty. Despite this diversity of organizing traditions, most international union bodies are organized by sector – such as the GUFs. As a result, they reflect a North European organizational culture rather than that of many Southern countries.

Working across such different national and union cultures and traditions pre-sents enormous challenges for international union bodies. This complexity requires large resource investments, which may not be available while the heterogeneity of the membership base compromises agreements about goals and strategies:

> *We have to work hard at reducing compartmentalization and making trade unionists, at all levels, feel that what happens internationally is something which involves them, which is directly relevant to them and which they can influence (Ryder, 2002b).*

It is unclear how the MR will address this problem. The Global Unions may facilitate communication between union bodies with different organizational cultures; but there is a danger that the cooperation will not be between 'equals'. Although there has been some consultation with Southern voices, the MR is an initiative that is largely originated and carried out at the ICFTU headquarters in Brussels. While this may be the most effective approach, there appears to be con-siderable confusion and lack of awareness about the MR among Southern union-ists, which contributes to a Southern perception of Northern domination of the international trade union movement.[4] Therefore, the education of members about its vision of globalization is an important challenge for the MR – it needs to per-suade members to downplay nationalism and participate in reforming globalization.

Strengthening transnational union work

The expansion of transnational union work requires the organizational growth of its international structures. While most of the movement has experienced a fall in mem-bership, transnational bodies such as the ICFTU have become stronger – having risen by 85 per cent since 1982 as they have grown to encompass affiliates in a wide range of former Eastern bloc and developing countries (ICFTU, 2001). Public Sec-tor International (PSI) – the worldwide umbrella of 560 unions representing public-sector employees (other than teachers) – has similarly had to cope with a tripling of its membership during the last 14 years, as well as related organizational challenges.

Transnationalization implies increasing complexity. As unions forge new transnational alliances, both within the movement and with external actors, inter-national union bodies must ensure that they have adequate systems to cope with the growth of languages, cultures and tasks. For example, as unions step up their transnational advocacy and seek to influence new targets, there are structural pressures – such as establishing advocacy offices in Washington, DC, that target the World Bank and the IMF.

To what extent should unions from different countries integrate their activities? More integration producing larger union structures provides economies of scale, greater bargaining strength and permits the development of specialist expertise, which would be difficult to develop by smaller unions. Such expertise includes information, communication, advocacy, management and legal knowledge – all essential for international advocacy and coordination. Another critical area is resource distribution. A larger and more centralized structure facilitates redistribution between rich and poor areas, enhancing overall resource-use efficiency. At the international level, redistribution can greatly facilitate the development of unions in new regions or countries.

The merger activity amongst GUFs illustrates the increasing transnationalization of the sector. When their job was largely to exchange information between national-level unions and to 'express solidarity', it was adequate to have small offices covering quite specific trades. However, as the tasks expanded to become more proactive and demanding, GUFs needed to employ more professional staff and to decentralize to regional offices around the world. Since they are resource poor, this has required pooling effort through widespread mergers. Now, there are just ten GUFs, some of whom embrace a wide range of related trades. This trend is illustrated by the newest GUF, Union Network International, created in 2000 out of various earlier union umbrellas covering post and telecommunications, insurance, banking and financial services, the retail sector, media, entertainment, graphic design, and information and communications technology (ICT) industries. It represents 15 million members and is, in effect, the union of the 'new economy'.

Mergers also create new problems. Larger organizations tend to be more bureaucratic and less flexible. Moreover, large union structures tend to face a more heterogeneous membership and find it more difficult to maintain high commitment and strong identity. Smaller unions are less bureaucratic and remain closer to the grassroots level. They are thus more adept at fostering participation and union identity. In order to remain flexible, therefore, delegation of authority to local levels is important. Decision-making needs to be located where the best information is. In flexible and heterogeneous working environments, this indicates the local level. But centralization is important in order to coordinate the different local units and to achieve economies of scale, bargaining strength and union solidarity. The challenge is achieving sufficient integration at the transnational level in order to capture the benefits of larger unions while retaining local autonomy.

The combination of contradictory pressures for centralization and decentralization, larger structures with flexibility and participation, and efficient resource allocation encourages organizations to adopt hybrid structures (Anheier and Themudo, 2002). Such structures include international federations and confederations – based on the principle of subsidiarity where the affiliates are the main power holders and the coordinating bodies exist to serve them. They can integrate the strengths of hierarchical organizations and loose networks (Lindenberg and Dobel, 1999), combining the economies of scale of a large organization with the flexibility and responsiveness of local decision-making.

The confederation structure can be quite flexible, allowing unions to have different levels of centralization depending upon the needs of the sector. PSI, for example, represents nationally bound public-sector employees. International networking doesn't strengthen their leverage over employers because, by definition, the employers are at national level. Hence, PSI is highly decentralized, with 25 regional and subregional offices. Its work focuses more on sharing information and advocacy within international institutions.

Therefore, the MR is examining ways of increasing transnational union unity and revising the international structure to accommodate growth while remaining flexible and effective.

Promoting democracy and participation

The advantages of restructuring are obvious: to take advantage of new opportunities offered by globalization while avoiding the constraints of traditional structures. The increased extent and complexity of transnational work calls for restructuring; but what structure works best? For membership organizations, organizational theory identifies two key challenges resulting from organizational growth: increasing effectiveness, on the one hand, and fostering democracy and participation, on the other (Anheier and Themudo, 2002). As mentioned above, to increase effectiveness, many union bodies are merging in order to take advantage of economies of scale. But the choice of organizational structure has as much to do with politics as economics. A leader of the ICFTU places much importance on the ability to foster internal democracy:

> *The strength of the ICFTU, its value, is that it is a truly global organization. Its representativity has never been greater. You will not find another example of a global organization which operates as effectively and with such extensive internal democracy. This does not mean simply being able to show that we have members in all the regions. What really matters is that we are able to put together and implement policies which reflect truly the views, the interests and the concerns of all our members (Ryder, 2002a).*

Federations and confederations also have the advantage of facilitating internal democracy (Handy, 1989). However, extensive internal democracy slows decision-making. Hence, the international confederation structure enhances internal democracy, but at the expense of faster and cheaper decision-making.

These dilemmas are compounded by organizational growth, adding new decision-making layers. The structure of the ICFTU is far removed from its shop-floor members (Moody, 1997). To influence an ICFTU decision, workers must influence their shop-floor representatives, who must influence their local or national union, who must – in turn – influence their GUF, who must influence the ICFTU. Therefore, few members, in practice, have any influence over the transnational structures, as is recognized by the ICFTU leader:

> *To be successful internationally, we really have to work at putting together a 'singleness,' a continuum of trade union actions that goes from local to global. This can be difficult to achieve. Even people who are active in the trade union movement in their own countries often regard international trade union work as something separate or different. Something in which they are probably not directly involved and may not have real influence on (Ryder, 2002b).*

Some of our interviewees agreed with this perception. This separation between international structures and local members is greatest for Southern members because of the distance and cultural differences. Many Southern unionists, while satisfied with some aspects of the international bodies, criticize their propensity to act as if they speak on behalf of the South without adequate consultation.[5]

International union bodies need to transnationalize further and to expand; but as they do so, they risk becoming more bureaucratic and removed from the grassroots – which could jeopardize their core support. They also need to ensure that both Northern and Southern interests are properly represented before they can claim any global representation.

Finding adequate resources

The growth of international union bodies requires new resources. Since they are primarily financed by dues from member unions, they need to persuade these members that such work is a priority; but they are also seeking new funding sources in a resource scarce environment. The MR recognizes this challenge. The newly reconfigured Global Unions need new resources in order to effectively address global labour-market issues or to build up an international campaign for workers' rights. The problem is that while ICFTU and GUF memberships have grown, most new members come from resource-poor developing and transition countries. Therefore, the ICFTU's income per individual member has declined by 22 per cent since 1994 (ICFTU, 2001).

New resources appear to be more readily available outside of the union movement (from the European Union (EU), liberal governments or various foundations and international institutions). The MR, itself, has largely been financed by donors. However, there is a risk that these new resources may contribute to separating transnational bodies from their grassroots constituencies by adding a new accountability to institutional funders, rather than union members, hence increasing the democracy deficit.

Some individuals question whether tapping such funding sources is healthy for the union movement. Martin and Ross (2001) argue, for example, that the ETUC has only been possible because of EU funds ('borrowed resources'), rather than the movement's own resources. Despite its important advocacy achievements, they argue, the ETUC is distanced from the grassroots level. Tarrow (2001) generalizes from such experience and observes that proximity to global governance structures commonly alienates the grassroots.

Limited sources, combined with increased demand for transnationalization, leads to chronic resource shortage. The strong merger activity within the movement is partly due to such shortages. Another likely outcome is increased competition within the union movement, perhaps impeding closer collaboration between transnational union bodies.

What leadership?

A final area of challenges relates to the leadership of the transnationalization process. Imaginative leadership is essential for building international umbrellas that are as representative as possible of the whole movement and that are best suited for responding effectively and equitably to complex world changes. To avoid leadership being North-biased and unrepresentative of the movement as a whole, the grassroots must be involved in the MR. With a strong tradition of social movement organizing, can union rank-and-file participation be adequately engaged in an international top-down initiative?

Moody (1997) argues that it can't and that there are too many top-down initiatives in the international trade-union sector. Many unions try to avoid this by concentrating on their own activities. Therefore, alongside the MR, there are various transnational bottom-up initiatives currently underway in the sector. Many transnational networks and alliances are being formed or are growing and are likely to become increasingly influential (Kidder, 2002). However, networks are normally based on personal contacts or shared occupations, such as dockers' networks or national networks. Although these initiatives don't solve all of the challenges and dilemmas of transnationalization, they often attract strong grassroots participation, in contrast to the more formal top-down initiatives.

MR organizers believe that top-down initiatives can promote member participation. The ICFTU general secretariat has largely conducted the MR. By doing so, the review has, effectively, gathered union leaders and opinion-makers who are aware of international processes, while leaving out national unions and grassroots activists, who are often unaware of the review's existence. This might be unavoidable given the ICFTU's 157 million members. As Giampiero Alhadeff – secretary general of Solidar, a labour-rights NGO – has stressed, involving people from the grassroots level in a global review might be 'wishful thinking'.[6]

Maybe involving every rank-and-file union member in a global exercise is unrealistic; but that does not legitimize just any top-down effort. In democratic organizations, leadership issues cannot be separated from questions of internal democracy. A top-down process will be successful if leaders are elected democratically and are *representative* of the grassroots. An international confederation may have democratic processes based on national delegates; but how democratic are these delegates? Within an international confederation, democracy is only as strong as the democracy at national level. However, the latter may be biased or entail little rank-and-file participation. This problem is illustrated – as is acknowledged by the MR – by the almost total absence of women in national delegate positions, despite the fact that women comprise about 40 per cent of all ICFTU members. Not surprisingly, women are also mostly absent from international leadership positions within trade union bodies (ICFTU, 2001). International bodies cannot adequately represent rank-and-file members if national bodies are themselves biased. To avoid that and to ensure leadership that truly represents grassroots interests, they must see that democratic procedures are in place not only at the international level, but also at the national and even shop-floor levels.

As with other challenges, unions must strike a balance between contradictory pressures. Therefore, while it is true that leadership must be representative and democratic, democracy at the global level may be cumbersome and slow. Lobbying and playing the 'media game' requires quick organizational deployments and statements of position. Effectiveness often calls for fast decision-making. The difficulty is deciding which decisions are to be taken by democratic processes and which delegated to leaders.

CONCLUDING REMARKS

As we have shown, trade unions face many challenges concerning transnationalization and adapting to a changing world. The flip side is that every challenge has the opportunity to increase the strength of the movement. Many of these challenges have counterparts in other international organizations and movements, which we believe are particularly relevant in the international trade union movement.

One important response to these challenges is the MR undertaken by the ICFTU and related union organizations. The Global Unions' family is the largest and, arguably, the most representative union umbrella in the world. Because of their size and resources, the ICFTU and the GUFs are best placed to facilitate the transnationalization and strengthening of the union movement towards a 'single and coherent voice'. The determination to do so is an indicator of where the international trade union movement – or, at least, a large part of it – is going. However, it is still too early to judge the impact of the MR. Because of the complex nature of restructuring a large global organization, there is no guarantee that it will adequately address all of the challenges that we present here.

As a top-down initiative, it risks reproducing traditional splits that have historically weakened the movement – between 'the West and the rest', North and South, nationalists and internationalists, formal and informal, top-down and bottom-up initiatives, and between lobbying and protest. One way forward may be to open up the dialogue as widely as possible: with its own members, with different international bodies, within different organizational levels, with the more informal and bottom-up initiatives, such as the so-called 'anti-globalization movement', and with the many transnational networks, created spontaneously. There are encouraging signs that the Global Unions network is already trying to do some of this.

Regardless of all the challenges described, the MR and the creation of Global Unions are two of the most important initiatives taken by the international trade union movement during the last few decades. They are also a sign of the unions' ability to adapt and embrace the opportunities and challenges of globalization.

NOTES

1   Telephone interview with Giampiero Alhadeff, secretary general of Solidar, 29 November 2002
2   Tim Noonan, ICFTU director of campaigns, 27 November 2002
3   Interview with Luis Corral, executive director of political affairs, Trade Union Congress of The Philippines, 23 October 2002, Manila
4   Telephone interview with Alan Leather, deputy general secretary of Public Services International (PSI), 27 November 2002
5   Interview with Luis Corral, executive director of political affairs, Trade Union Congress of The Philippines, 23 October 2002, Manila
6   Telephone interview with Giampiero Alhadeff, secretary general of Solidar, 29 November 2002

Chapter 4

Campaign to Increase Access to HIV/AIDS Drugs

Tasneem Mowjee

This chapter outlines the campaign undertaken by national and international non-governmental organizations (NGOs and INGOs) to reduce the price of HIV/AIDS drugs in developing countries and thereby increase access to treatment. After providing background information on the issue, the chapter highlights the cases of South Africa and Brazil, where there have been legal disputes about the price of HIV/AIDS treatment but where the governments have adopted very different approaches to improving access. Although the issues of local production of medicines and patent protection have also arisen in countries such as Thailand and India, this chapter focuses on the cases of Brazil and South Africa because they offer an interesting contrast in the position of the government and the role of civil society organizations (CSOs). The chapter then discusses various aspects of the NGO campaign and concludes with a brief outline of the future plans of the NGOs.

BACKGROUND

The *World Health Report 2000* states that 11 million people a year die in poor countries of infectious diseases. Of these, HIV/AIDS is the second largest killer – responsible for 2.6 million deaths (pneumonia accounts for 3.9 million deaths).[1] The HIV/AIDS pandemic is particularly acute in sub-Saharan Africa where the Joint United Nations Programme on HIV/AIDS (UNAIDS) estimates that 28 million of the 40 million people currently infected with HIV worldwide live. In 2001, AIDS killed 3 million people and is now the single leading cause of death in Africa. Currently, it is estimated that one third of the world's population lacks access to essential medicines (though in the poorest areas of Africa and Asia this figure increases to half).[2] While NGOs acknowledge that a number of factors prevent people from obtaining life-saving medicines, price is one critical factor in access to the antiretroviral (ARV) treatment necessary for combating HIV/AIDS. In the US and Europe, ARV treatment costs US$10,000 per patient per year. However, through the use of a number of strategies, the Brazilian government has been able to reduce this to US$3000 per patient per year, which has helped it to provide free treatment to 95,000 people.[3]

NGOs involved in the campaign have expressed concern that the World Trade Organization's (WTO's) rules on intellectual property will increase the cost of essential medicines and further restrict the access of poor people. Under the Trade-Related Aspects of Intellectual Property Rights (TRIPS) agreement, member countries must grant patent protection to pharmaceutical patent holders for at least 20 years. Under this agreement, most countries were obliged to pass national legislation guaranteeing patent protection for 20 years by 2000, while least developed countries were given until 2006 to comply (this was extended to 2016 by the Doha Declaration in November 2001). However, they are still required to grant exclusive marketing rights to patent holders. WTO members who fail to comply face the threat of trade sanctions, as determined by the WTO Dispute Settlement Board (Oxfam, 2001). NGOs argue that restricting the right of governments to allow the production and/or import of low-cost copies of drugs is likely to reduce competition and thus increase the prices of essential medicines.[4] For example, the introduction of generic ARVs into the global market since September 2000 is believed to have led to a dramatic reduction in prices. In Brazil, generic production reduced ARV prices by around 80 per cent. By contrast, the price of drugs not facing generic competition fell by 9 per cent.[5] Thus, one of the major aims of the campaign has been to have the TRIPS agreement interpreted so as to protect the rights of Southern governments to develop appropriate public health policies and to promote the access of poor people to treatment, particularly for HIV/AIDS.

The TRIPS agreement does contain safeguards that permit governments to modify patent protection to protect public health interests. These include compulsory licensing and parallel importing. Compulsory licences permit the production of generic products without the consent of patent holders, though the latter are paid compensation. Licences may be issued by public bodies for various reasons and are commonly used by developed countries such as the US.[6] Both private and public organizations can apply for compulsory licenses. When a patented product is sold at different prices in different markets, parallel importing allows governments to import it from another country where it is being sold more cheaply. For example, Mozambique can buy Bayer's Ciprofloxacin in India at one fiftieth of the price that Bayer charges in Mozambique, due to generic competition.[7]

The compulsory licence issue was highlighted by the anthrax terror campaign following 11 September. The demand for Cipro (the Bayer drug to combat anthrax) tripled when the first case was reported at a newspaper office in Florida, then doubled again after the outbreak spread to New York and Washington, DC, as panic-buying set in.[8] In mid October 2001, the Canadian health minister announced that the government would override the Cipro patent (which did not expire until 2004), and would order almost 1 million tablets of a generic version of the drug from the Canadian firm Apotex, in order to build a national stockpile in case of biological attack.[9] The US government came under pressure from senators and consumer lobby groups to follow Canada's example.[10] However, Bayer greatly increased its production of Cipro and agreed a price with the government, so the US did not issue a compulsory licence (although it could have obtained the drug far more cheaply).[11] Furthermore, the Canadian government withdrew its licence a few days after issuing it.

Some press articles pointed out that the possibility of the use of compulsory licensing by the US government undermined its strong stance on patent rights at the WTO. The *Guardian*, for example, questioned:[12]

> *What constitutes a public health emergency? Three dead and a dozen infected with anthrax is enough to prompt rethinking in Washington about its previously staunch defence of drug companies' patent rights... Calls in Washington for the drugs industry to put people ahead of profits during the current crisis must be raising some mirthless laughs in the capitals of sub-Saharan Africa. With a real emergency on their hands – 25 million people infected with AIDS and 17 million already killed by the disease – African governments have faced implacable opposition from Washington in their quest for cheaper drugs. The US regularly threatens trade sanctions on governments that consider importing or licensing cheaper copies of patented remedies.*

An Oxfam interviewee noted that the US government's position on Cipro made developing countries angrier about the US stance, but it also strengthened their WTO bargaining position. This case also put the issue of TRIPS and pricing policies back on the agenda before the WTO's Fourth Ministerial Conference in Doha. Following intense lobbying by NGOs involved in the campaign, as well as Southern demands, Doha resulted in the adoption of a Declaration on the TRIPS Agreement and Public Health (WT/MIN(01)/DEC/2) on 14 November 2001, stating:

> *...the TRIPS agreement does not, and should not, prevent members from taking measures to protect public health. Accordingly, while reiterating our commitment to the TRIPS agreement, we affirm that the agreement can, and should, be interpreted and implemented in a manner supportive of WTO members' right to protect public health and, in particular, to promote access to medicines for all.*[13]

However, the declaration failed to resolve one issue – how countries with insufficient pharmaceutical manufacturing capacity can use compulsory licences. Developing countries had requested the WTO to authorize them to import generic medicines; but the conference deferred the issue to the TRIPS council, which has been unable to find a solution as of April 2003.[14] There has also been concern about the extent to which Southern governments will be able to use the flexibility provided by the declaration. This is partly due to the tentative language of the declaration (the use of 'should' rather than 'must', or other stronger terms) and partly due to Southern governments' 'fear of arm-twisting by the major governments or by the pharmaceutical corporations' (Raghavan, 2001). The cases of Brazil and South Africa, described below, are widely regarded as examples of such pressure being brought to bear.

THE BRAZIL EXPERIENCE

Brazil's 1988 constitution establishes an integral right to health through prevention and assistance. Therefore, Brazil has a public health system that provides free services. The government's policy of prescribing free ARVs – together with information campaigns, voluntary testing and counselling – reduced AIDS mortality by 51 per cent between 1996 and 1999, reduced the hospitalization rate by 80 per cent, sharply reduced the rate of mother-to-child transmission of the disease, and considerably lowered the incidence of HIV.[15] The strength of the government's commitment is reflected in its proposal to the United Nations Commission on Human Rights (UNCHR) that affordable access to HIV/AIDS drugs be made a basic human right. This resolution was passed on 23 April 2001 by 52 of the council's 53 voting members (with just the US abstaining). In order to afford free treatment, between 1996 and 2000, the Brazilian government strove to reduce the cost of ARV treatment by 80 per cent through the local manufacture of generic drugs and bulk purchases of imported drugs (Oxfam, 2001a). Of the 12 drugs provided to patients, Brazil produces 8 as generics and has negotiated a 70 per cent price reduction for 3 with the manufacturer Merck.

These achievements have led Brazil to be hailed as a model for other countries by the United Nations (UN). Even a GlaxoSmithKline (GSK) interviewee praised its political will. Nevertheless, pharmaceutical companies have accused the government of excessive price control and not respecting patent rights on treatments for HIV/AIDS and other diseases. They have threatened to take legal action or withdraw from the country (Oxfam, 2001b). In addition, the US government has used trade sanctions and took Brazil to the WTO's dispute settlement process.

The dispute between the two governments originated in a petition filed on 11 June 1987 by the US Pharmaceutical Manufacturers Association, complaining of Brazil's lack of patent protection for pharmaceuticals as an unreasonable practice that burdens or restricts US commerce. On 23 July the US trade representative (USTR) initiated an investigation and requested consultations with Brazil. These brought no resolution. On 21 July 1988, the US president determined Brazil's policy to be unreasonable and directed the USTR to hold public hearings on certain products exported from Brazil (held on 8–9 September). On 20

October, President Reagan used Section 301 of the 1974 Trade Relations Act to levy 100 per cent tariff increases on certain paper products and consumer electronics items. On 26 June 1990, the Brazilian government announced that it would introduce legislation to provide patent protection for pharmaceutical products and the process of their production by 20 March 1991. The USTR then deemed Brazil to be taking satisfactory measures and, on 27 June 1990, the sanctions were removed. However, the USTR announced that she would closely monitor the Brazilian government's efforts to enact such legislation.[16]

In 1993, the USTR placed Brazil on the Special 301 Priority Watch List due to perceived deficiencies in Brazilian intellectual property (IP) law (Manoochehri, 2001). The US government publishes an annual *Special 301* report that aims to 'detail the adequacy and effectiveness of intellectual property protection' in other countries. This includes information on WTO disputes and reviews of policies in various countries, and places countries on the Priority Watch List or regular Watch List. According to Love (1999), countries are put on these lists by having laws, policies or practices that the US government doesn't like, considers important and is trying to change through bilateral pressure. Simply being on the list is regarded as a trade sanction because it implies that the US government sees the country as an investment risk. However, Love (1999) argues that the government is likely to apply bilateral pressure on the topics mentioned in its list, which Southern governments find difficult to resist.

Manoochehri (2001) describes how this pressure from the USTR prompted the Brazilian government to enter into talks with the US in order to resolve the dispute. By mid 1996, Brazil had passed legislation to give stronger patent monopolies to computing and pharmaceutical firms. However, this stopped short of what the USTR wanted, as it required pharmaceutical products qualifying for patent protection to be partially produced locally within three years. Failing this, the government could issue a compulsory licence (unless the patent holder can show that local production is not feasible). Therefore, in January 2001, the US submitted a request to the WTO to mediate its case that Brazil was in violation of the TRIPS agreement.

WTO acceded to this request, but a dispute resolution panel was not appointed. This has been interpreted as a sign of US reluctance to pursue the case in the face of severe criticism from NGOs.[17] According to an article in the *Guardian,* 'The dispute had become a symbol of perceived intimidation by the US and pharmaceutical multinationals against developing countries that sought to obtain cheaper and wider access to essential medicines'.[18] Then, on 25 June 2001, at the start of a three-day UN General Assembly Special Session on HIV/ AIDS, the US government withdrew its case. The USTR, Robert Zoellick, argued that 'litigating this dispute before a WTO dispute panel has not been the most constructive way to address our differences, especially since Brazil has never actually used the provision at issue'.[19] Instead, the two governments agreed to use the recently established US–Brazil Consultative Mechanism as a way of finding 'creative solutions for trade and investment issues of mutual concern'. Under the terms of the agreement, Brazil undertook to provide advance notice to the US government before applying against a US firm the specific provision in its law that was the basis for the dispute.[20]

While the US presented the agreement as involving 'consultation', Brazil insisted that it onl1 requires 'talks' in the context of an existing joint 'Consultative Mechanism'.[21] Hence, despite appearing to have caved in to pressure to consult the US before applying the disputed clause, the Brazilian government defiantly stated in its press communiqué that 'Brazil maintains its conviction that Article 68 is fully consistent with the TRIPS agreement and an important instrument available to the government, in particular in its efforts to increase access of the population to medicines and to combat diseases such as AIDS'.[22]

Though other Southern governments and NGOs welcomed the US government's withdrawal, many are concerned that no precedent was set. Furthermore, James Love, of the US Consumer Project on Technology (CPT) and a leading campaigner on the TRIPS issue, has argued that giving the US government the right to be consulted on each compulsory licensing request 'is not helpful... At some point, we have to respect national sovereignty...let Brazil continue its difficult and costly efforts to treat poor AIDS patients'.[23] However, according to an interviewee from Oxfam's Brazil office, the agreement was just a formality and has not prevented the government from threatening to issue compulsory licences without consulting the US. Although the threat was issued against a Swiss company, Hoffman la Roche, the patent for the drug is held by the US-based Merck Sharp & Dohme. A direct threat to Merck had already resulted in an almost 70 per cent reduction in the price of its AIDS drug efavirenz.[24] According to a Brazilian government press release, six months of negotiations with Roche failed to result in a satisfactory price reduction.[25] Therefore, in August 2001, shortly before the September WTO TRIPS council meeting to discuss the conflict between health and patents, minister of health José Serra decided to override the patent. Within a week, Roche had accepted the government's demand to reduce the price of the drug by a further 40 per cent and to save the Brazilian government US$35.4 million per year.[26]

The Brazilian government's decision to provide free AIDS treatment and its stance against the pharmaceutical companies and the US government are in stark contrast to the actions of the South African government. The pharmaceutical companies have attempted to portray Brazil's position as a result of domestic politics and the (unsuccessful) bid of the health minister, José Serra, to succeed President Cardoso;[27] but interviewees suggested other reasons. According to the head of one Brazilian NGO, the constitutional right to health has been an important factor as it enables citizens to sue the government for treatment. This was the product of a powerful health movement before HIV/AIDS became prominent. Secondly, Brazil has had a tradition of promoting locally produced drugs for free distribution and, again, the case of AIDS is an example rather than an exception. Then, when the Brazilian parliament approved a law obliging the government to treat all HIV/AIDS patients, it was implemented vigorously, partly due to the social movement around AIDS in Brazil and to civil society organization (CSO) pressure. When HIV was first found in Brazil, those infected were mainly intellectuals and artists from the middle classes who had a greater capacity to mobilize and pressure the government. Television has also played a role in creating sensitivity about the issue of AIDS by, for example, showing people dying of AIDS because of inadequate hospital facilities. In addition, many government officials working on the AIDS programme began their careers within NGOs and have, therefore, been more activist in their approach. Finally, the forceful personality of the former health minister, José Serra, led him to adopt a tough stance with both pharmaceutical and tobacco companies.

SOUTH AFRICA'S EXPERIENCE

South Africa's constitution charges the government with the responsibility of making health care more accessible to the poor.[28] On 31 October 1997, the South African National Assembly passed the Medicines and Related Substances Control Amendment Act No 90 of 1997 (the Medicines Act). This law amended a 1965 act and contained a range of measures aimed at making medicines more affordable and improved the functioning of the Medicines Control Council (MCC). This was done in order to address existing inequities in the health system that had persisted from the apartheid era and due to a long-term problem with high drug prices.[29] On 18 February 1998, the South African Pharmaceutical Manufacturers' Association (PMA) and 40 multinational pharmaceutical companies took legal action to have certain crucial sections declared unconstitutional and to prevent the president and minister of health from implementing them.[30] This included Section 15C, which allowed for parallel importing and compulsory licensing. According to the Aids Law Project (ALP), many of the contested measures were already standard practice in developed countries and complied with the TRIPS agreement. They regard the legal action as an attempt by the PMA to achieve a number of objectives, such as having the ambiguities in the TRIPS agreement (particularly regarding parallel importation) interpreted in a restrictive way and to deter other developing countries from similar action. Implementation of the act was thereby stopped.

Between February 1998, when the PMA initiated legal action, and 10 November 2000, the date of the hearing, there were several developments. In 1998 the pharmaceutical companies succeeded in having South Africa placed on the USTR 301 Watch List, though it was removed a year later following pressure from AIDS activists in the US and demonstrations outside US embassies in South Africa, led by Treatment Action Campaign (TAC), a South African NGO in the forefront of the campaign to promote access to HIV/AIDS treatment. President Bill Clinton also signed an 'executive order' recognizing the rights of African countries to pass legislation to promote better, more affordable, health care without interference from the US, as long as it was TRIPS-compliant (as noted by Heywood, 2001, although this did not extend to developing countries in Latin America and Asia).

In South Africa itself the court case stagnated. The pharmaceutical companies benefited from this inertia because measures that would have drastically reduced the price of many medicines (as well as their profitability) were delayed.

TAC was established in December 1998. Between 1999 and 2001, it frequently held demonstrations demanding that the PMA withdraw the case. Although it was unable to tackle the issue more directly (because it lacked the capacity), TAC initiated other campaigns, such as a treatment literacy campaign and a campaign to prevent mother-to-child transmission of HIV/AIDS (see Soal, 2001). TAC also lobbied Pfizer Inc in 2000 to demand a price reduction of its anti-fungal medicine Diflucan/Fluconazole. This led, in October 2000, to TAC Chairperson Zackie Achmat bringing back 3000 tablets of a bio-equivalent generic fluconazole (Biozole) from a trip to Thailand. At a press conference on 18 October, TAC announced the launch of its 'Christopher Moraka defiance campaign against patent abuse and profiteering'.[31] This led to an outcry as the public realized how generic competition could reduce drug prices. The issue dominated news headlines for a week and led to television and radio discussions. This not only helped to educate the public, but also to build sympathy and support for TAC across the social and political spectrum. In addition, although TAC had technically broken the law, the MCC granted it an exemption to import the generic medicine from Thailand for use by a clinic run by Médecins Sans Frontières (MSF) in Cape Town. According to TAC, the campaign also influenced the decision of Pfizer to donate Diflucan for use in the public sector. TAC argues that its various campaigns also helped prepare South African civil society for the broader mobilization required for the court case.

By early 2001, following the success of the defiance campaign, TAC decided to intervene in the court case, the hearing of which had been set for March 2001 (though the South African government did not draw public attention to this). On 11 January 2001, the PMA's head of scientific and regulatory affairs, Maureen Kirkman, informed TAC of the dates. TAC held discussions with senior lawyers about whether it should aim to join as a party. It was advised that this would seriously delay the hearing. Therefore, it decided to seek permission to intervene as *amicus curiae*.[32] This was endorsed by the TAC national executive committee, which met on 15–16 January at a clinic run by MSF in Khayelitsha in Cape Town. Spirits and confidence were high at the meeting, as TAC had just imported a second batch of Fluconazole tablets from Thailand in the glare of publicity (they were brought in by a local soap star).

TAC's objective was to overcome the inertia around the case and to draw international attention to the dates. At a press conference on 16 January, TAC announced its *amicus* decision and started to mobilize an international campaign demanding the withdrawal of the pharmaceutical companies. TAC called for a Global Day of Action against the pharmaceutical companies on 5 March 2001, the first day of the court case. This received significant attention from the local and international media.

Between January and March there was intense campaigning activity in South Africa and abroad. TAC's international allies mobilized support and some INGOs put pressure directly on the companies and on Northern governments.

On 4 March, the Congress of South African Trade Unions (COSATU) and TAC held an all night vigil outside the court, and TAC leaders used the opportunity to have a workshop with the most senior officials of COSATU on the legal and political issues posed by the case. On 5 March, 5000 people marched past the Pretoria High Court and handed in a memorandum at the US embassy. There were also worldwide demonstrations, and over 250 organizations from 35 countries signed a petition opposing the legal action; this was published on 8 March. On 6 March the court gave the pharmaceutical companies until 28 March to answer TAC's founding affidavit. The government and TAC were then given until 10 April to respond. The case was effectively postponed until 18 April. MSF started an international petition that collected 250,000 signatures and proved crucial in persuading the European Union (EU) and the Dutch government to call for the case to be dropped.

TAC filed its arguments on 17 April. Faced with the solidarity of CSOs and international public opposition, a number of the PMA member companies started reconsidering their position. The damage to their reputation was highlighted by the UN Secretary General Kofi Annan's reported remark to President Mbeki that the case had cast the pharmaceutical industry 'in the role of evil empire trying to thwart the Third World's efforts to get affordable medicines' ('The Call that Won the Drugs Battle', *The Sunday Times,* 22 April 2001). On 18 April, the PMA requested an adjournment and after 24 hours of intensive internal negotiations its legal team announced that its clients were unconditionally withdrawing their case against the government and would bear all costs (except those of the *amicus*).

Despite this apparent victory in the court case, some have questioned what was actually achieved. The withdrawal of the PMA meant that there would be no binding legal precedent in the form of a judgement. In addition, it did not follow that the government would actually implement the act to import cheaper drugs and improve the access of AIDS sufferers to treatment (ICTSD, 2001).

Nevertheless, TAC argues that its intervention in the case and the international campaign achieved a great deal. Firstly, the three-year legal battle that had prevented the government from implementing the act had been resolved. Secondly, the international attention greatly strengthened support for the argument that commodities such as essential medicines should be treated differently under patent law. This was, undoubtedly, one of the factors resulting in the Doha declaration described earlier. Thirdly, the case demonstrated how CSOs could help to bring the world's most powerful multinational corporations to account (see 'Aids Charity Has Drug Makers on the Run', *Guardian*, 18 April 2001). At the national level, TAC's campaign mobilized civil society and demonstrated that alliances could be forged between lawyers, doctors and various other groups.

As the description of the PMA court case demonstrates, the South African government adopted a very passive stance compared to that of the Brazilian government.

According to a TAC interviewee, this was because the government was 'caught between a rock and a hard place'. It wanted to be seen to be making medicines more affordable, particularly for important constituencies representing poor people. But there were splits in the government – especially at the senior level – about the impact that this would have on big business's perception of it. Furthermore, TAC's focus on ARVs and medicines relating specifically to HIV made the government uncomfortable (because of the dissident view of AIDS held by President Mbeke and the minister of health).[33]

THE INTERNATIONAL CAMPAIGN

Numerous organizations have been involved in the campaign to reduce the price of HIV/AIDS drugs. At the international level, these include NGOs such as Oxfam, MSF, Voluntary Service Overseas (VSO), CPT, Health Gap, Third World Network (TWN) and Health Action International. At the national level, TAC has been the leading NGO in South Africa, while there are a large number of AIDS NGOs in Brazil (such as Associação Brasileira Interdisciplinar Aids and Grupo de Incentivo à Vida de São Paulo). However, rather than a formal network, this has been a loose coalition of national and international NGOs that became involved in the campaign at different times (although some of the INGOs, such as Oxfam, MSF and TWN, regard themselves as strategic allies, undertaking joint actions around key WTO events). The NGOs have collaborated when their interests coincided, particularly to share information and on joint press releases or statements, and have worked on their own campaigns at other times. There have also been strong personal links between individuals in the larger organizations involved in the campaign. One example of cooperation between NGOs was the Global Day of Action on 5 March 2001, called for by TAC to mark the first day of the court case. TAC's INGO allies – including MSF, Oxfam, the Health Gap Coalition (in the US), and Action for Southern Africa (ACTSA, UK) – then mobilized support. Demonstrations were held in 30 cities around the world, including in Brazil, The Philippines, the US, the UK, Kenya, Thailand, France, Italy, Denmark, Australia and Germany.

NGOs have had different reasons for becoming involved in the campaign. For example, Oxfam has approached the issue as one of trade rather than health (though it is working increasingly on the issue, Oxfam does not have programmes specifically for people with HIV/AIDS). It has researched the impact of trade rules on poor countries and has planned a trade campaign for several years (finally launched in April 2002). It regards intellectual property (IP) as particularly crucial in trade issues and access to medicines as a stark example of how trade rules hurt poor people. Like Oxfam, TWN was interested in the broader issue of TRIPS – development and the erosion of developing country sovereignty – not just the public health aspect of TRIPS. MSF, on the other hand, became aware of the restricted access to essential treatment through its direct experience with HIV/AIDS programmes. TAC was established on 10 December 1998 (Human

Rights Day) by AIDS sufferers who had lost friends and colleagues to the disease.[34] The personal dedication to the cause is strengthened by TAC's policy of having people with HIV as its leaders. HIV-positive people have also been spokespeople for TAC, as they can talk from direct experience, which is far more powerful than charitable sentiments. Due to the individual nature of the NGO campaigns and their different motivations, NGOs have their own names for their campaigns. For example, Oxfam's is known as the Cut the Cost campaign, while MSF has a Campaign for Access to Essential Medicines.

According to an Oxfam interviewee, there has not always been total agreement between the main NGOs on policy issues such as reform of TRIPS. Oxfam has been keen to press for change and emphasized the overall development aspects of the agreement, whereas MSF has focused more on strengthening the health safeguards. Similarly, VSO has stressed the issue of pricing, rather than patenting rules. There have also been situations when an NGO's mandate precluded support for a particular position. Oxfam, for example, felt that it could not argue against the patenting of genes unless it could demonstrate a clear impact on poverty, as this was a religious/ethical issue. However, the Oxfam interviewee argued that these were differences of emphasis and tactics and that there has been substantial agreement on the overall campaign and no major tension between the NGOs.

Organizations such as Oxfam, Consumers International (CI) and TWN believe that NGOs are increasingly focusing on global rules because international decision-making has become more centralized and more influential with regard to the actions of national governments. This applies to the International Monetary Fund (IMF), the World Bank and the International Standards Organization (ISO), not just the WTO. Nor are global rules a recent phenomenon. As a WTO secretariat staff member pointed out, government interest in intellectual property protection dates back to the Paris Convention for the Protection of Industrial Property, signed in 1883. The TRIPS agreement was negotiated during the 1980s, with the substance of the text agreed by 1991 (though the agreement was not adopted until 1994). The fact that the EU, as a whole, rather than individual member states, determines trade policy has also driven NGOs to work internationally. Therefore, NGOs such as Oxfam GB need to influence other European governments besides the UK.

Relationships with governments

Some interviewees noted that the relationship of INGOs with Southern governments, not just other CSOs, played an important part in the campaign. Southern governments have, historically, been wary of Northern NGOs because of the latter's criticism of them on issues such as the environment, child labour and human rights. However, on the issue of TRIPS and access to medicines, there has been a coincidence of interest between many Southern governments and Northern and Southern NGOs. As a result, an Oxfam interviewee believed that Southern governments are more receptive to both domestic and Northern NGOs. The latter have provided moral and technical support to Southern governments. According to an NGO respondent, this is because – in order to change the policy of a multilateral institution – lobbying Northern governments is insufficient. Southern governments must want the change, as well. He argued that there was progress at the ministerial conference in Doha because developing countries emphasized the TRIPS and health issue. They were helped by public support for the campaign, particularly in the North.

However, the relationship between Southern NGOs and their governments has not always been cordial. In the case of South Africa, the relationship between TAC and the government has been mixed. Although the media emphasized the 'alliance' between the two, TAC argues that, in reality, there was little contact between them.[35] On 1 February 2001, a TAC/ALP delegation met with the director-general of the health department to discuss the pharmaceutical companies' court case against the government. TAC received a positive response to its request to join the case, although the final government position depended upon consent from all of the respondents (including the president's office, with which the TAC has had a poor relationship, primarily due to President Mbeke's views on AIDS). However, the ministry of health realized that TAC's intervention would be just one step in its campaign for treatment access and that it would increasingly criticize the government's HIV policy. This has indeed been the case, with TAC taking the government to the constitutional court on a treatment programme to prevent mother-to-child transmission of HIV and winning the case.

After victory in the court case, TAC felt excluded by the African National Congress (ANC) – for example, from acknowledgement at a 'victory rally' held in Pretoria on 19 April. Similarly, while the minister of health congratulated the INGOs, such as Oxfam and ACTSA, she apparently chided them in private for working with TAC. This attitude may indicate a concern amongst ANC leaders and some ministers that TAC had hijacked the court case and focused attention on access to antiretroviral drugs. A TAC interviewee attributed it directly to support for the dissident view within the ANC, although he added that, in private, there is much support for TAC amongst senior ANC leaders. He argued that it is 'the clique' around the president that echoes his views on AIDS, which is the source of much of the conflict.

In Brazil, where the government has been proactive in providing free treatment to AIDS sufferers and where local NGOs play a vital role in service delivery, the relationship between NGOs and the government has generally been good. There are three levels of government in Brazil (federal, state and city), and the federal government has funded NGO activities (from a World Bank loan, one tenth of which was set aside specifically for NGOs). The federal government has a department devoted to managing relations with AIDS NGOs, which means that there is constant institutional dialogue regarding implementation. Since the head of this department, as well as several other staff members, originally worked for NGOs, they are sympathizers. The NGOs, for their part, supported the government when the US lodged its TRIPS dispute with Brazil at the WTO. They organized public demonstrations in front of US consulates in major cities such as São Paulo, Recife and Rio de Janeiro in 2001. They also met with the consuls, requesting them to drop the case against the government and arguing that local production of medicines is important in a poor country such as Brazil, particularly when the devaluation of its currency made the purchase of imported drugs even more expensive. They also wrote statements and travelled abroad to defend their government's position. Furthermore, the NGOs held demonstrations before the Doha ministerial, particularly outside of the Japanese and Canadian consulates because these countries supported the US position.

Nevertheless, the relationship has had acrimonious moments. For example, while AIDS NGOs in Brazil have endorsed government actions with which they agreed (such as a recent campaign targeting gay people), they have not hesitated to criticize it on issues such as the lack of research into the causes of AIDS mortality and the impact of AIDS on different vulnerable groups. They have also used their constitutional right to sue the government to secure access to newer and better drugs. The government, too, has been critical of NGOs. During its dispute with the US government, at a public conference, the coordinator of the AIDS programme suggested that the NGOs had not been as supportive as the government would have liked, and certainly not as constant in their support as INGOs. However, one interviewee attributed this criticism to a specific disagreement. The Brazilian government had decided to place advertisements in US papers and wanted the support of the Brazilian NGOs. Since the NGOs were not consulted at the beginning or allowed to make any changes to the text of the advertisements, they refused to participate.

Relationships with pharmaceutical companies

Since one aim of the campaign has been to get pharmaceutical companies to reduce the price of HIV/AIDS drugs, NGOs have engaged in dialogue with, and lobbied, the companies. For example, Oxfam has produced reports on the performance of individual companies, such as GlaxoSmithKline (GSK) and Pfizer. It has often been hard hitting, though it is keen to praise exemplars as well as to criticize laggards. Although the report on GSK (published in February 2001) was discussed with the company, a company representative said that they were disappointed with it because they had already implemented many of the recommendations and had told Oxfam that they would be implementing the rest. GSK subsequently published its policy in June 2001 in a document entitled *Facing the Challenge*. Oxfam has also undertaken publicity stunts, such as handing out medicine packets with leaflets outlining the campaign at GSK's annual general meeting (AGM), and encouraged supporters to write to the GSK chair.

The NGOs have more often been in direct conflict with the pharmaceutical companies, accusing them of profiteering at the expense of the lives of poor people (as described in the South Africa case). The companies have responded by underlining the importance of research and development (R&D) in producing more effective treatments, as well as preventative drugs such as vaccines. A GSK spokesperson explained:

*We've got an HIV/AIDS vaccine that is just going through human
clinical trials this year. It's still five, seven, ten years from being available. That's the issue with pharmaceuticals. It takes, on average, 10 to
15 years and costs, on average, US$800 million to do it. It's very time
consuming, risky and expensive.[36]*

However, he admitted that the companies had not been able to communicate 'the
complexity of the R&D development process and the need for IP protection' in
a way that countered the emotion of the accusations against them. The industry
has come to feel that 'all the emotion is on the NGO side of the argument and
all the rationality is on the industry side', so that it needs to counter NGO campaigns with more emotion.

Nevertheless, both the NGOs and pharmaceutical companies have tried to
engage in dialogue. According to a GSK interviewee, the company consulted
NGOs such as Oxfam, MSF and VSO (as well as other stakeholders) regarding
its policy for developing countries and the role of donations. NGOs have met
with the companies to discuss specific issues. For example, Mark Heywood,
TAC's deputy chairperson, met senior GSK representatives in November 2000
to discuss the need to resolve the pending court case between the pharmaceutical
companies and the South African government. Although the Brazilian government has not included NGOs in talks with pharmaceutical companies regarding
prices, the NGOs took the initiative, in 1997, to arrange a meeting with companies such as Roche and GSK who had a monopoly on AIDS drugs. They
requested the companies to reduce their prices, but their proposal was rejected.

In addition to trying to influence pharmaceutical companies directly, NGOs
have worked with the media. A TAC interviewee pointed out that mainstream
media coverage of the campaign played a very important part in getting the companies to withdraw from the court case. NGOs were able to work with the media
and provide an alternative line of argument, raising the case's profile. The por-
trayal of the companies as putting profits before human lives in the international
media embarrassed them in their key markets and amongst their shareholders,
pressuring them into withdrawing.

A GSK interviewee highlighted the apparent favouring of NGOs over pharmaceutical companies in the media. According to him, the company highlighted
a number of inaccuracies in Oxfam's report at the time of its launch. Oxfam's
response was, 'Well, if you're unhappy with things in there, go into the media and
criticize us, attack us for it because we want to generate as much publicity as possible about this issue.' However, the company felt it was in a no-win situation:

*Big, multinational drugs baron, GSK, cannot attack little old Oxfam in
the media because the best that will happen is that the media will ignore
it; the worst that will happen is that we'll be lambasted for doing it.*

In addition to the relations between NGOs and pharmaceutical companies
described above, a number of Brazilian AIDS NGOs have received funding from

social programmes run by the companies (although some have refused such funding). The NGOs who have received funding have not reacted uniformly. While some have remained activist and critical of the companies, others appear to have become more supportive of industry interests. For a period, pharmaceutical companies seemed to cease funding the NGOs, which some attributed to the NGOs' defence of the government position. However, the companies still provide assistance to NGOs.

Relationships with other groups

Some NGOs in the campaign have forged alliances beyond their traditional partners. For example, Oxfam has obtained the support of 'establishment figures' in the media who believe that WTO rules restrict the free market and that TRIPS supports anti-competitive behaviour. Scientists such as Sir John Sulston, co-founder of the human genome project, have supported Oxfam's campaign because they have experienced practical problems with patent rules. As a result, 12 Royal Society members wrote to the *Financial Times* on the second day of Oxfam's campaign, stating that they shared its concerns about patent rules. The British Medical Association and the Royal College of Nursing in the UK, as well as health workers in other countries, have also supported the campaign, as have social investors. As ethical investment has become more mainstream, the large financial houses have established sections for this. As part of managing pensions and other funds, financial companies undertake risk assessments, including reputational risk. Therefore, Oxfam launched its report on GSK in London with the social investment community.

In addition, Oxfam's position has been supported by some within the WTO who are not allies, but who believe that the WTO should never have been given responsibility for TRIPS (although it is too late to change this). Some within the UK government, particularly the UK Department for International Development, accept that TRIPS does not benefit developing countries and have questioned government policy (although others, such as staff within the patent office, have been more sympathetic to corporate interests). Although Oxfam does not have 'moles' within the pharmaceutical companies, it has received support from people within the industry or retired people with inside knowledge of target companies. Furthermore, a policy advisor to Glaxo before its merger with SmithKline Beecham came to work for Oxfam, advising on corporate social responsibility issues. However, an Oxfam interviewee regretted that it had not developed sufficient contact with unions in the pharmaceutical companies as a mechanism to present its arguments to staff.

TAC, too, has consciously engaged with a broad spectrum of organizations. It has established a close working relationship with trade unions of teachers and health workers. Before TAC was formed, its leaders worked for organizations such as the AIDS Law Project (ALP). From 1994, this established relations with the trade union movement, particularly because of ALP's efforts to combat discrimination in the work place and to improve access for people with AIDS to employee benefits. Therefore, from the very beginning, TAC understood the political importance of the Congress of South African Trade Unions (COSATU) as an ally. Despite some organizational problems, COSATU is still regarded as the most organized, cohesive and justice-seeking CSO in the country. It also has 2 million members, many of whom are vulnerable to HIV, and therefore has been a key TAC partner. However, it has not always agreed with TAC's strategies. According to a TAC interviewee, COSATU has been very critical of its defiance campaigns and did not support its legal action against the government because it believes that there are other ways of achieving the same objectives. Other South African groups have also criticized TAC's defiance campaign. The director of an NGO, Africa Fighting Malaria, stresses that revenue generated from patents is necessary for further R&D.[37]

One of TAC's stated objectives is to 'improve the affordability and quality of health-care access for all'. As its campaign developed, TAC realized that it was not going to improve access without improvements in health services and changes in peoples' attitudes to health. Therefore, it has deliberately built alliances with organizations that boost South Africa's capacity to provide health services. This has included developing relations with junior doctors and medical organizations. Health workers are critical for implementing AIDS treatment programmes; but in South Africa, public health-care workers are poorly paid and work in terrible conditions. Therefore, TAC believes, any campaign for treatment must stress investment in the health care system and better wages and conditions for doctors and nurses. Not all health workers' unions are members of COSATU as there are two other union federations, and TAC also works with them. Its approach has been to work through the public health system, which needs to be improved, rather than promoting the creation of a parallel system for AIDS treatment. Additionally, TAC has worked with organizations such as the HIV Clinicians' Association and the South African Medical Association in order to ensure medical rigour.

TAC has also worked with churches, particularly the Anglican Church and the South African Catholic Bishops Conference (with the latter, it has temporarily put aside differences on issues such as the use of condoms). TAC's rationale is that many individuals – particularly amongst the poor and those affected by HIV – belong to churches, and so the latter can help to remove the stigma associated with HIV and convey information to large audiences. Churches worked hand-in-hand with trade unions during apartheid. Today, TAC seeks to involve them in tackling new social issues.

The role of information and communications technology

Information and communications technology (ICT) has played a key role in helping NGOs to share information and coordinate their efforts, using individual NGO websites as well as e-mail listservs such as ip-health. Organizations place information about their activities on the listserv, which is immediately disseminated globally. The Consumer Project on Technology (CPT) website is particularly well known for making a wealth of papers and documents available. TAC has used its website to make court papers available immediately after filing. The ability to supply accurate information has helped TAC to establish good relations with the media. It has also enhanced transparency and accountability, which was important when the South African government accused TAC of being funded by the pharmaceutical companies.

However, an NGO respondent pointed out that working internationally could be time consuming and frustrating because of different time zones and getting reports published in different languages. In addition, messages must resonate in different languages and cultures. Therefore, a common message needs to be balanced by diversity so that it contains the same core points, but sufficient flexibility, in order to adapt to different contexts. Consultation with partner organizations to agree the text of petitions or statements can also be time consuming and increase transaction costs. However, this is balanced by a greater sense of ownership amongst participating NGOs.

CONCLUSIONS

The effort to reduce HIV/AIDS drugs prices in developing countries worked as a campaign in bringing together grassroots groups such as TAC and various Brazilian NGOs with well-established INGOs. The network's informal nature enabled the organizations to cooperate on common interests while working separately on aspects of individual concern. For example, while TAC focused on access to ARV treatment and improving health care in South Africa, the INGOs developed wider campaigns, such as trade (Oxfam) or access to essential medicines (MSF). NGOs have also tried to ensure that their activities are complementary, so while the Consumer Project on Technology (CPT) has disseminated vast quantities of information and numerous documents through its website, others have drawn on this information for their campaigning activities. Furthermore, while MSF has focused more on direct HIV/AIDS work, the issue has been just one aspect of Oxfam's wider trade campaign.

ICT also played an important role in bringing a wide range of organizations together by enabling them to share information quickly and to make large quantities of information available on websites.

However, the different emphases and activities meant that – without a clear reason to come together, such as the South African court case or WTO events – NGOs have tended to focus on different agendas and individual campaigns. Oxfam, for instance, has had its trade campaign, while MSF has worked to promote research into new treatments for neglected tropical diseases. TAC is now building on its legal successes – for example, by successfully promoting the mother-to-child-transmission treatment case. It is now pressing for the measures to be implemented. Furthermore, although the success against the Pharmaceutical Manufacturers' Association (PMA) has contributed to 'substantial, even drastic, price reductions', medicines are still priced beyond the means of most South Africans. Therefore, TAC is launching a new legal case through the Competition Commission, initiating an investigation into its allegation that the companies have abused their patents, over-pricing medicines, aided by a lack of competition. To start its pressure, TAC is requesting meetings with all of the major companies operating in South Africa. Finally, because the attitude of the president and the health minister prevents an effective response to HIV/AIDS, TAC is working towards getting a national treatment plan.

The cases of South Africa and Brazil are interesting because of the very different approaches of the governments to both the pharmaceutical companies and local NGOs. This chapter has explained these differences and how they have led to different results – notably, that drug prices and levels of access to HIV/AIDS treatment are very different in the two countries. This underlines the important role of the state. In Brazil, local NGOs have not been invited by the government to participate in talks relating to drug prices, so their direct role in the campaign to reduce prices has been limited. Nevertheless, the proactive stance of the Brazilian government has offered a different role to NGOs – supporting the government in its position vis-à-vis the pharmaceutical companies and the US government. The government has also established a national council to consult with NGOs and academics, and has acknowledged NGOs' roles in HIV/AIDS treatment programmes (most recently, at the conference in Barcelona on HIV/AIDS, 7–12 July 2002). One Brazilian interviewee argued that 'a strong government leads to a strong civil society because they can work together'.

However, the relationship of Brazilian NGOs and their government is changing. This is because funding from the World Bank loan will soon end and NGOs will have to obtain funds from other public sources – more difficult, due to government bureaucracy. Also, as the government has outsourced most AIDS prevention and assistance activities to NGOs, they are greatly concerned about how the change in funding will affect prevention activities, particularly of NGOs who depend on public funds.

The case studies presented here also suggest that the INGOs – together with the support they mustered from leading scientists, journalists, health professional associations and politicians worldwide – have not only strengthened the campaigns at the national level, but have enabled these to be springboards for launching a 'generic' campaign to modify WTO patent rules, allowing cheaper access to life-saving drugs in all poor countries. The INGOs have not only facilitated exchanges between grassroots activists working on a common issue internationally – thereby greatly strengthening these national campaigns – but have also used ground-level information from a few national campaigns to give greater credibility to their global case. This therefore illustrates a powerful symbiosis between the local- and global-level activists.

NOTES

1   Cited in 'Cut the Cost: Patent Injustice – How World Trade Rules Threaten the Health of Poor People', Oxfam, February 2001; see www.oxfam.org.uk.
2   From the Médecins Sans Frontières (MSF) 'Access to Essential Medicines' campaign website: www.accessmed-msf.org/index.asp.
3   Based on Oxfam (2001b); see References at the end of this book.
4   Cited in 'Cut the Cost: Patent Injustice – How World Trade Rules Threaten the Health of Poor People', Oxfam, February 2001; see www.oxfam.org.uk.

5   From the Médecins Sans Frontières (MSF) 'Access to Essential Medicines' campaign website: www.accessmed-msf.org/index.asp.

6   Examples of US compulsory licences use are cited in the 'Health GAP Statement on Brazil's Intention to Issue a Compulsory Licence for Nelfinavir' (22 August 2001) at www.cptech.org/ip/health/c/brazil/hgap-brazil08222001 and in a listserv message from James Love, CPT, 24 August 2001 (see www.cptech.org/ip/health).

7   From the Médecins Sans Frontières (MSF) 'Access to Essential Medicines' campaign website: www.accessmed-msf.org/index.asp.

8   Heather Stewart, Charlotte Denny and Andrew Clark (2001) 'Bayer bows to pressure on anthrax antidote', *Guardian*, 23 October

9   According to Nick Mathiason, 'Anthrax Antidote? We'll Buy the Lot', *Observer*, 21 October 2001

10   Based on Sarah Left (2001) 'Row looming over anthrax drug patent', *Guardian*, 22 October

11   Prices cited in Heather Stewart, Charlotte Denny and Andrew Clark (2001) 'Bayer bows to pressure on anthrax antidote', *Guardian*, 23 October

12   'Patient rights versus patent rights', Notebook in *Guardian*, 23 October 2001

13   Available from the WTO website: www.wto.org

14   Based on 'Green Light to Put Public Health First at WTO Ministerial Conference in Doha', joint statement by MSF, Oxfam, Third World Network, CPT, Consumers International, Health Action International and The Network, 11 November 2001. Available from Oxfam News Releases on Oxfam's website: www.oxfam.org.uk.

15   From the Médecins Sans Frontières (MSF) 'Access to Essential Medicines' campaign website: www.accessmed-msf.org/index.asp; Oxfam (2001b); and joint NGO statement by TAC, Oxfam and MSF on 31 August 2001 on 'Discrimination in Media Reporting on Brazil', available from the CPT website: www.cptech.

16   Based on information from the CPT website: www.cptech.

17   According to an article from *WTO Reporter* (2001) 'United States Drops WTO Case Against Brazil Over HIV/AIDS Patent Law', 26 June, available at www.cptech.org/ip/health/c/brazil/bna06262001.

18   Peter Capella (2001) 'Brazil Wins HIV Drug Concession from US: Complaint to WTO on Patent Law Withdrawn', *Guardian*, 26 June

19   Available at www.ustr.gov/releases/2001/06/01-46: press release by the Office of US Trade Representative, Geneva, 25 June 2001

20   According to a USTR press release, 25 June 2001, 'United States and Brazil Agree to Use the Newly Created Consultative Mechanism to Promote Cooperation on HIV/AIDS and Address WTO Patent Dispute'.

21   In 'US Beats a (Tactical) Retreat over Brazil's Patent Law' by Chakravarthi Raghavan. Article first published in the *South–North Development Monitor* (SUNS); see www.twnside.org.sg/title/tactical.

22   Text of communiqué available at: www.cptech.org/ip/health/c/brazil/brazilstatement06252001.

23   In 'US Beats a (Tactical) Retreat over Brazil's Patent Law' by Chakravarthi Raghavan. Article first published in the *South–North Development Monitor* (SUNS); see www.twnside.org.sg/title/tactical.

24   According to an article from *WTO Reporter* (2001) 'United States Drops WTO Case Against Brazil Over HIV/AIDS Patent Law', 26 June, available at www.cptech.org/ip/health/c/brazil/bna06262001, and 'Ministry of Health Announces Compulsory Licensing of Nelfinavir Patent', Brazilian Ministry of Health press release available at www.cptech.org/ ip/health/c/brazil/nelf08222001.

25 'Ministry of Health Announces Compulsory Licensing of Nelfinavir Patent', Brazilian Ministry of Health press release available at www.cptech.org/ip/health/c/brazil/nelf08222001.

26 'Roche and the Brazilian Ministry of Health Reach Agreement for Supply of HIV Drug Viracept: Brazilian Government Honours Patent for Viracept', Roche Press Release on 31 August 2001; see www.roche.com/med-corp-detail-2001?id=689; and *Washington Post* (2001) 'Swiss Company Agrees to Cut Price of AIDS Drug', 1 September

27 According to Chakravarthi Raghavan, 'US Beats a (Tactical) Retreat over Brazil's Patent Law'. Article first published in the *South–North Development Monitor* (SUNS); see www.twnside.org.sg/title/tactical.

28 The description of the lawsuit between the pharmaceutical companies and the South African government and the role of TAC is based on Heywood (2001).

29 See Heywood (2001) for a detailed description of the inequities in South African health care and reasons for the high price of medicines.

30 The pharmaceutical companies included the five who lead in the HIV/AIDS field: Merck & Co; GSK; Bristol-Myers Squibb; Roche; and Boehringer Ingelheim.

31 The campaign is named after a TAC volunteer who died in July 2000 from AIDS-related illnesses that can be treated by Pfizer's drug Diflucan (fluconazole).

32 The term '*amicus curiae*' means 'friend of the court'. In South Africa, to be admitted as an *amicus*, the applicant must demonstrate that he or she can provide insight and argument that does not already exist in court papers and that the input is not erroneous, vexatious or repetitive. Unless special permission is sought, the *amicus* must confine himself or herself to points of law and not introduce new evidence that might be disputed (Heywood, 2001).

33 According to Mark Heywood of TAC, the dissidents' view has two main components. Firstly, although they accept that acquired immune deficiency syndrome (AIDS) exists, they believe that there is no hard scientific evidence that it is caused by HIV or any other virus. President Thabo Mbeke argues that other factors, such as poverty, cause AIDS. While TAC agrees that poverty worsens people's immune systems, it believes that it is nonsense to suggest that AIDS has no viral cause. Secondly, they claim that ARVs are poisonous and are the cause of death, not a virus. President Mbeke, in particular, has been responsible for popularizing these arguments, which have impacted upon government health policy. Why the dissident view has widespread support is discussed in Robins (2002).

34 For a full description of events leading up to TAC's establishment, see Soal (2001).

35 Based on Heywood (2001).

36 It should be noted that industry estimates of R&D costs vary and have been disputed. For example, an e-mail message from Professor Michael Davis (michael.davis@law.csuohio.edu), 28 February 2002, cited on the CPT website, says:

> *Ten years ago when I started working in this field, Pharma said it cost about US$100 million per drug. About five years ago, they had upped that to US$200 million. Within a year or two after that, they were up to US$300 million and just last year they were making the outrageous claim that it cost US$500 million. Now, it costs US$800 million. Puhleeze, as they say! Before we go any further with this, is it possible we could demand some audited numbers – audited by somebody disinterested?*

37 Richard Tren (2002) 'The Boys from Brazil', posted on the ip-health listserv on 25 February; see www.lists.essential.org/pipermail/ip-health/2002-February/002719.

Chapter 5

Jubilee 2000: Laying the Foundations for a Social Movement

Paola Grenier

Each campaign is finite, and there is always another campaign to enlist in when the first fails or goes rancid. The realized impurity of a movement can destroy the person who has identified himself with that movement; but the impurity of a campaign can be taken in one's stride: such impurity is just what one expects of something finite and mortal (Rorty, 1998: 118–119).

INTRODUCTION: WHAT WAS JUBILEE 2000?

Jubilee 2000 has been hailed as one of the most successful global campaigns on economic and social justice, focusing on debt relief for the poorest countries in the world.[1] This chapter is about how its origins as a focused and imaginative campaign led to its prominence and successes, and at the same time sowed the seeds for friction and conflict.

The public profile of Jubilee 2000 masks the complex development from a small and informal campaign, based at Keele University in the north-west of England, into a broad-based coalition with organizations active in 69 countries and individuals in 166 countries. It mobilized millions of people and hundreds of organizations, impacting on the policies, and thinking, of both national governments and multilateral institutions. Based on a biblical reference for debt relief as a new beginning, Jubilee provided a spiritual message for the millennium. It was a five-year campaign that played an important part in laying the foundations for a broad and diverse emerging social movement concerning debt relief.

Jubilee 2000's form is multidimensional, and has evolved over time. Jubilee 2000 was originally a UK-based campaign calling specifically for the 'cancellation by the year 2000 of the unpayable debt owed by the world's poorest countries under a fair and transparent process' (Hanson and Travis, 1999; Barrett, 2000). This was the founding aim of the Jubilee 2000 Coalition UK that brought together 110 UK organizations. The UK office also provided the inspiration and leadership for the international campaign network – Jubilee 2000 – a loose transnational network of organizations, groups and individuals with the common objective of debt relief. The development of the international network was a stage in the emergence of a transnational social movement, linking domestic and international protests and engaging a range of actors who had not before been involved in debt campaigning. Figure 5.1 (see p88) maps this evolution from a UK coalition to an international network, and then to a broader and more diverse movement, though at times the stages coincide and overlap.

The Jubilee 2000 Coalition UK and the campaign focus were all time-limited and ceased to exist in those particular forms on 31 December 2000, after barely five years of operating. By this point, commitments to bilateral and multilateral debt relief totalled US$110 billion, and some actual relief (about US$12 billion) had been obtained for 20 countries (Barrett, 2000: 38).[2] Though this fell well short of the original objective of relief of the unpayable debt for 52 countries, totalling US$375 billion, it was still a significant achievement in terms of economic benefit to some of the poorest nations. More significantly, the message of debt relief had been widely adopted within the target institutions – the multilaterals and the G7 governments – as well as by many individuals and civil society organizations (CSOs) internationally.

The winding up of the UK Coalition left a gap in terms of leadership and coordination for the international network. Nevertheless, since the millennium, CSOs, politicians and others have continued to campaign on debt relief, albeit more loosely coordinated, within an emerging social movement with multiple messages, rather than as a campaign with a single objective.

Jubilee's rapid rise and short life make it an interesting and tightly delineated example of the development of present-day transnational civil society.

This case study tracks the emergence and development of Jubilee 2000. It is based on interviews with key leaders of Jubilee 2000 UK, questionnaires to national campaigns, documents relating to Jubilee, press articles, internet sites and observations at meetings. The following section focuses on the context of debt as a global issue and the origins of Jubilee 2000 UK. The third section, 'Forging the coalition', looks at the creation of the broader coalition in the UK and covers its development into a transnational network, as well as the challenges and opportunities that were experienced. The fourth section, 'The end of 2000', looks at the contentious way in which the campaign ended and provides an overview of the forms in which Jubilee and the debt campaigns have continued since 2000. The final section provides some concluding thoughts and comments on Jubilee.

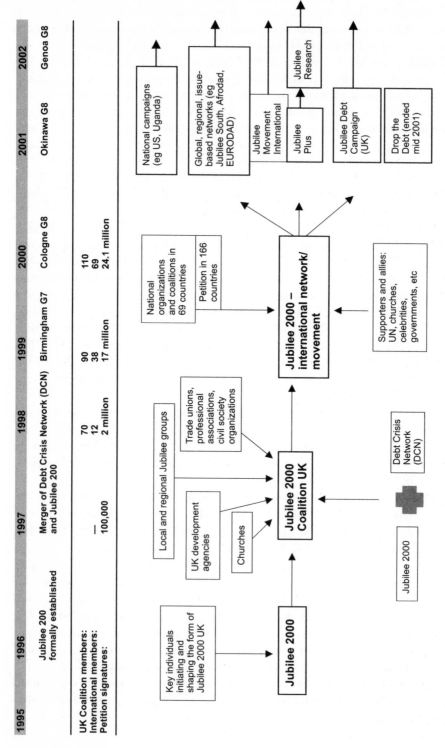

Figure 5.1 *Jubilee 2000 – evolution timeline*

THE CONTEXT AND ORIGINS OF JUBILEE 2000

Jubilee 2000 brought together the historical message of the biblical jubilee and the principles behind that, with the particular context of the developing-world debt crisis of the 1990s. This section looks at the issue of debt and how Jubilee 2000 evolved from an idea seeking to address the debt problems into an active and organized campaign.

Debt as a global issue

The Jubilee concept was first conceived in 1990 as the debt owed by some of the poorest countries was reaching a crisis (Dent and Peters, 1999). Following an earlier crisis in 1982 when Mexico defaulted on its loans, there was some reform of the debt regime, largely focusing on middle-income countries. The debts of the poorer countries did not threaten the global economic system and were therefore not a focus for reform. The development non-governmental organizations (NGOs) noticed how those countries, mostly in Africa, were cutting basic services and investment in infrastructure in order to service their debts – hence creating severe social problems. Campaigns were mounted in the North and South to raise awareness of this; but progress in changing policy was slow.[3]

Sovereign debt is a global issue, based on economic interdependence between countries. The poorest countries' debts were with the World Bank, International Monetary Fund (IMF), other multilateral institutions, and individual Organization for Economic Cooperation and Development (OECD) governments. Debt, therefore, highlighted the roles, responsibilities and governance of the multilateral institutions, as well as national governments. One of the challenges for debt campaigners was a displaced accountability, where Northern creditors – largely the G7 countries – were accountable to their own citizens and not to those in debtor countries. This defined debt as a global issue requiring campaigning at both national and international levels.

The global nature of the debt problem contributed to the way in which the Jubilee campaign took shape. At its birth in the early 1990s, there was considerable momentum and expertise behind debt campaigns in a few countries, especially in the UK and The Netherlands, and international coordination was emerging – though it was still limited.

The origins of Jubilee 2000

Martin Dent, a retired political scientist at Keele University, initiated the Jubilee idea in 1990. At this very early stage some fundamental choices were made that formed the philosophical and strategic basis for the future campaign (interviews: Lovett and Dent; Dent and Peters, 1999). The focus was the one-off relief of the unpayable debts of the poorest countries. It therefore avoided the moral hazards of pressing for debt relief for countries who were able to pay, and also for recurring debt relief for poorer countries. This was critical in obtaining credibility with the financial institutions.

Dent drew on the idea of jubilee, a biblical message that had already had significant historical impact through the anti-slavery movement and US liberation:

> *And ye shall hallow the fiftieth year, and proclaim liberty throughout all the land unto all the inhabitants thereof: it shall be a jubilee unto you; and ye shall return every man unto his possession, and ye shall return every man unto his family Leviticus 25 (10).*

Essentially, the jubilee message is to free all slaves, forgive all debts and return all dispossessed land every 50 years. This was brought to life in a modern context as a message of one-off debt relief (Dent and Peters, 1999). The millennium was the obvious deadline; and the name Jubilee 2000 was born. The spiritual and biblical nature of the message meant that Jubilee was more than a campaign target or slogan; it had an appeal with religious leaders (including the Pope and the Archbishop of Canterbury) and churchgoers, as well as with the general public (Jubilee 2000 Coalition, 2001).

During the early 1990s, Jubilee 2000 was a loose, informal and somewhat chaotic group, of which Martin Dent, Bill Peters (a retired diplomat) and Isabel Carter (of Tearfund) were the core individuals. Their main activities were attending conferences, writing letters and promoting a petition that started in 1990 with 200 students from Keele and came to have significant international impact.

Another key future determinant was that Dent started attending meetings of the Debt Crisis Network (DCN) in 1991. This was an informal network of UK development agencies that coordinated and shared information on debt campaigning and, occasionally, partnered on specific campaigns. In 1994, Ann Pettifor was employed by DCN to step up its work. Some people in the network recognized the inspirational potential of Jubilee, though others thought it lacked credibility. The next stage, through 1995, involved Ann Pettifor working persistently with Jubilee 2000 to develop the idea into a wider, more strategic campaign.

Establishing Jubilee 2000 as an organization

Jubilee 2000 was officially launched in April 1996 as a new and independent charity. Isabel Carter was 'almost entirely responsible for getting Jubilee 2000 off the ground' (interview: Pettifor). Feeling inspired by a vision from God, she formally registered the organization with the Charity Commission, raised some funding and found an office within Christian Aid (Hanson and Travis, 1999; Barrett, 2000). Ann Pettifor was employed as part-time coordinator alongside her DCN role.

Within its first year, Jubilee 2000 gained high-profile support, with the Most Reverend Desmond Tutu as its president. The campaign gained pace within the churches, in particular. The petition became a powerful campaign tool as it mobilized people and organizations both in the UK and internationally (Hanson and Travis, 1999). In April 1997, Jubilee 2000 launched the 1000-day countdown to the millennium in a widely reported central London event, attended by 400 activists (Barrett, 2000). By this point, Jubilee's potential became evident, and the development agencies involved in DCN started taking Jubilee 2000 more seriously.

Jubilee's founding characteristics and strategies shaped its future in three ways and were the basis for the tensions that emerged. Firstly, its campaign message involved framing debt remission in popular, understandable terms as a part of the one-off celebration of the millennium. This attracted people and provided a powerful deadline around which to gain momentum and build urgency. It also led to disagreements and disillusionment when the deadline came and not all of the debt had been written off. Secondly, it was a broad collaborative effort that aimed to mobilize mass support internationally for debt relief. It therefore encompassed a diversity of opinions and vested interests that were difficult to hold together, even at the beginning. Thirdly, Jubilee originated in the UK. While the wisdom of extending internationally became quickly apparent, its UK origins were always strongly present and Jubilee UK provided the leadership for the international campaign. These three characteristics are explored in greater detail below.

FORGING THE COALITION

Following its successes in 1996–1997, Jubilee 2000's priority was to rapidly broaden its support base within the UK, while at the same time developing the international Jubilee movement. This section looks at how Jubilee's UK origins, its collaborative nature and its focus on the millennium deadline fuelled internal tensions, both in the UK and internationally.

Building the UK coalition

The successes of Jubilee 2000 led Ed Mayo, chair of DCN, and a few others to start thinking about closer cooperation. In 1997, Jubilee 2000 merged with DCN. This was a critical step in bringing together the Jubilee idea with the resources, networks and expertise of the development agencies. The merged organization restructured itself as an umbrella body and was renamed the Jubilee 2000 Coalition UK. It was officially launched on 13 October 1997, consisting of 70 organizations (Hanson and Travis, 1999; Barrett, 2000).

The merged organization adopted a fairly standard organizational structure – with staff, trustees, patrons, a president, an office and budgets. It was both a registered charity and a company, as is standard practice in the UK. As a coalition, it had an organizational membership base, consisting of the UK development agencies, the regional/local Jubilee groups in the UK and other coalition members. Most significantly, the organization was formally British and the trustees were therefore representatives of the UK coalition members.

The millennium became an important aspect of the organizational form, as well as the campaign deadline. As is the case for many campaigns at the early stages, it was considered important to avoid creating another NGO that would become institutionalized when the original campaign deadline had passed (interviews: Pettifor and Lovett; Bunting, 2000). Jubilee also wanted to work constructively with the development agencies, and not to be seen as competing with them. The solution was to establish a time-limited organization – 'a short-life, temporary volatile entity' – that would exist for the duration of the campaign until 31 December 2000 (Marks, 2000). Staff contracts therefore ran until that date:

> *The time limit – that was one of the really useful things. Although it created stress and pressure, it also gave everyone the excuse: we can't worry about structures now, we can't worry about getting the process absolutely right; what we have to do is to build the pressure and get a result because we haven't got very long (interview: Lovett).*

While deadlines are common in campaigns, marking such a clear end point for both the campaign and the organization was to become highly contentious within the Jubilee membership nationally and (especially) internationally.

As well as its time-bound nature, the Jubilee Coalition was collaborative and heterogeneous. This was both a strength and a weakness, and gave rise to a number of overlapping tensions. It brought increased legitimacy, resources and supporters, at the same time as disagreement and competing interests and perspectives. This was notable as organizational culture differences grew between Jubilee – the new and small campaign group, that was highly flexible and personal in nature – and the large, formal and well-established development agencies (interviews: Pettifor and Owuso). In effect, Jubilee operated at a more grassroots level, with local activists breaking down the divisions between agencies at a local level and creating unity from the bottom up:

> *The relationship with these institutions [the development NGOs] was always complex because as institutions they are quite inflexible; they are big ships and they can't change their steerage very easily (interview: Pettifor).*

In addition, while the development agencies were cooperating within the Jubilee coalition, on the whole they worked independently and were often competing with each other. Taken together, this meant that Jubilee was not a wholly cohesive and collaborative effort, and there were many ongoing challenges in the internal running of the campaign.

From its launch in 1997, the Jubilee Coalition quickly became a high-profile campaign in the UK and, increasingly, internationally, gaining credibility with the institutions and the people whom it was targeting. Highlights were the 70,000-strong human chain formed around the G8 summit in Birmingham in May 1998; the 50,000-strong protest at the Cologne summit in 1999; and the 65,000 e-mails sent one day in the summer of 2000, resulting in the Italian government closing its e-mail account (Barrett, 2000). In addition to these mass events, Jubilee also met directly with policy-makers and political leaders, including UK Prime Minister Tony Blair, the heads of the IMF and the World Bank, and leaders from the South. It gained committed support from the *Guardian* newspaper, and was featured regularly in papers, magazines and on the radio.

However, Jubilee's successes also deepened its tensions with the UK development agencies. Even though the agencies were formally represented on its board, the secretariat was the driving force behind what had become a popular and an increasingly international campaign. As Jubilee became more successful, it was seen, more often, as competing for funds, media coverage and public profile (interview: Moulds):

> *They [some of the biggest aid agencies] have become anxious that the success of the campaign weakens their profile among supporters and fund raising (Bunting, 2000).*

In terms of staff relationships, the policy experts in the development agencies had misgivings about the way in which the coalition involved people without debt expertise in its campaigning (interview: Pettifor). This raised concerns about weakening the credibility of the agencies' policy work, and whether efforts to popularize the issue would erode good relations with the UK government, the World Bank and the IMF. These tensions reflected the differences in organizational structures, culture and priorities mentioned earlier. There were also tensions related to particular personalities and personal relationships: 'What is this – a soap opera or a political movement? Well, it's both. And that is not necessarily bad' (interview: Moulds).

As much as Jubilee depended upon the development agencies for support, it also challenged their ways of working, their interests and their expertise, and encountered jealousy and – at times – resistance. The following sub-section examines the emergence of the international campaign and how the UK Coalition provided leadership to this, as well as the emerging social movement.

Shaping the campaign internationally

The Jubilee 2000 Coalition UK inspired the international movement, developing and providing leadership to the network of Jubilee campaigns in different countries. It was the three defining aspects of Jubilee outlined earlier – its popular focused message; its diversity; and its UK origins and leadership – that made the international campaign successful, but also led to the difficulties and problems that made it increasingly difficult to hold together.

This first aspect is the systematic and astute way in which Jubilee 2000 UK framed the issue of debt and created a highly targeted campaign focus:

> *Designing a campaign is like looking at a diamond. The specialists, they look at the diamonds for two years before they cut them and then they get the maximum reflection from the diamonds. So, you would have to cut the problem in the way that would get maximum effect. And we cut the debt problem to get maximum reflection (interview: Pettifor).*

The campaign message stemmed from the original jubilee concept, first promoted by Dent and Peters during the early 1990s – the one-off remission of the unpayable debt of the poorest countries. Politically, the message was positioned to 'be radical enough to mobilize people but not so radical that you were marginalized' (interview: Pettifor). It carefully presented debt in social, human and common-sense terms that made it accessible and emotive for the general public in both the North and South:

> *For me, what they did better than anyone else, better than their coalition members, was this way of articulating the issue, often in very punchy short sentences in a way that converted supporters (interview: Moulds).*

Jubilee's analysis emphasized the co-responsibility of the creditor and debtor countries. Creditors had, at times, supported corrupt regimes and used loans to pursue inappropriate commercial agendas, while debtors, occasionally, practised bad economic management and, sometimes, corruption. Theirs was not a call for debt 'forgiveness' but for debt remission and relief: 'Our incurring of debt has not primarily been our fault and hence "forgiveness" is not what we are seeking but justice' (Zambian church leaders, August 1998, in Barrett, 2000: 14).

The campaign targets were similarly carefully defined. Initially, Jubilee 2000 UK focused on the seemingly unaccountable World Bank and the IMF, although recognizing that the G7 governments were the key decision-makers and financiers behind them.[4] The specific target for policy reform that was adopted was the Heavily Indebted Poorer Countries Initiative (HIPC), launched in the autumn of 1996, which sought debt relief for the poorest countries. HIPC followed from the reformist stance adopted by the World Bank under its then new president, James Wolfensohn, coupled with effective NGO campaigns on debt reform (Scholte, 2001; Bauck, 2001). HIPC identified 42 of the poorest heavily indebted countries as eligible for debt relief providing that they comply with economic conditionalities or 'structural adjustment programmes' (SAPs). These condition-alities were deeply resented in the South for requiring six years of compliance with demanding, and often socially damaging, economic reforms before a debtor received relief.

Jubilee 2000's campaign objectives were to reform HIPC, including speed-ing it up and extending it from 42 to 52 countries, as well as removing SAP con-ditionalities. Implicitly, it sought to reform the institutions, rather than the more radical approach of abolishing them (Scholte, 2001; Desai and Said, 2001). These tight campaign demands were powerful for mobilizing public opinion; but the reformist stance, together with difficulties in agreeing what alternative condi-tionalities would be appropriate, became areas of disagreement and conflict in the international coalition.

The international campaign that targeted the multilaterals was paralleled by national campaigns. There was growing political will in some creditor countries for helping poorer countries who couldn't repay their debts (Bauck, 2001; Hut-ton, 2000). The long history of debt campaigning in the UK was reflected by the leading role that the UK government had played in promoting debt relief under successive chancellors of the exchequer since 1987.[5] Strong campaigns developed in a similar way in Canada and The Netherlands, where campaigns had been effective and governments were open to debt relief. In contrast, there was minimal campaigning in Japan, whose government was politically the least receptive to debt relief.

The second aspect of the international campaign was mobilizing mass support for the message. Ann Pettifor, director of Jubilee 2000 Coalition UK, gave an extraordinary impetus to developing the campaign internationally by addressing meetings and conferences around the world. She was widely interviewed by the media, prompting organizations and individuals to join. By 1998, over 60 national campaigns had been organized – 69 by the end of 2000:

> *The purpose of the coalition-building was simple: to harness the broadest possible social forces to challenge the much more powerful forces of the international financial institutions (Barrett, 2000: 6).*

Jubilee worked largely through existing church and political networks. Its message had a resonance in the South (interview: Owuso), and churches were particularly important in mobilizing support. Its transnational nature gave it a powerful voice and legitimacy with international institutions, the media and national governments:

> *It was an extraordinary coalition of groups, ranging from aid agencies and churches to the British Medical Association, the music industry and the Mothers' Union. This formula was replicated in each country, forming an enormous civil network which commanded considerable respect at the World Bank and the International Monetary Fund (IMF) (Bunting, 2000).*

The petition was the mechanism for signing up to the campaign and was a primary campaign focus (interview: Pettifor; Barrett, 2000). It gave Jubilee 2000 a mandate, backed by millions of individuals, 'to cancel the unpayable debt of the most impoverished nations… We are looking for a new beginning to celebrate the millennium' (Jubilee Coalition, petition website). The petition reached 166 countries, breaking a world record with 24.2 million signatures, and enabled activists to get involved in countries where there wasn't a full-blown campaign.

The internet and e-mail were important tools for Jubilee in communicating internationally, helping with consultation and decision-making (questionnaire responses: Jubilee groups in Ireland, Zambia, Burundi, Cameroon and Ecuador). Policy and research materials were 'universally praised' (Marks, 2000) and provided Southern organizations, in particular, with dependable information and arguments. Jubilee was a pioneer in using the internet as a campaigning and communication tool, with its own website since 1995 (interview: Pettifor). Such early use may have been to Jubilee's advantage, predating the flood of information and e-mails that has ensued (questionnaire response: Jubilee groups in Ireland).

The third aspect was that, formally, there was no central or lead organization, though, in practice, Jubilee 2000 UK filled this role for various reasons. It was the founder and originator of the Jubilee debt-relief concept; it initiated the campaign, the petition and the international coalition; it was the best-resourced

Jubilee (interviews: Pettifor and Lovett); it had a charismatic and highly committed director (Jubilee 2000 Coalition UK, 2001) – 'she was perceived in the movement as the driving force, for better or for worse' (interview: Lovett); it recruited international figures and celebrities; and the major media and global institutions related to the London office as the international mouthpiece. Even though it was not formally elected as international network leader, it had a great deal of legitimacy in that position. Most tellingly, national groups generally followed its lead. In spite of this, leadership of the campaign was increasingly contested, resulting in serious rifts within the North and between North and South.

Jubilee 2000 UK set the basic campaign direction, the focus and the strategies: 'We had to make sure that it was exciting enough that everybody else would want to be there' (interview: Pettifor). It would then inform the international network what events and activities Jubilee 2000 UK was undertaking, but left it up to each group to decide whether to join in. This approach allowed an incredible energy, resourcefulness and imagination to evolve – from blow-up 'loan sharks', to rickshaw rides, trumpet calls and e-mail campaigns from mountain tops (Barrett, 2000). Every country and every group did things slightly differently, having their own identity, as well as being part of a bigger whole.

The international campaign was boosted by two critical events. The first was the promotion of Jubilee by the pop star Bono and the retired boxer Mohammed Ali at the Brit Awards in February 1999. Through this televised show, Jubilee's message was broadcast internationally to millions of people; this gave the campaign international popular recognition and took it to another level (interview: Lovett). The second event was a significant breakthrough at the G8 summit in Cologne in June 1999, when US$100 billion was committed to debt relief. Both of these events provided evidence of Jubilee's effectiveness and heightened Southern campaigners' confidence in their involvement (interview: Owuso).

The process of crafting the campaign strategy was a daily challenge, at all times seeking maximum opportunities internationally (interview: Pettifor). As the campaign momentum grew, and as greater numbers became involved, internal tensions came increasingly to the fore.

Success and growing tensions

This section explores the processes within the Jubilee movement, especially North–South relationships, as these can be the most testing aspect of a transnational coalition (Kekk and Sikkink, 1998). It then looks, in turn, at communications between Jubilee members, the structure and governance of the international network, and pressures to develop greater Southern leadership.

Firstly, what were the communications challenges within Jubilee? Southern campaigners were not directly involved in the formation of Jubilee 2000 UK during 1996–1997 – it was a 'British invention that then went worldwide' (interview: Kewsi Owuso). Nevertheless, they were increasingly involved as the campaign evolved. The North–South links were generally considered to be positive and 'enlightened' compared with many other such NGO relationships (interviews: Lovett and Owuso).

A meeting in Rome in November 1998, attended by 38 Jubilee groups (equally from North and South), provided the first major opportunity to air different national perspectives. There was extensive debate and dissension around campaign objectives (Collins, 2001; interview: Pettifor). At the end, a statement was agreed that, while generally consistent with earlier Jubilee 2000 UK statements, put greater emphasis on creditors' responsibility for supporting corrupt regimes and for damaging conditionalities (Jubilee Call, website). Opinions vary as to whether this meeting was a success or a failure. There was certainly significant North–South friction, as well as healthy debate, with some serious disagreement that was left unresolved.

Also debated was Jubilee's reformist, rather than radical, stance. It sought to change relationships between richer and poorer countries through existing frameworks and opportunities, and did not advocate dismantling the World Bank and the IMF (interview: Lovett). This created consternation with certain Southern groups, who took a more radical, abolitionist position. These debates reflect the tension between solidarity around campaign objectives and welcoming pluralism and debate within the movement. Jubilee was both unifying and plural, though this was difficult to sustain – 'a social movement need not be rooted in a consensus to achieve an effective solidarity' (Grint, 1997: 291).

Apart from occasional meetings, such as in Rome and at summits, most communication was by e-mail. While this was essential in facilitating international communications, it was 'impersonal' and revealed the power and resource imbalances between North and South (Collins et al, 2001: 143). These imbalances led to concerns about the structure and governance of the network, which had always been loose and transnational. The Rome meeting debated establishing a formal international governance structure; but it decided against this largely because the participants viewed Jubilee as a social movement for which high levels of regulation and strict membership criteria would be inappropriate.

Jubilee 2000 worked with existing organizations and networks who chose their own activities, expressing solidarity with the Jubilee message by signing the petition (Barrett, 2000; interviews: Lovett and Pettifor). The particular benefits of this were high levels of creativity and local ownership, as activities were locally originated and resourced:

> *The informality of the more or less autonomous local, national and international coalitions could have been a weakness. But, in the end, it gave room for creative and spontaneous action and greater flexibility (Barrett, 2000: 7).*

However, the resulting loose and informal network at times proved a 'messy and entirely unsatisfactory way of working together' (interview: Lovett). There were no formal processes for consultation within the coalition, let alone global decision-making. Internally, the Jubilee 2000 Coalition UK adapted its organizational structure in its last year to give equal prominence to working with the international network as the campaign focused on the G7 countries (interview: Owuso).

It retained leadership of the international campaign and – even though it was responsive to the global network – technically its primary accountabilities were to its domestic coalition members.

In spite of these shortcomings, Jubilee 2000 created a 'platform for the people in the South to make their case', rather than the more common pattern of Northern agencies speaking on their behalf (Jubilee 2000 Coalition UK, 2001):

> *One thing which it [Jubilee 2000] did really well: it was always a very dynamic interface between the work of the [Northern] agencies and what we are doing in the South (Owuso, 2002).*

In terms of North–South relationships, the fact that the locus of leadership was in the North was contentious. There were growing calls for more Southern leadership – first at the Rome meeting and also at a South–South Jubilee 2000 meeting prior to the 1999 Cologne G8 summit (Collins et al, 2001). However, there were no governance processes in place to deal with this formally. Jubilee 2000 focused on the campaign aims and on the deadline, and 'lip service' was paid to developing Southern leadership (interviews: Lovett and Owuso). Jubilee 2000 UK remained the voice of the global movement (interview: Owuso). There was a sense that Jubilee was 'created in the North by middle-class white people, which was then offered' to the South, though this was more problematic for some groups than others (interview: Moulds), and quite remarkable leadership emerged in many of the national campaigns – for example, in Uganda, Bolivia and Peru – which in turn created regional hubs.

These tensions contributed to a serious conflict within the Jubilee movement, centering on a leadership challenge from a network of individuals and groups in Africa and Latin America known as Jubilee South. These were intellectuals and left-wing political activists, some of who were present at the Rome meeting, though some Southern groups also sought to distance themselves from Jubilee South's radical stance. The organization was later formalized at a meeting in South Africa in November 1999. It took on the Jubilee name and adopted the Jubilee message; yet, it sought to challenge the Jubilee 2000 campaign from within. It promoted the illegitimacy of debt, called for reparations and the righting of colonial wrongs, and presented a rejectionist position towards the global financial institutions. It also envisaged a much longer campaign, without the millennium deadline:

> *The Jubilee concept, for some of us – if not all of us – in the South, has a far-reaching meaning than the limited concept applied in the North…a meaning that embraces the whole of the economic aspects of our lives (statement at the South–South summit in South Africa, by Mandlate, 1999).*

Events in the US created the opportunity for Jubilee South to gain greater credibility and to challenge the Northern leadership. Congressman Jim Leach introduced a bill into the US Congress in March 1999, promoting additional debt relief by the US while retaining adjustment programmes. Jubilee 2000/USA supported the Leach bill, and this proved to be highly contentious within the US, between Southern and Northern campaigns, and within the Jubilee movement as a whole. Southern groups had fiercely rejected SAPs at the Rome meeting, and they therefore felt that their voice had been ignored by the Northern campaigns. This gave Jubilee South legitimacy in voicing these concerns and in criticizing the North in general, even though Jubilee 2000/USA was also criticized by other Northern campaigns, including Jubilee 2000 UK. This was, essentially, an ideological clash, with Jubilee South taking advantage of the Leach bill to assert leadership over the international movement, framing it as a clash between the North and South and thereby undermining the leadership provided by Jubilee 2000 UK.

In fact, Jubilee 2000 UK worked hard to stop Jubilee 2000/USA from supporting the Leach bill under the Jubilee banner, and went so far as to try to 'unite the whole world against the Americans' (interview: Pettifor). Within Jubilee 2000/USA, there was 'a rift that almost tore the coalition apart' and, in the end, it did not support the bill (Bauck, 2001). Jubilee was unable to fully resolve the issue, as it kept its focus on the campaign deadline, and this became 'the outstanding division that was left at the end of 2000' (interview: Lovett).

This situation was further complicated as Jubilee South gained profile and credibility in the North as a genuine voice from the South, and it reflected broader North–South iniquities:

> *If you are in Ghana and you see the slave forts, it's a part of your heritage. The idea that you are doing someone a favour by not paying these debts is just outrageous. If only decent books of accounts had been kept, what price, how much, would the North actually owe you – billions! So you can very much understand their position and you can very much understand the position of the people in the North who sit around wisely and talk about political realities and conditionalities and all that. And both are absolutely right (interview: Moulds).*

The Jubilee Coalition UK had no control or legal rights over the use of the name Jubilee or over who joined the network. When the Leach bill issue threatened to tear the movement apart, intense social pressure was brought to bear. The form of control was social, and was based on informal relationships and trust, rather than on formal structures and hierarchies. This allowed for a more organic development of the movement, including national and context-specific campaigns, but also laid it open to power struggles, internal dissent and the pursuit of alternative agendas.

The strengths of Jubilee 2000 internationally as a broad-based, loose coalition also proved to be its main weaknesses. The high level of autonomy and control amongst network members fostered local ownership, creativity, initiative and resource mobilization, and brought together a very diverse range of people and organizations. However, as the campaign grew and gained the attention of the media, global institutions and public opinion, there was increasing dissent around objectives, as well as internal power struggles and the pursuit of other agendas. During 2000, Jubilee's momentum became harder to control and was unfocused. By the end of 2000, the Jubilee Coalition was clearly running out of time as a unified campaign (Marks, 2000):

> *It was beginning to look like it was just about to fragment; you could say just 'hang on'. All those tensions you could actually just bottle for a fixed period (interview: Moulds).*

THE END OF 2000: FRAGMENTATION AND MOVING ON

The Jubilee 2000 UK Coalition and the international campaign that it coordinated ended on 31 December 2000 amidst celebration of its successes and confusion regarding its future. The campaign had reached a hiatus; thereafter, the energy invested inevitably dropped off. This section focuses on that period, the controversy surrounding its ending, and the ways in which campaigning has continued internationally, based on Jubilee's achievements and legacies.

The decision to end

The deadline was an important feature for Jubilee 2000 in the UK and the millennium focus had a particular saliency in the UK, with its Millennium Dome and Millennium Bridge. Yet, the millennium did not have the same significance in many other countries, and the cultural assumption that it did created conflict within the international network. Jubilee campaigns elsewhere promoted one-off debt cancellation and did not envisage stopping at the end of 2000. Jubilee 2000 UK may not have been clear about this when encouraging groups to join (interview: Owuso). As the deadline approached, there was growing disagreement about winding up, even amongst people who had signed up to the original vision (interviews: Pettifor and Lovett):

> *There has been an implicit assumption by the vast majority of those involved in Jubilee 2000 South Africa that the campaign will continue beyond the year 2000 (Dor, 2001).*

There were strong reasons to end the campaign as it was originally conceived. The deadline was inherent to Jubilee 2000's identity and the way in which it had developed; and the movement was displaying growing internal tensions and fragmentation pressures, making it difficult to sustain itself in its current form (interviews: Lovett, Pettifor and Moulds): 'There was much recognition that the shared vision is running out of time' (Marks, 2000).

On the other hand, there were many reasons for it to continue. Jubilee 2000 was gaining ground and momentum, but had not achieved its full objectives – 'people felt that the need to achieve the original aims was more important than standing by the deadline' (Marks, 2000).[6] It had inspired an array of groups to join the campaign, and these groups needed international coordination, information and networking. In particular, the Southern groups gained an international voice and access to expertise through the Jubilee coalition, and, in some cases, had only got going in 2000.

On a personal level, emotional attachment and commitment to the cause meant that many people were reluctant to let go and were experiencing a 'grieving process' (interviews: Pettifor and Lovett):

> *If you compared Jubilee 2000 to a football team, it would be the only football team that was in the lead at half time which decides to abandon the game (Owuso, 2002).*

The trustees of the Jubilee 2000 Coalition UK had been considering the issue for about eight months prior to the end date. However, it was difficult to concentrate on this as the millennium deadline loomed and the priority was to maximize debt-relief commitments: 'It's very difficult to focus on the last chance and the far horizon at the same time'; because of the loose nature of the international coalition, there was no clear method for engaging activists more widely on this key decision, resulting in a 'contentious' and 'chaotic' process (interview: Lovett). There was a swift review, based on a written or e-mailed questionnaire, sent to UK coalition members and the international network. While this did not allow for detailed discussion, the strong and consistent message was that members wanted coordinated campaigning to continue in some form (Marks, 2000).

The Jubilee 2000 Coalition UK was officially wound up, and the Jubilee 2000 campaign effectively ended, with the passing of the millennium; but three new organizations were immediately created in the UK (see the following sub-sections), reflecting the expressed desire for continuation. Many of the national campaigns in the international movement also continued.

Legacies of Jubilee 2000

Jubilee 2000's achievements and internal disputes left three legacies. At the time of publication, the campaign's transition from Jubilee 2000 is still underway, and how it will develop in future years is uncertain.

Firstly, Jubilee 2000 was a focused campaign that nurtured an emergent social movement with a broad composition and a diversity of aims within the overall issue of debt. The ending of the campaign left the movement without clear international leadership; but it did feature a number of diverse organizations and people loosely networked regionally and globally (interviews: Pettifor, Owuso and Lovett). Involvement with Jubilee had presented opportunities – particularly in the South – for strengthening organizations, increasing expertise and heightening legitimacy, both at home and internationally. Jubilee bridged political divides in the South as well as the North, enabling CSOs to play new and significant roles in some of the political processes, especially in Africa (interview: Owuso):

> *The Uganda Debt Network has used the knowledge and confidence gained in its efforts to improve the terms of the HIPC arrangement for Uganda as a basis to launch a campaign for greater transparency of the national budget (Scholte, 2001: 98).*

At the same time it has left the South with the legacy of a campaign that was determined and defined in the North.

Secondly, there were the emotional legacies linked to controversy surrounding the winding-up controversy and the unresolved conflict with Jubilee South. Feelings of betrayal were particularly strong amongst Southern organizations who had not been so bound to the deadline. There was some confusion about Jubilee's aims and focus, following the conflict with Jubilee South, which 'caused a huge split from which the movement has never really properly recovered' (interview: Pettifor).

The third legacy stemmed from Jubilee's high profile, which generated a perception that the campaign had succeeded in solving the debt problem. Hence, since the end of 2000, it has been increasingly difficult to maintain the profile and raise funding for ongoing debt campaigns, and the development agencies have moved on to prioritize other campaigns, such as HIV/AIDS and trade justice, where they believe they can make more of an impact (interviews: Moulds and Lovett). Jubilee's success also prompted government and multilateral institutions to adopt the language of the debt campaigners (but not the spirit or substance), and has resulted in new policies in the form of the enhanced HIPC and the Poverty Reduction Strategy Paper (PRSP) process. This has reflected increased interest in ensuring that debt relief goes to poverty reduction, not in helping developing world elites. However, many campaigners now regard HIPC as fundamentally flawed and see the PRSPs as masking privatization agendas. As a result, new campaigns are struggling to find ways of challenging debt policies in ever more complex ways.

Post-2000 campaigning

Jubilee debt campaigns since 2000 are best understood as comprising an emergent social movement, which manages to sustain a broad focus on debt but with a dispersed, rather than centralized, leadership. As such, it is difficult to map precisely its international presence and forms. There are, certainly, organizations and coalitions who campaign on debt in many countries. There are formal, informal and evolving networks between people and groups internationally, regionally, around specific topics, and within broader development networks. These are outlined below, focusing first on the UK and then internationally.

UK campaigns

The three follow-up organizations to Jubilee 2000 Coalition UK, created at the end of 2000 and working on different aspects of the issue, have had an uncertain time. Not only was the momentum diffused, but the political climate also changed.

Drop the Debt was a six-month campaign that focused specifically on the G8 Genoa summit in June 2001. In practice, changes in the Italian and US governments meant that there was much less political sympathy for debt cancellation than anticipated, and the violence of the anti-globalization protests in Genoa eclipsed the issue of debt and left a negative feeling for many campaigners (Verdict on Genoa Summit, 2001). Drop the Debt ceased to exist as planned, without having made tangible progress.

The Jubilee Debt Campaign (JDC) was formed in 2001 as a UK network of agencies and local/regional groups working on debt – an equivalent to the original UK Debt Crisis Network, closely linked with the development agencies and with an office within War on Want. It plays more of a coordinating function than providing leadership to the groups involved and has sought to clarify its role in the wake of Jubilee 2000. It has developed campaign strategy, materials and an improved website in order to provide support and coordination to the many active local groups, and has struggled to obtain funding and media profile.

The third organization that was established was Jubilee Plus, which changed its name in early 2002 to Jubilee Research. This is based within the New Economics Foundation – an independent think tank – and provides policy analysis, research and monitoring of debt. It also promotes particular policy agendas – for example, around proposals for a national insolvency and arbitration process. Jubilee Research also hosts the website for a nascent international network called Jubilee Movement International (JMI).

National and international campaigns

Internationally, there remains a strong commitment to debt campaigning. From various lists on websites and internet searches it is possible to identify 47 countries with ongoing Jubilee campaigns, compared with the 69 that existed at the height of Jubilee (websites of Jubilee USA Network and JMI). It is striking that almost all of the Northern campaigns have active websites, whereas the Southern ones rarely do.

Table 5.1 *Evolving status of Jubilee 2000 groups*

	Original members of Jubilee 2000	Operating campaigns – August 2002	Campaigns with websites – August 2002
North	23	19	17
South	46	28	2 (+ 1 that is not current)
Total	69	47	19

Many national campaigns appear to have become more confident and effective and have broadened their campaign priorities (interviews: Lovett and Owuso). While there is much consensus regarding what the key issues are, they are multiple and complex compared with the simple Jubilee aim. Many organizations continue to focus on HIPC, particularly given the very slow progress that has been made since 2000. By September 2002, six countries had reached completion point, only four more than at the end of 2000 (IMF and World Bank, 2002). A further 20 were due to receive debt relief within the next three years. Of those 26, it was anticipated that between 13 and 22 will still have unsustainable debts after HIPC, as measured by the debt ratios used by the World Bank and IMF, and will require additional relief and support (Clarke et al, 2002; Denny and Elliott, 2002; IMF and World Bank, 2002). HIPC is increasingly considered ineffective, and campaigns therefore tend to focus on other opportunities.

A second very common campaign theme in both the North and South is for a fair and transparent arbitration process. The economic crisis in Argentina has given this proposal a particular relevance, and the IMF and World Bank are increasingly receptive to the idea.

The most notable difference between Northern and Southern groups is that the latter mostly target their own country's debt and directly related issues, whereas Northern campaigns target creditor nations, generic debt issues and, in some cases, form campaign partnerships with heavily indebted countries. At a national level, debt is often associated with issues of economic and social justice, such as corruption, poverty relief, HIV/AIDS, trade, reparations and the need for sovereign insolvency laws:

> *A lot of the Southern campaigns in Africa and Latin America are driving forward with the original vision, but obviously without the millennium peg – mobilizing and pushing for debt cancellation, but also very much focusing increasingly on their own governments to push for any proceeds from debt cancellation to be used in the interests of ordinary people and fighting poverty (interview: Lovett).*

Importantly, campaigns in the less politically receptive Northern countries, such as the US and Japan, seem to be growing in strength.

International coordination and networking remain ambiguous. Jubilee Movement International is serviced by Jubilee Research in the UK, and is presented as a Southern-led network. It has met twice: in April 2001 in Mali, when it was formed, and in March 2002 in Ecuador. However, it is not considered particularly strong or effective (interviews: Pettifor and Owuso). Jubilee South continues to exist as a Southern network, and was active at the World Social Forum in Porte Alegre in February 2002, though it is difficult to assess its current strength. The African Forum and Network on Debt and Development (AFRODAD) and a similar network of debt campaigners in West African network, also exist, and there may be an emerging Andean network. A handful of Northern and Southern groups have created a network focusing on 'odious debts'. Undoubtedly the strongest regional network continues to be the European Network on Debt and Development (EURODAD), which predated Jubilee and continues to operate out of Brussels.

While Jubilee campaigns continue, there is a clear lack of international leadership and active coordination. The solution is thought to be the adoption of an overarching campaign objective around which to mobilize internationally (interview: Pettifor), and the question remains as to where the locus of leadership would lie. But the lack of resources in the Southern groups remains marked, and harshly illustrates the differing capacities between North and South to access the globalizing world and to provide global leadership.

Jubilee 2000 elevated debt on the agenda of both CSOs and the official institutions. It has also sown the seeds for a potential global social movement, with expertise, a language, campaigning skills, networks and a strong presence in both the North and South. The remaining issue is whether the collective action that was so apparent in Jubilee 2000 can be sustained in new forms in order to make the shift from a transnational campaigning network, led from the UK, to a truly global social movement with cycles of focused campaigning (Tarrow, 1998):

> *Membership in a movement requires the ability to see particular campaigns or particular goals as parts of something much bigger, and as having little meaning in themselves (Rorty, 1998: 115).*

CONCLUSIONS

What is the nature and form of Jubilee 2000 and the ensuing Jubilee movement, and to what extent is the movement an example of transnational activism?

Jubilee defines and refers to itself as an international movement, rooted in and inspiring domestic change throughout the world (Collins, 2001; Marks, 2000; Barrett, 2000; interviews: Pettifor and Lovett; JMI website). This is consistent with Tarrow's definition of a transnational social movement as:

> *...socially mobilized groups with constituents in at least two states, engaged in sustained contentious interaction with power-holders in at least one state other than their own, or against an international institution or a multinational economic actor (Tarrow, 2001: 11).*

Jubilee was certainly engaged in contentious politics at the level of both the nation state and multilateral institutions. The pattern of interactions are illustrated in Figure 5.2, and show how national campaigns used their transnational links to gain force domestically and with multilateral institutions. The problem, in this case, is not that expressed by Kekk and Sikkink (1998) – domestic campaigns being blocked from effectively challenging their national governments – but that campaigns in debtor countries don't have a direct way of challenging the creditor countries through existing national and international structures. As a result, the necessary leverage to bring about change requires Northern activism and North–South solidarity. This is an attempt to clarify the nature of the relationships between the movement and global structures, as suggested by Tarrow (1998).

Whether the contentious interactions around debt relief will be sustained as 'cycles of contention' (Tarrow, 1998: 7) remains to be seen. This chapter therefore presents Jubilee and the debt campaigns as an *emergent* social movement,

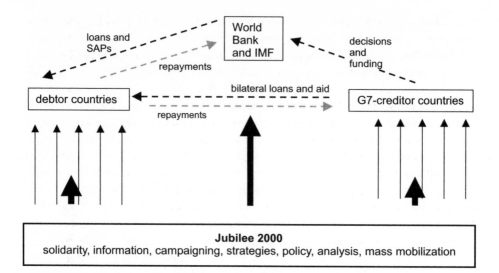

Source: adapted from Kekk and Sikkik (1998)

Figure 5.2 *Points of influence of Jubilee 2000*

rather than as an established one. Critically, will Jubilee be able 'to tap more deep-rooted feelings of solidarity or identity' that are necessary for building a sustainable social movement (Tarrow, 1998: 5)? For some, Jubilee did tap into a notion of the 'global citizen' – someone who identifies with the world and seeks to address inequalities and injustices (Barrett, 2000) as a response to globalization and the increasing opportunities to travel, experience and learn about other countries (Dent and Peters, 1999). However, international movements are clearly not new phenomena. There is a long history of people who have linked up, and supported each other, internationally on issues of social and economic justice. If the notion of global citizenship has significance within Jubilee, it is in marking a shift away from a paternalistic sense of the Northern countries providing support and resources to the Southern countries, and towards an understanding based on North–South equality. Jubilee did emphasize co-responsibility between North and South, as well as justice rather than charity or forgiveness. However, in practice it was hard to live up to these principles, and, at times, Jubilee reflected the same 'North–South imbalances that it criticizes...in terms of access to resources, information and global decision-making' (Collins, 2001: 147).

Another important way in which Jubilee created solidarity was through the religious aspects of its message. Through congregations and the church-based development agencies, Jubilee tapped into a sense of identity and solidarity based on spirituality. The Christian churches were vital to Jubilee and, especially, to its impact internationally, as were the messages from religious leaders. There are strands within Jubilee that have the potential to create sustained North–South solidarity around identities rooted in global citizenship and spirituality – potential foundations for a sustained transnational social movement. But these are not yet well formed, and it isn't clear whether they provide strong enough solidarity.

Such solidarity could provide an indication of the emergence of de Senillosa's (1998) concept of a fifth generation of North–South NGO relationships. He sees the proliferation of a range of different networks crossing North–South and regional boundaries as a new stage in the evolution of these relationships, which started with emergency aid, followed by providing development expertise and technical assistance. North–South partnerships then ensued, followed by attempts to empower the South through lobbying efforts in the North. In reality, Jubilee 2000 did not create wholly equal solidarity relationships between the North and South. However, there are indications in the ongoing development of the movement that different networks are slowly forming that could lead to greater equality. But this is taking place within an environment in which Northern NGOs still have far greater access to decision-makers, resources and communication technology.

Questions of identity and solidarity bring us to the processes underpinning Jubilee – its leadership and governance. At the core of Jubilee 2000 was a tension between the leadership of the campaign, based in the UK office, and its development into a transnational movement. Within the UK, the organization and governance were formalized; but there were still tensions – in particular, the development agencies felt threatened by the international profile and funding that Jubilee 2000 attracted. These agencies are made up of a cosmopolitan class of well-educated and well-travelled development professionals. Jubilee, on the other hand, was a popular movement under a broad banner, challenging global inequality through debt relief. The organizational culture of Jubilee was markedly different from that of the agencies: 'Jubilee provided a space to be creative, to take risks…it had a different feel and atmosphere' (interview: Owuso). This striking difference between the feel and organizational culture of Jubilee and the development agencies, as a whole, illustrates the distinction that Tarrow (2001) draws between organizations engaged in 'contentious politics' and those that are more established and have developed 'routine transactions'.

Internationally, leadership was exercised through informal social processes based on solidarity, personal relationships, trust and informal communications. While Jubilee aimed at being a broad and diverse movement, the leadership was not able to hold together the extremes of Jubilee 2000/USA's support of the Leach bill, with the leftist intellectual Jubilee South and its radical agenda. Within the US movement, support for the bill could be justified due to the fact that it opened a door to debt relief in a country whose government had consistently opposed it. However, within the global movement this was unacceptable because of the more widespread rejection of structural adjustment programme (SAP) conditions. Grint (2000: 420) commented that 'the trick of leadership – and the real invention – is to develop followers who privately resolve the problems leaders have caused or cannot resolve'. The conflict can therefore be seen as not having been adequately dealt with by the membership because the movement failed to overcome the inherent tensions between Northern and Southern groups, resulting from the imbalances in resources and power. This weakness also reinforced, in some people's eyes, Jubilee South's position as a legitimate Southern voice. Jubilee may have been 'enlightened' compared to many other North–South relationships; yet, it was certainly not equal (interview: Owuso). The introduction of more formal processes became inevitable, and since the end of 2000, and the formation of new networks such as Jubilee Movement International (JMI), there has been more attention to formal governance.

The problems faced by Jubilee are typical of an entrepreneurial approach that needs to become more institutionalized. A conscious decision was made early on to use the campaign as a way of building a social movement, rather than a formal organization or network. The critical questions now are whether such a movement can grow and gain force, and whether it can do this as a more equal movement, expressing solidarity and justice between North and South despite its history as a Northern-initiated campaign:

> *This is part of a living process. Those who follow us in this task must have not just a specific legacy of debt forgiven, but also a living legacy of a heightened consciousness among many people in the world of the need to close the gap between rich and poor, in order to ensure a fairer distribution of the world's resources (Dent and Peters, 1999).*

NOTES

1   The developing world debt crisis is largely regarded as being concerned with the debts of developing country governments to foreign sources. This debt includes debt borrowed from other governments or from inter-governmental institutions (especially the World Bank and the IMF). Private debts through commercial institutions are not very significant for the poorer developing countries.

2   Bilateral debt is between two national governments. Multilateral debt is lent by a multilateral institution, typically the IMF or the World Bank, to a national government; the richer countries provide the capital, as well as bilateral loans. Most significant are the G7 group of richest countries: the US, the UK, France, Italy, Germany, Japan and Canada.

3   This division into North and South is useful in illustrating the differing impacts of globalization; but some countries do not fall neatly into one category or the other.

4   The G7 governments were key targets for Jubilee. Therefore, they organized protests and campaigns around the G8 summits. The G8 countries include Russia, though Russia was not a significant creditor or target for Jubilee.

5   The UK chancellor of the exchequer is the finance minister.

6   The amount of debt relief obtained by the end of the Jubilee campaign is difficult to assess accurately. US$100 billion of multilateral debt was committed following the Cologne summit, of which US$45 billion was new. About US$10 billion in bilateral debt was also committed by G7 countries following Cologne. However, in terms of debt relief delivered, by the end of 2000, two countries had reached completion point and were receiving debt relief under HIPC and 20 countries were at the decision point. Looking beyond the end of 2000, even by the autumn of 2002, only six countries had reached completion point, and, in most cases, the debts were again considered unsustainable, even with relief. A further 20 countries were at decision point, facing a similar debt sustainability problem.

Chapter 6

The Age of Protest: Internet-Based 'Dot Causes' and the 'Anti-Globalization' Movement

John Clark and Nuno Themudo

INTRODUCTION: CIVIL SOCIETY AND THE WAY OF THE WEB

Two new phenomena have emerged within civil society during recent years. Both have important implications for development policy and practice. The first is the birth of cause-promoting groups whose organizational realm falls largely within internet space; we call these 'dot causes'. The second is the growth of mass protest against global capitalism that is often characterized by disruptive and sometimes violent direct-action tactics. The emergence of dot causes and the anti-global capitalism movement (hereafter called the 'Movement') are distinct; they are not two sides of the same coin. However, they are concurrent, and there is a strong link between them that merits study in order to better understand the distinctive confidence, diversity and power of the Movement. This chapter explores how they inter-relate.

There is a strong contemporary trend for civil society organizations (CSOs) to build stronger and more formal transnational networks for international advocacy, propelled by need and opportunity in the globalizing world. The growth of the internet and information technologies is revolutionizing civil society advocacy (see O'Brien et al, 2001; Smith, 1997) and is facilitating the formation of networks and coalitions (see Keck and Sikkink, 1998; Smith, 1997). These organizational forms have lowered the costs of advocacy, enabling the entry of new participants and increasing the potential for greater effectiveness, which offers competition, as well as opportunities, to more conventional 'bricks and mortar' CSOs and new challenges to policy-makers. There are, to date, very few academic studies of this issue.[1] We seek to address this gap by focusing on a new type of advocacy network: the dot cause.

The term 'dot cause' can apply to any citizen group who promotes social causes and chiefly mobilizes support through its website. Such groups fit Keck and Sikkink's (1998: 2) definition of 'transnational advocacy networks' as including 'those relevant actors working internationally on an issue, who are bound together by shared values, a common discourse and dense exchanges of information and services'. In social movements, dot causes can be important mobilizing structures, attracting new support, coordinating collective action and producing and disseminating new framings, as is examined below.

As 'virtual' actors, dot causes arguably constitute a new type of organization in the development arena. Some of the earliest examples were the Free Burma campaign, starting in 1995, followed by campaigns against Shell in Ogoniland and against McDonalds (O'Neill, 1999). The degree of virtualization and lack of physical presence is exemplified by the anecdote that when the Coalition to Ban Landmines (a dot cause) was awarded the Nobel Prize, it did not have a bank account to receive the award money (Mekata, 2000). Although some dot causes mobilize solely in 'virtual space' (such as Protest, OneWorld and IndyNews), others combine it with local/national meetings (for example, the Association for the Taxation of Financial Transactions for the Aid of Citizens – ATTAC – and Globalise Resistance). In all cases, internet communications play a critical role in resource and people mobilization, and in coordinating 'real' physical action, such as street protests.

Their chief weaknesses are, firstly, that – in relying on the internet – they have inherently weak mechanisms of information quality control and, secondly, they do not (yet) offer an alternative to 'face time' in decision-making or designing strategies for campaigns and events. They support, but do not replace, more traditional advocacy and campaigning efforts, although they provide a central *meeting point* for the concentration of social energy.

Dot causes can be networks of groups or individuals. They are often offshoots of existing CSOs or umbrellas of CSOs who share common objectives. Internet mediation of a global campaign can powerfully extend the reach of the core organizers of such campaigns. The best-known example of this is the International Campaign to Ban Landmines (ICBL). This is a largely internet-mediated umbrella of initially 50 (rising to several hundred) CSOs concerned with armaments, and humanitarian and human rights issues (Mekata, 2000). Most of the practical organization was conducted at the national or local level by the component CSOs. However, the international coordination and common-strategy development of ICBL enabled the whole to become much more than the sum of the parts (and for this the network received the Nobel Peace Prize in 1997). The successful campaign to oppose an Organization for Economic Cooperation and Development (OECD) proposed multilateral agreement on investment was, similarly, an internet-mediated coordination of up to 600 non-governmental organizations (NGOs) in over 70 countries throughout the world (Kobrin, 1998).

When the primary participants in a dot cause are individual citizens, rather than CSOs, however, different dynamics arise. The dot cause is no longer simply a 'wholesaler', providing member CSOs with information and action ideas for use with their constituencies. It now becomes a 'retailer' – directly communicating with the public and providing a deliberative space in which interested citizens devise analysis and strategy. Dot causes are products of modern information and communications technology (ICT) that facilitates and reduces the costs of sharing information, linking together like-minded people and promoting events. Since communications are pivotal, dot causes are transforming civil society advocacy and will present growing challenges and opportunities for more conventional 'bricks-and-mortar' CSOs, as well as for policy-makers.

One dot cause that attempts to draw links between web-activists and popular movements is People's Global Action (PGA), which sees itself as a coordination mechanism, not an organization. It is not registered anywhere and has no spokespeople, but it does have a manifesto. Its main activities are to coordinate anti-free trade and anti-World Trade Organization (WTO) activities around the world, and to organize a conference on these themes every two years. Its website is its main point of contact with its supporters and the outside world. Globalise Resistance and Reclaim the Streets are other dot causes that participate in the Movement.

Today's protest Movement is historically the first social movement that has dot causes as important mobilization structures. The next two sections discuss some basic features that this creates. We then use a social movement analysis to examine the emergence and growth of the Movement, and the role of dot causes in it. We conclude by discussing the implications of our analysis and critical questions posed for academics, civil society and policy-makers.

THE ANTI-GLOBAL CAPITALISM MOVEMENT

The Movement now attracts much attention from the public, policy-makers and academics alike. By bringing to prominence issues of globalization and global inequality (Giddens, 2001), and by mobilizing thousands to protest against the current regime of global governance, it played a major role in the collapse of the 1999 WTO ministerial negotiations in Seattle (Desai and Said, 2001b). The Indian environmental activist Vandana Shiva argues: 'a new threshold was crossed in Seattle – a watershed towards the creation of a global citizen-based and citizen-driven democratic order' (*Guardian*, 8 December 1999). While the attribution of policy changes to social movement action is plagued with uncertainty (Giuni, 1999), we believe that the Movement has already had an important impact upon institutions of global governance and the development processes. The recent implied support given by the German and former French prime ministers Gerhard Schroder and Lionel Jospin to the Movement's argument for a Tobin tax on foreign-exchange transactions (*Financial Times*, 11 September 2001) illustrates this.

Inter-governmental organizations and their agendas are modifying in response to pressure by global social movements (O'Brien et al, 2001). The fact that they engage at all with these movements demonstrates civil society power: global governance no longer rests solely with governments (O'Brien et al, 2001) but includes actors such as social movements (Khagram et al, 2002).

Today's protest movement fits the definition of a transnational social movement, as '[a set] of actors with common purposes and solidarities linked across country boundaries that have the capacity to generate coordinated and sustained social mobilization in more than one country to publicly influence social change' (Khagram et al, 2002: 5). It is extremely diverse (and, hence, generalizations have to be used with caution) and combines a variety of organizational forms and ideological positions in relation to globalization. It has transnational sources of problems, transnational processes of collective action and transnational outcomes. Moreover, it has been called a 'movement of movements' (Harding, 2002) because it combines elements from older social movements, such as labour, environmental, feminist, and peace movements (Desai and Said, 2001b), as well as NGOs, church and neighbourhood groups. The Movement's key organizational nodes, however, are networks of individuals and organizations primarily interacting via the internet (that is, dot causes).

The diversity means that the Movement is hard to define with precision, as is its composition. Some key groups float in and out of its boundaries, depending upon the issue at hand. Established NGOs such as Oxfam, Jubilee 2000 and Friends of the Earth (FOE) would say they are not *part* of the Movement, though they may have sympathy with it. They focus on many of the same issues and are to be found at the same global events, often promoting similar arguments; but they are often critical of the tactics and black-and-white analysis of the more headline-grabbing direct-action components. Yet, there clearly is a symbiosis. The mass protests have elevated the issues in the eye of the public, politicians and the media, while the analysis of the established NGOs and trade unions have added greatly to the Movement's credibility. The combination of well-researched evidence with mass mobilization and citizen outrage has proved compelling. Each without the other would be unlikely to succeed.

This multifaceted nature leads to a terminological difficulty: the mainstream press generally talks of the 'anti-globalization movement'. Many prefer the title 'anti-capitalism' (for example, Desai and Said, 2001b). More recently, there have been attempts by some within the Movement to base definitions on its proposals, rather than on its oppositional character. Therefore, in the 2002 World Social Forum (WSF; see Chapter 7), a declaration was approved by participants that the Movement should strive for, and be called, the Movement for (Global) Peace and Social Justice. Because of this terminological confusion, Klein (2001a) chooses just to call it 'the Movement', which is also our preference.

Policy-makers have so far found it difficult to respond to the Movement. They largely dismissed what some see as its precursor – the massive street protests greeting the annual meetings of the International Monetary Fund (IMF) and the World Bank in Berlin in 1988, and in Madrid in 1994, since few in government or the media took them seriously and closure of the meetings was not threatened. However, since then, the disparate groups of protesters have come together, albeit loosely, to form a broad movement that has gained strength and attracted lively media attention.

The turning point was the Seattle protest in 1999. Ironically, as discussed below, the WTO negotiations failed largely due to rifts between governments rather than the Movement's persuasiveness or levels of protest. However, public opinion largely credited the power of protest, which added to citizen support for such protests (since they seemed effective), as well as to the resolve of policy-makers not to allow this disparate movement to derail future global talks. This set the battle stage for the 2001 summit meeting of the G7 countries in Genoa. Around 100,000 protesters took part and 20,000 police and military personnel were deployed (Harris et al, 2001). Thus, the Movement attracted enormous attention.

A consequent strategy of policy-makers is to avoid, rather than curb, such demonstrations. As a result, the 2001 WTO ministerial meeting was held in Doha, Qatar.[2] Protesters portrayed the use of an undemocratic venue as a ploy to neutralize them, and it did, apparently, attenuate the demonstrations at the venue itself. However, the whole negotiation process was closely monitored in 'real time' by activists, and was publicly disseminated via websites such as those of the World Development Movement (WDM) and IndyNews (IndyNews website). These alternative perspectives fostered a more critical citizen response than could have been possible through using traditional mass media alone. Furthermore, national demonstrations were held in more than 100 cities in 30 countries (Protest website), mobilizing more people overall than Seattle did (George, 2002). Their underlying message to policy-makers was that 'you can run, but you can't hide!'

The events of 11 September had an immediate curbing effect on the Movement, taking a lot of its previously gained political space. Some protest events were cancelled or turned into marches for peace, and some groups – strongly critical of the US government – softened their tone or went into hibernation. Not surprisingly, the media has dedicated very little attention to the Movement since the war in Afghanistan (Taylor, 2002; George, 2002). There was some early speculation of its terminal decline; but recent events reveal otherwise. In particular, the mass participation of about 60,000 people and the global media coverage of the second WSF show that it is far from dead. In the next section we examine some of the key features of the Movement.

NEO-ANARCHISM AND THE LEADERSHIP DILEMMA

The methods of mobilizing any social movement influence its characteristics and effectiveness, and vice versa (McAdam et al, 1996; Khagram et al, 2002). As will be explored below, dot causes play an important role in the organization of the Movement.[3] And this, we argue, explains many of its characteristics, as well as its rapid growth, particularly at the transnational level.

The internet provides much more than an exchange of information. It allows conferences and conversations to be held instantaneously between North and South, East and West, and from this a truly global movement has been spawned (Harding, 2002). 'The protest in Seattle was not an isolated, spontaneous event, but rather a conscious tactic of an increasingly coordinated and powerful movement against globalization' (Khagram et al, 2002).

The individual dot causes that are most prominent in the broader Movement (such as Globalize Resistance, the Wombles and Reclaim the Streets, as well as the coalitions organizing protests against the IMF, WTO or G8 meetings) are not so much web-based organizations as organizational spaces. Based on the internet, they are virtual meeting spaces for communities of interest, and facilitate identity formation at a global level (see Warkentin, 2001). These dot causes, collectively, offer a loose ideological framework (a rejection of global capitalism and today's structures of global governance); learning and exploration opportunities (especially web-links to like-minded sites); illustrations of citizens' actions (particularly, step-by-step guides to direct action); the ability to bypass the traditional media; and mobilization for large-scale events into which individual groups of activists can plug their actions (such as the international protests and days of action).

In 'virtual' organizations, the lack of sustained physical contact reduces the organization's ability to generate trust (Handy, 1995). 'The necessary trust to seriously discuss agenda setting, strategies and risk management cannot be developed by e-mail alone (if it is available)' (Jordan and Van Tuijl, 2000: 2065). On the other hand, the strength of a network is directly proportional to membership, frequency of exchanges and the trust generated between network members (Keck and Sikkink, 1998). Dot causes therefore need to find alternative ways of generating trust and bonding, such as creating a network of 'affinity groups' who meet face-to-face and developing a shared culture and language of ideological radicalism.

Unlike most CSOs and social movements, dot causes do not offer leadership (or clear spokespeople), explicit political alternatives or detailed action strategy. Herein lies the dilemma. To succeed, social movements usually need strong leadership; yet, the internet medium – and the protest Movement that it has helped to spawn – eschews strong leadership. Instead, the Movement celebrates equality; followers are urged to be leaders, to think for themselves and to act as they choose. 'Arguably, the web helps those who so wish to defy leadership and formal organization and, instead, promote their own initiatives' (Scholte, 2001: 2). We believe that this neo-anarchism (lack of leaders, common goals or unified strategy) is an inevitable feature of the internet-mediation of citizens' action, distinguishing it from more traditional movements. For example, the goals and strategies of the environmental and women's movement of the 1970s and 1980s were well defined, and many of its leaders are still household names today.

The nub of the dilemma is that the internet is a better medium for disseminating information and opinions than for building trust, developing coherence and resolving controversies. Such dissemination is an essential starting point for devising campaign strategies; but civil society has not yet discovered an alternative to face-to-face meetings for planning strategy. It is common for dot causes to set a date and place for a day of public demonstrations, and then encourage adherents to come on a self-selecting basis to a planning meeting for the actual events – or simply to get together with like-minded activists and devise something to bring to the day of action. The outcome is more like a 'carnival' than an organized protest.

To be more assertive would endanger the democratic characteristic of the Movement. Since there aren't conventional forums from which leadership can emerge or be validated, it has made a hallmark of rejecting leadership. As networks, dot causes offer a space for communication – not control – and any collective action that ensues is the result of individual commitment and participation.

The extreme of leadership rejection is illustrated by one dot cause:

> *Who is in charge of Subversive Enterprises, International? No one...*
> *Each member of Subversive Enterprises, International is responsible for*
> *their own actions, and their own leadership... No one is higher than*
> *anyone else. No one is lower than anyone else. We are a network, not a*
> *bureaucracy. Feel free to consider yourself a member right now... The*
> *only reason this 'organization' was formed, was that we hoped that*
> *individuals like yourself (-selves) might be more encouraged to take*
> *action if you knew that there were others out there like you, with similar*
> *interests and goals. You want to start you own chapter/branch/franchise*
> *of Subversive Enterprises, International? Go right ahead. We would*
> *prefer that your agendas be somewhat compatible with ours, but anything*
> *goes. (Subversive Enterprises International website).*

Such inherent anarchism has three consequences for the Movement and its components. Firstly, the most prominent figureheads are independent commentators or 'interpreters' of the Movement, rather than leaders or spokespeople. Naomi Klein, Lori Wallach, George Monbiot, Waldon Bello, Vandana Shiva and Noreena Hertz are radical journalists and authors who are sympathetic to the demonstrators but do not claim to 'speak on behalf of' the Movement, still less lead it. As discussed below, an important source of inspiration for the Movement is 'Subcomandante Marcos' in Mexico, who has positioned himself as a poetic, philosophical advocate of the Zapatista cause but energetically denies any pretension to leadership (hence the lowly title he has assigned himself).

Secondly, though the infrastructure of the mass protests is well planned (including training sessions in direct action; technical assistance in the manufacture of giant puppets; legal services for those arrested; catering; accommodation; and crèche facilities), the component events are left up to smaller groups of activists, as is the choice of target (the specific injustice of global capitalism to be resisted). The net effect is that these events, and the Movement more broadly, do not promote one *specific* cause, as have other modern social movements – such as women's movements, the environment movement, peasants' movements or gay/lesbian rights movements. Its protagonists are not so much marketers of a 'brand' (a particular ideology or cause) as the organizers of a 'protest mall', a one-stop shop for multifocused demonstrators – all and sundry are invited to come, browse and participate in whichever stall most attracts them.

Thirdly, tactical schisms split the Movement. Many are strong advocates of non-violence, eschewing damage to property and the use of physical force or threatening behaviour. Conversely, others (such as Global Action) retaliate that these activists are irrelevant and promote the use of violent tactics (quaintly described in one website as 'projectile reasoning') – claiming that nothing would have been achieved at Seattle had it not been for the violence (Cockburn and St Clair, undated). Being predicated on each activist group deciding for itself what action to take, it follows that everything goes. There are no rules. Even though the large majority might opt for non-violent activities, a few will often take the violent course. Since the latter command most of the media attention and determine the policing strategy adopted for the overall event, the Movement has become characterized by violence. This split over tactics was evident in Genoa and has become more apparent in the aftermath of 11 September.

Much has changed in the Movement between the street protests of Berlin in 1988 and those of Seattle in 1999 and beyond. West Berlin's conditions for protest were extraordinary. The protest was considered the centre of the leftist and alternative movements in West Germany, and 80,000 people demonstrated. The next year, the IMF–World Bank meetings were held in Washington, DC, and only a handful of protesters gathered (Gerhards and Rucht, 1992: 570). But ten years later about 50,000 attended the Seattle protests (*Financial Times*, 4 December 1999) – the largest public demonstration in the US on an international issue in a generation. More importantly, unlike a decade before, Seattle was followed by other mass protests in Washington, DC, in 2000; Prague in 2000; Gothenburg in 2000; Genoa in 2001; and Florence in 2002 – not to mention a myriad of protests taking place during Mayday or the 2001 WTO ministerial meeting. In Seattle, over 1500 groups lent support for the protests (*The Economist*, 11 December 1999), compared to around 133 in Berlin (Gerhards and Rucht, 1992). Interestingly, both the Berlin and Seattle protests comprised mostly local and national protesters; but Seattle attained an international character because groups throughout the world could hear about it and participate indirectly via the web (Nauthton, 2001). Between 1988 and 2002 the internet revolutionized communications. However, the role of the internet, in general, and of dot causes, in particular, in this growth and transformation remains largely unexplored. We will now try to address this gap.

SOCIAL MOVEMENT ANALYSIS

From the rich theoretical landscape of social movement theory, we find the eclectic approach of McAdam, McCarthy and Zald (1996) most useful. McAdam et al (1996) study social movements by focusing on three factors:

- the structure of political opportunities and constraints;
- the collective processes of interpretation, attribution and social construction that mediate between opportunity and action (ie framing processes); and
- the forms of organization, informal as well as formal (ie mobilizing structures).

We discuss each in turn, although all of these factors are inter-related (McAdam et al, 1996: 8–9).

As mobilizing structures, dot causes may play a number of roles in the Movement:

- helping to create a transnational awareness of shared interests or conflicts;
- providing a network outside of people's neighbourhoods, social groups and political allegiances;
- strengthening transnational collective identities and frames; and
- helping to identify political opportunities and resources at both national and international levels (see Tarrow, 2001: 13).

We will show that the way in which dot causes play these roles have implications for the definition of the Movement.

Political opportunities

Political opportunities refer to the 'external conditions in the political sphere that help [a movement's] emergence and development' (McAdam et al, 1996). Dot causes seek out and exploit political opportunities to further their cause – particularly political pressure points that arise at international and national levels. Four developments in the political opportunities structure have been of particular relevance.

The first is the increasing tension between governments concerning global governance and the management of globalization. Divisions between North and South, and between Europe and the US, have become manifest, as has a dwindling public faith in the fairness of unrestrained markets. Widening disparities both within and between countries has sharpened concerns about exclusion, and the rapid contagion of economic crisis has called into question whether capital markets (at least) need more, rather than less, regulation (Stiglitz, 2002; Wade, 2001).

Secondly, the internet has allowed previously opaque processes of intergovernmental negotiations to become demystified and accessible. Citizens now feel quite well informed and empowered to intervene in these processes. Dot causes provide the opportunity. They can communicate to wide audiences information that would otherwise be politically 'filtered' by vested interests. By providing evidence of poor performance and malpractice, dot causes have helped a more confident movement capable of mobilizing thousands to grow.

Thirdly, throughout much of the world there is a profound loss of faith in traditional institutions of democracy, particularly as citizens are increasingly concerned that decisions affecting their lives are not taken in national parliaments but in transnational governmental or corporate forums. This 'democracy deficit' presents a lacuna into which globally organized citizens' movements seek to step (Boggs, 2001; O'Brien et al, 2001).

Fourthly, there is a general reluctance of Western states to repress the protests. Effective mobilization requires national as well as international political opportunity, and this varies widely across the globe. The Movement has, undoubtedly, been stronger in countries of 'tolerant regimes' and sometimes 'weak regimes' with little propensity for repression (see Tilly, 1978).

These four developments contributed to the drama of protests surrounding the 1990 WTO ministerial meeting in Seattle. A failure of the European Union (EU) and US trade negotiators to agree on basic objectives left the talks in disarray. Those negotiators, together with other G8 counterparts, spent much time behind closed doors trying to resolve their differences, leaving developing country negotiators feeling angry and politically marginalized. The leading economies preached free markets and the global good, but appeared to adopt strategies based on narrow, short-term self-interest. In particular, it appeared that the US government sought a fully open global market for its exporters, investors and service providers, but was not prepared to relinquish any of its own protectionist policies (Oxfam, 2002). The WTO appeared to both developing countries and citizens' groups as a vehicle for global Americanization. The ensuing confusion – all but a handful of negotiators were excluded from the pivotal deliberations – underscored CSOs' condemnation of the governance of globalization (and of WTO specifically), and appeared to confirm a widespread public alarm about the failure of democratic institutions to affect decisions of life-shaping importance.

Against this unedifying backdrop, and the relative unwillingness of the US Clinton administration to repress the protests, the Movement (broadly defined to include the dot causes, NGOs and trade unions who urged their supporters to demonstrate) staged the 'Battle of Seattle'. The protesters' deep conviction that something was very wrong with the WTO process hit a chord. Disgruntled negotiators from developing countries added credence to this case, as did the presence, on the streets, of trade unionists, churchgoers, environmentalists and human rights activists, alongside more anarchic protesters. That thousands of people demanded justice and a new approach struck many as a prescient and appropriate public response. And the violence perpetrated by some of the protesters, together with police over-reaction, guaranteed global mass-media coverage. Globalization became a clearly contested political issue.

Subsequently, almost any high-level inter-governmental meeting has been seen by the Movement as a political opportunity to promote it. With relative ease of travel (except to places where civil liberties are restricted and to meetings convened at short notice), it has proved possible to mobilize thousands of people to gather for counter-protests at these events. The guaranteed presence of journalists from around the world – who are captives of the meetings, all thirsting for new angles – provides plenty of opportunity to get alternative views across. And for those seeking adventure, the prospect of disrupting the official meetings, if only for an hour or two, provides an enticing goal. Thus, opportunities facilitate social movement action; but this action also fosters opportunities (Tarrow, 1996).

Cultural framings

Cultural framings refer to the presence of shared cultural models that facilitate mobilization. Social movements connect people with causes through developing collective identities and a community of interest around a shared condition. Framing, as McAdam et al (1996: 6) describe, is about 'the conscious strategic efforts by groups of people to fashion shared understandings of the world and of themselves that legitimate and motivate collective action'.

The roots of social movements lie in shared experience and a shared sense of grievance (McAdam et al, 1996). In today's Movement, the grievances are so many and so diverse (ranging from worry about job security, corporate greed, developing world debt and HIV/AIDS, to concerns of war 'against terrorism', cultural take-over and environmental destruction) that there is little common thread other than the conviction that the current globalization process lies behind it all. This 'cluster-of-movements' characteristic (Desai and Said, 2001b) adds to the plurality of visions and standpoints – a diversity magnified by it being a trans-national movement. This loose definition of grievance, and the consequent lack of consensus about goals, is a defining feature of the Movement.

In general, social movements tend to be anti-systemic (O'Brien et al, 2001) and involve marginalized groups wanting some political change (see O'Brien et al, 2000; Smith et al, 1997). Today's Movement is strongly 'counter-cultural' (Kriesi, 1996: 158), organizing *against* a cultural template rather than *for* specific public goods. What unites its different elements is not a demand for specific reforms, but the rejection of 'global capitalism' and its influence on culture and human relations (Klein, 2000). This is the Movement's 'master frame' to which all group and individual frames are pegged. There may be agreement on specific injustices stemming from today's management of globalization; but there is considerable disagreement on the extent to which the current system is condemned and – more so – on what should be put in its place. It is, as Subcomandante Marcos has put it, a movement of 'one big no and many small yesses'. As an alternative and cheap new medium, dot causes have greatly contributed to this ideological pluralism, giving voice to many previously unheard groups.

Although the Movement is defined by counter-cultural motivations, some constituents have instrumentalist goals. Many within it strive for specific collective goods, such as debt relief, cheap generic drugs for HIV/AIDS and the reduction of carbon emission. These instrumentalist groupings tend to be more moderate, while the more counter-cultural groups tend to be more radical. Because of their low level of institutionalization, dot causes frequently populate the more radical zone, while traditional CSOs tend to be more instrumental.

One of the most important influences for this new civil society dynamic has been the Zapatistas National Liberation Army (EZLN) in Mexico. This popular uprising has aspired not to speak on behalf of the indigenous people of Chiapas, but to allow them to speak for themselves. It declares no leader (Subcomandante Marcos describes himself as just a conduit through which the communities express themselves). It has an inclusive and pro-democracy ethos, but beyond this is highly plural. Every community decides for itself; the poorest peasant is the true comandante (De Leon, 2001). Its central message is a new form of democracy (akin to old anarchism). It puts great premium on skilful communications, particularly using the internet. Its messages are not dull polemics, but are witty, poetic, spiritual and designed to be inspirational. 'It is often said that the Zapatistas' best weapon was the internet; but their true secret weapon was their language' (Klein,

2001b). The Zapatista movement has directly influenced the anti-capitalist movement worldwide through its frames and outreach. There are now estimated to be 45,000 Zapatista-related websites in 26 countries (Klein, 2001b).

With their ability to facilitate communications, dot causes have a pivotal role in producing and disseminating critical or subversive framings, and in promoting new collective identities, such as the Zapatista message. Mobilizing anger against the 'legitimacy gap' of global governance institutions such as the IMF, the World Bank or the WTO illustrates this. The Movement requires sustainable alternative media that emphasize solidarity rather than self-interest. Dot causes that inhabit the internet provide such media.

The paradox is that the strength of the Movement is also its weakness. Its multifaceted nature and diverse strategies encourage and empower a wide diversity of adherents; but these adherents connect personally with the Movement in widely differing ways. The young middle class of the US or Europe might be anxious about an approaching global environmental Armageddon, or feel alienated from political processes over which they have no say. Trade union members feel threatened by the drift towards flexible labour markets and the ease with which transnational corporations shift production from one country to another. Peasants in the South feel threatened by the pressure for agricultural markets to be opened to (probably subsidized) foods from rich countries, while Northern protectionism denies them the chance to export reciprocally. Southern factory workers fear that introducing labour and environmental standards in world trade will present an excuse for banning the importation of their products. Each group within the broad Movement has its distinctive personal connection with the core issue; but these connections are so diverse as to be frequently contradictory (Desai and Said, 2001a).

For many, the internet has democratized communications. By providing an alternative and cheaper medium, dot causes have helped to increase the pluralism of the globalization debate. However, the stark inequalities of access to new information technology – the digital divide – casts a shadow over the ability of these networks to truly democratize communications at the global level. New frames are being produced and disseminated; but there is a danger that they contain a strong Western bias. Undeniably, however, dot causes represent a new form of participation and increase the pluralism of political debate.

Mobilizing structures

Mobilizing structures comprise both conventional (formal and informal) and 'virtual' organizations and networks that facilitate collective action and social movement formation. In the case of the Movement, they include both traditional CSOs, such as trade unions and environmental groups; but a pivotal role is played by the new phenomenon of dot causes. These offer reduced costs of communication, greater diversity of concerns, increased prospects for generating widespread action of these concerns, and maximum outreach, including to new constituencies. The ability to network in a society facilitates mobilization (Tilly, 1978), and dot causes undoubtedly enhance this.

Dot causes gain influence by offering alternative mass media and sources of information (see Keck and Sikkink, 1998: 19). To communicate, protest movements rely on both traditional and novel mass communications. Until recently, widespread dissemination was very expensive – either directly (paying for mailings, posters or advertisements) or indirectly (newspapers that promote a radical cause risk losing advertising revenue; television stations that are regarded as politically biased risk loss of franchise; and political parties who champion fringe causes risk loss of donations and members). Today, completely new channels are available at very low cost, such as the dot causes and the alternative news websites – for example, the Independent Media Centre (in English) or Nodo50 (in Spanish). These are also more convenient, more convincing and more interactive for a growing slice of the population, particularly the youth, than is the traditional mass media.

Hence, for the Mayday 2001 protests in London, millions of people received information, as well as political propaganda, from the wide array of websites promoting protests or direct action (including Mayday Monopoly, London Mayday, Mayday Conference, the Wombles, Globalize Resistance, Direct Action, Reclaim the Streets, People's Global Action, Guerrilla Gardening, Primal Seeds and anarchist sites). Groups seeking to change public opinion didn't need newspapers and other old means of communications to mobilize support; they were betting on new communications, and they didn't trust media that depend, directly or indirectly, on capitalism.[4]

Dot causes bypass the 'middle man' of conventional social mobilization. Many see little need for national or regional sections, local groups or other structures, and there is a direct and two-way link from the organizers to the supporters – so that the supporters become the organizers. Anyone can post their views and experience, enter a chat-room and perhaps become part of the leadership; the periphery becomes the core.

Dot causes tend to be highly horizontal, voluntary and extremely fluid – traits that generate both strengths and weaknesses. Dot causes, having neither the reputation of established CSOs to defend nor structured processes of public accountability, may not have the same standards of ethics and accuracy. They tend to promote single issues but collectively are quite plural. On any given cause there are large numbers of websites or dot causes (usually hyper-linked) presenting a veritable market-place of causes and opinions. The strength of specific websites depends upon their direct appeal (the test of the market). These traits shape the type of movement generated. Disdain of leaders makes dot causes less vulnerable to cooptation, but also reduces their ability to promote clear alternatives.

As a global cause, the Movement needs strong Southern participation, which is only practicable via electronic communications, and through this the involvement of Southern activists has increased (Warkentin, 2001). Although the internet permits global mobilization, in practice there are still many physical, monetary and cultural obstacles.

Unequal familiarity with new technology and access to resources leads to a North–South tension. Many Southern activists see events such as Seattle and global social movements as very Northern (or US) dominated (O'Brien et al, 2001), focusing primarily on issues of Northern concern (for example, the protection of the US environment, US jobs and US markets; US citizens wanting to have clear consciences about child labour; and reducing pressures for illegal migration). They are angry that issues of concern to the South (such as the way in which agriculture is dealt with in WTO talks) are not addressed. And events that are largely Southern organized (such as the citizens actions at the UN Conference on Trade and Development – UNCTAD – meetings in Thailand in 2000 and the first World Social Forum – WSF) attract very few Northerners.

Although information on the number of visitors to dot-cause websites is scant, it is evident that many are very effective disseminators. The Mexican Zapatista movement claims that over 2 million visitors have visited its site, 1 million in 2001 alone (EZLN website). ATTAC's website received 16,000–20,000 hits per hour during Porto Alegre in 2002. Normally, it gets over 1000 visitors per day (George, 2002). An independent counter of site visitors claims that Nodo50.org (a Spanish dot cause) has received 825,004 visits between September 1997 and December 2001 (Nedstat website). Furthermore, there is a profusion of such dot causes. Estimating numbers is difficult; but one indicator is that over 50,000 web pages contain the term 'anti-globalization' (Google website). Dot causes also tend to be well linked between them and to other websites. For example, ATTAC has over 3000 internet links to its website (Google website).

Though not without difficulties, the Movement powerfully illustrates the potential that dot causes have in bringing together actors who would not normally share the same stage (for example, the anti-landmines campaign). This is partly because the internet enables the participation of CSOs from far-flung corners of the world (the 'defeat of distance'); but also because this medium is particularly conducive to transient partnerships – the alliance of politically and culturally very different CSOs for a specific, perhaps time-bound, purpose. This 'blending of ideology' is tacitly accepted for reasons of expediency because it entails no commitment beyond the specific cause at hand, and because it entails little impact on the component CSOs' own style and support base. Depending upon the task at hand, this can be both a strength and a weakness of dot causes.

CONCLUSIONS AND ISSUES FOR CONSIDERATION

Dot causes are networks – mobilizing structures – that promote cultural framings and exploit political opportunities in order to generate collective action. The neo-anarchist nature of the Movement and the chaotic nature of the internet combine to generate great variety. Dot causes can vary from an individual's website to the complex transnational sites of networks such as Ya Basta!

Though new, there are signs of tension within the governance and management of dot causes, paralleling those found in traditional CSOs. The leadership dilemma presents a particular problem for both dot causes and the Movement. Where leaders are in evidence, they tend to be self-appointed, with poorly defined accountability and an unclear mandate, and their process decisions are often resented. In the first WSF, many participants were angry with the strict control of the organizers and with the fact that although anyone could organize a workshop, only a chosen few (mostly white men in their 50s) got to speak from the main platform. Klein speaks of the 'yawning democratic deficit' and describes how some participants even staged a protest against the organizers (Klein, 2001c).

Decision-making tends to rest on fluid leadership and haphazard processes – such as whoever turns up to a particular meeting. This may be fine when it comes to organizing multicause protests or critiquing 'the system', but does not lend itself to building consensus on alternatives (other than a vaguely defined new grassroots democracy). There is agreement on what is wrong with the world, but not on what should be put in its place. The two WSFs were intended to address this gap but have had limited success in this regard (see Chapter 7).

However, the specific targets of injustice make powerful campaigns: unjust trade, developing world debt and global governance. Through these, the Movement is trying to influence the main players and rules of development.

Our exploration of the Movement and the dot causes that mobilize for it suggests various questions for future consideration.

Questions for researchers

Some critical questions about dot causes and their role in the Movement deserve further research.

How can theory account for the emergence of the Movement?

Most social movement scholarship suggests that transnational social movements are hard to sustain (for example, Khagram et al, 2002; McCarthy, 1997; Tarrow, 2001); yet, today's vocal and, apparently, durable protest Movement seems to contradict this. We suggest that the roles of dot causes in the Movement provide critical clues to help explain its strength and longevity.

What is the impact of the Movement and of dot causes on world development?

Business interests have traditionally had much more access to institutions of global governance than CSOs, but this may be changing. Dot causes and other CSOs have increased pluralism in development policy-making, demanding that these institutions be accountable for the impact of their policies on women, the environment, the poor and labour (O'Brien et al, 2001). How successful are these demands? How is this changing global governance? Who is empowered to participate? Are Southern concerns promoted as energetically as Northern interests? As the profile of the typical internet user is young, white, male and English-speaking, the contribution of dot causes to global democracy and pluralism is inevitably limited (Scholte, 2001). Is a 'digital divide' emerging within global civil society? Who chooses the agenda that is promoted?

Can dot causes be effective, in the long run, with a weak local base of support?

Jordan and Van Tuijl (2000) argue that the 'iron law of transnational advocacy' is that NGOs must maintain their local links in order to be successful transnationally. While some dot causes have 'affinity groups', they rely mainly on virtual communications between members and between groups. Can, and should, dot causes attempt to build geographically located constituencies? Can epistemic communities replace geographical communities in advocacy and collective action? Are dot causes more effective as wholesalers to other groups, or as retailers to individual members?

Questions for civil society organizations

For many existing CSOs, the new virtual organizations pose many dilemmas and questions.

Should they cooperate or distance themselves?

Expediency suggests cooperation with dot causes that share aims, concerns and analysis on specific issues; but overall style and agreement on tactics are also important. Most CSOs find that the informality and radical counter-cultural stance of most dot causes makes structured cooperation difficult.

How compatible are the goals?

A social movement is more likely to be successful if its component groups share compatible goals; otherwise, it will be split by internal dissent (McAdam et al, 1996). CSOs operating within the Movement must compare their own organizational goals with those of others in the Movement. If there is basic compatibility, collaboration will be more sustainable.

Does the Movement's radicalism open up or close down political space?

Because social movements normally try to influence policy on behalf of marginalized and resource-poor groups, they frequently use disruptive tactics (McCarthy, 1997). Does such radicalism increase the potency of more moderate elements within the Movement, at least in terms of their dialogue with officials, or does it lead to officials developing a 'bunker mentality' regarding civil society? In the stretched spectrum of political views, are traditional CSOs comfortable with no longer being the radical David battling the Goliath of corporations and governments – especially when the newcomers often depict them as being 'part of the system'?

How serious is the tactical schism?

Different elements of a social movement must reach basic agreement on means as well as goals. Those seeking to dialogue with policy-makers perceive a need to distance themselves from both the carnival and carnage aspects of mass protests. Yet, they know only too well that the popular appeal and the media attention generated by the Movement have elevated causes that they espouse beyond their dreams, and that this opens up space for them to advance their proposals. Many traditional CSOs find it difficult to decide whether to endorse demonstrations and encourage their supporters to take part, knowing there may be violence and attacks on property.

Some, such as Oxfam, find themselves critical of the critics: 'the isolationist and protectionist tendencies on display at Seattle, Washington and other public demonstrations against the international order show that short-sightedness and selfishness are not exclusive to politics, bureaucracy or business' (Oxfam International, 2000). Jubilee 2000 and the World Development Movement (WDM) have found that anarchist groups' campaigns on developing world debt present more problems than opportunities (for example, in Prague) as they constricted the space for lobbying and made many supporters feel 'used' by the demonstrators (Pettifor, 2001; WDM, 2001).

Friends of the Earth (FOE), however, welcomes the protests, though it does not actually encourage its supporters to take part. How else, it asks, would we be having such a wide debate about the WTO or genetically modified organisms (GMOs)? FOE sees a symbiosis between protesters set on confrontation and those striking deals with business. FOE benefits from the elevation of issues on the public agenda, while the protesters draw credibility from FOE's serious research and policy analysis.

Some argue that closer links should be forged between protesters and campaigning NGOs (Woods, 2000) and that a failure to do so will render these mass anti-globalization protests a wasted opportunity – little more than 'political tourism'. It is important to recognize, Woods (2000) argues, that protesters and NGOs are employing different tactics but that tactical diversity is essential. Others comment, however, that in this age of civil society ascendancy, CSOs who engage in transnational advocacy need to boost their own legitimacy and accountability (for example, Florini, 2000). Forming close links with the radical fringe might fuel the backlash of criticism to which CSOs are increasingly subject.

Questions for policy-makers

Dot causes and the Movement, in general, have done much to create the public perception of a democratic deficit in institutions of global governance. On the other hand, good relations with social movement organizations 'may make for smoother acceptance of an expanding governing role of [these] institutions' (O'Brien et al, 2001: 20). Three critical questions for policy-makers are as follows.

How can the violence, disruption and negative press be contained?

A reliance on ever-stronger police and military presence adds to the media spectacle and is, therefore, what the violent demonstrators really want; it also risks loss of life and is expensive. Conversely, holding key international meetings in locations that are hard for citizens to reach contributes to a sense of exclusion and a widening gulf between decision-makers and the public. The ideal is to revert to easy-access locations, but with agreements reached with protesters to cooperate with the police in order to ensure that no violence or property damage occurs and to facilitate the arrest of violators. This necessitates responsibility on the part of the protest organizers, but also calls for better discipline on the part of policy-makers. No such deal could be possible without a *quid pro quo* of giving more airtime, within the meeting itself, to civil society members and Southern voices, and of giving more attention to social concerns.

How best to build dialogue with the Movement?

Though policy-makers in most countries now regularly talk with CSOs, this tends to be about quite specific policy issues and is restricted to the more-established CSOs. Policy-makers must recognize that there is a mounting popular clamour for social justice and environmentalism to be inherent in the way that globalization is managed. Hence, policy-makers need to engage at a senior and serious level with CSO leaders, including those who play pivotal roles in shaping public opinion – not just those with whom policy-makers feel comfortable. Exclusion of prominent but radical voices will give the impression of a 'divide-and-rule' tactic (though exclusion of those who continue to advocate violent or highly disruptive tactics might be justifiable). Policy-makers need to work with civil society in order to build a common view of what has been called 'ethical globalization' (Clark, 2001).

Will the Movement match the challenges facing it?

Will the Movement grow in power or simply disintegrate? What will be the role of dot causes in the future? It is too soon to tell; but whatever its course, the Movement has already started a public debate that will have enduring consequences for globalization and world development.

NOTES

1　For a survey of the brief literature on new technologies and civil society advocacy, see O'Neill (1999), Warkentin (2001) and Naughton (2001).

2　The avoidance strategy has continued. For example, the 2002 G8 meeting was held in Kananaskis, a remote area of Canada.

3　The evidence for this claim is diverse, including activists in the protest movement (for example, Klein, 2000; Evan Henshaw-Plath in the Protest website); media analysis (for example, *Financial Times*, 30 April 1998; *The Economist*, 11 December 1999; *El País* website, 'Anti-globalization' section); government agencies (Canadian Security Intelligence Service, 2000); as well as anti-globalization websites themselves (for example, the IndyNews and Globalise Resistance websites).

4　To be sure, the Movement still needs the traditional mass media in order to reach a wider public and to influence public opinion. But the growth of the internet has led to the creation of an alternative communications medium with the potential to reach thousands, or even millions, without using traditional mass media.

Chapter 7

World Social Forum: Making Another World Possible?

Günther Schönleitner

The World Social Forum (WSF) in 2002 in Porto Alegre was the second annual international gathering of transnational civil society in counterpoint to the World Economic Forum (WEF) of business leaders and the political elite in Davos. Its emergence is, in various ways, remarkable. Firstly, its scale makes it one of the most impressive and truly global examples of transnational civic activism. Secondly, it attempts to transform a heterogeneous global protest movement into a positive-cause protagonist of global policy change, enabling the movement to come together for the first time in order to define its own agenda rather than merely reacting to agendas set by governments. The WSF sees itself as recasting the WEF. Within two years, Grzybowski (2002) celebrates, *they* have become seen as 'anti-Porto Alegre'. Thirdly, the WSF functions as an intermediate structure that inter-links citizens and civil society organizations (CSOs) from different countries, playing a potentially crucial bridging role for the formation of transnational social movements.

Yet, the WSF also reflects the tensions and contradictions inherent in forging the collective endeavours of many heterogeneous civil society actors across country boundaries. The WSF slogan – 'another world is possible' – is essentially empty. This 'other' world could be better or worse than today's, depending upon subjective value judgements. The fact that the WSF has failed to present a positive-value slogan epitomizes the dilemmas it faces in managing the tension between a diversity of actors and values and clarity in defining alternatives to neo-liberal globalization. This chapter describes how the WSF has responded to these tensions and contradictions, the structures and governance it has evolved, and the challenges it faces as it strives to become a truly global process.[1]

The chapter is divided into six sections. The first examines the emergence of the WSF and its founding mandate. The second discusses how this translated into WSF's organizational structures, and the tensions and dilemmas that appeared within its evolution. The third section examines the WSF's boundaries – who is in and who is out – and describes the diversity of actors, highlighting the most important internal divisions. The fourth describes four underlying functions of the WSF, and how these aim to bridge the contradiction between maximizing diversity and generating coherent alternatives to neo-liberal globalization. This highlights a major internal schism between two camps with conflicting views on the nature of the WSF project. The fifth section discusses efforts to transform the WSF into a permanent and decentralized venture. The final section examines the WSF's organizational form, arguing that it currently combines elements of international non-governmental organizations (INGOs), transnational social movements and networks; the likely evolutionary path will depend upon up-coming decisions concerning its mandate.

THE EMERGENCE OF THE WORLD SOCIAL FORUM

The essential context of the WSF's emergence is the international movement against neo-liberal globalization and the rise of international bodies of global governance. These geopolitical phenomena have intensified the globalization of civic activism by expanding the scope of questions that can only be addressed by working globally. The WSF charter explicitly states its opposition to neo-liberal globalization as a defining characteristic of its participants. The anti-globalization movement has clearly conveyed what it is opposed to, but has found it difficult to explain what it actually stands for. Hence, the public perceive it to have a 'character of protest and resistance, as if there were no alternative proposals' (interview: Tibúrcio).

The WSF was created to address this lack of a coherent alternative vision, and to strengthen the proactive, rather than the reactive, capacity of the movement. Any attempt to produce such alternatives in a closed circle of activists and intellectuals would have been seen as illegitimate; it had to be a broad-based exercise. But assembling global civil society for such a task would face formidable obstacles. What would motivate and mobilize civil society actors to participate, without attracting some but alienating others? What would make it exciting and media worthy? How can one combine the unifying effects of confronting a common enemy with the less unifying task of visioning a 'new world'? And who would take the lead?

The idea to create a World *Social* Forum in opposition to, but inspired by, the World *Economic* Forum, was born by Oded Grajew of CIVES, the Brazilian Association of Entrepreneurs for Citizenship. It developed in discussions between Grajew, Francisco Whitaker of the Brazilian Commission for Peace and Justice (CBJP), linked to the Catholic Church, and Bernard Cassen of the Association for the Taxation of Financial Transactions for the Aid of Citizens (ATTAC-France; see Chapter 8). It would build on the 'anti' character of the movement by using 'anti-Davos' as a unifying polarization. The metaphor of oppositions – economic versus social; North versus South – of the two forums was highly symbolic, galvanized the movement and attracted international media attention. The forum idea was attractive because it is open ended:

> *In Davos… they haven't reached agreements. They haven't made declarations. It has been a forum for thinking, and it has been successful. Our intention is [similar], although [our]…perspective is to rethink the world from the point of view of society (interview: Grzybowski).*

A forum allows the huge diversity of civil society actors comprising the movement to come together, while imposing minimal commitments and common standards. The charter of principles defines the WSF as 'an open meeting place for reflective thinking, democratic debate of ideas, formulation of proposals, free exchange of experiences, and inter-linking for effective action'. The response of both civil society and the media to the WSF has been massive and growing, as figures from the WSF secretariat attest (see Table 7.1).

Table 7.1 *Numbers participating in World Social Forums*

	Delegates	Registered civil society organizations (CSOs)	Countries represented	Accredited journalists
WSF 2001	4702	1396[2]	117	1870
WSF 2002	12274	4909	123	3356

When cautious estimates of the non-delegate participants ('listeners') are included, these figures rise to 10,000 in 2001, and 50,000 in 2002. As Oliveira points out in interview: 'everything indicates that the diverse organizations of civil society were potentially lacking such a space, because the idea spread like fire in the hayloft'. Why was the response so massive? The novelty of the WSF is that it provides a multi-issue arena for debate within civil society, for combining protest with learning, for building bridges between themes and sectors, and for fostering new networking opportunities.

A study on the WSF 2001 by the Fundação Perseu Abramo (FPA) suggests that it may be this multifaceted character of the forum or, as Naomi Klein puts it, a 'strange hybrid' of a model United Nations (UN) teach-in, political convention and a party (Klein, 2001: 2) that the participants liked. They cited the most important reasons for participating as protesting against neo-liberal globalization (34 per cent of respondents); listening to, and learning from, speakers and the invited contributors (22 per cent); and exchanging experiences with activists of common causes (19 per cent). At the same time, 72 per cent of respondents found the forum to be 'very important' for formulating alternatives to neo-liberalism. However, fewer felt that it actually fulfilled this function: 47 per cent found the WSF 'very pro-positive' and 27 per cent 'more or less' so. Unfortunately, no such study is available on the second WSF.

What triggered the WSF? It is part of a broader dialectic opposition to neo-liberalism and a search for what might follow it (interview: Sader). It responds dialectically to the WEF and to triumphalist proclamations of the 'end of history':

> *The difference of the WSF relative to Seattle is that it is not about specific negotiations; it's about a perspective. Therefore, the WEF is the counterpoint... If the WEF didn't exist, would we? I don't think so. The counter-position is a law of life. [The WEF], in fact, proposed counter-socialism. They were successful, but they have created an enemy – us. In all social struggles you first create an enemy. Who will we create over time (interview: Grzybowski)?*

The impressive response to the WSF suggests that the lack of coherent 'pro-' positions has been a widespread concern among activists, and reflects the secular rise of global civil society that 'both feeds on and reacts to globalization' (Anheier et al, 2001: 7). The internet has been a major tool of mobilization. The WSF's website made information widely accessible in four languages. During the second WSF, it received about 500,000 visitors per day (interview: Mondonça). The registration of delegates and the planning of workshops were achieved through the web; the e-mail bulletins keep delegates and others updated; and almost all internal communication and external liaison has been done via internet and mobile phones. Without modern information and communications technology (ICT), the WSF would hardly be possible in its current form.

How can highly heterogeneous global forums instigate global policy change? WEF played a significant role in promoting the neo-liberal agenda of the 1980s and 1990s by forging an intellectual alternative based on neo-classical economic theory and its faith in market mechanisms. The alternative the WSF is seeking is based on less clear theoretical foundations, focusing on grassroots democracy and citizen choice. It therefore must accommodate a heterogeneous movement of, in Subcomandante Marcos's words, 'one big no and many small yesses' (see Chapter 6). How has the WSF designed structures, processes and activities to generate such alternatives, and what tensions and contradictions have surfaced?

BUILDING ORGANIZATIONAL STRUCTURES

The WSF was initiated by a heterogeneous group of eight Brazilian CSOs comprising the organizing committee (OC). It was assembled by Grajew and Whitaker in order to build a strong Brazilian foundation for their idea (Whitaker, 2001). It makes decisions through a principle of consensus and includes a social movement, a union federation, a federation of non-governmental organizations (NGOs), the Brazilian branch of ATTAC, an organization linked to the Catholic Church, an association of progressive entrepreneurs, a research institute, and a human rights organization.[3] The WSF secretariat is accountable to the OC and currently comprises ten administrative staff in São Paulo. The WSF does not have a legal identity; all contracts are concluded in the name of the Brazilian Association of

Non-Governmental Organizations (ABONG), and the brand 'World Social Forum' has been registered – in Brazil and internationally – in the name of ABONG.

The OC has spawned 34 mobilization committees (MCs) in 28 countries, 19 regional MCs in Brazil, and has helped to create the Brazilian Council (BC), comprising approximately 100 CSOs. However, both the mobilization committees and the BC only have consultative functions. Some OC members complain that the BC makes more demands (for example, for travel tickets) than suggestions and practical contributions, and they devote little time to it (interview: Grzybowski). The MCs contribute considerably by mobilizing support and disseminating information about the WSF. Some Brazilian MCs sought participation 'in the direction of the forum' (interview: Marques), and want the OC transformed into an elected body (FSM-Comité Mineiro, 2002). As one MC representative put it: 'The forum must not be owned by some people because they have invented it' (interview: Marques). The OC has resisted this as unworkable 'democratism and assemblyism'.

The OC perceives itself as a facilitator of a horizontal process, rather than the executive leadership of the forum. According to the WSF charter, the forum does not represent anybody; nobody should exert leadership or speak on its behalf. As the WSF is not meant to be a decision-making body, there are no final declarations or approved positions. In practice, the OC has been much more than the organizer of two forums. It has played a political role in establishing the methodology, drafting the 'charter of principles', choosing the conference venue, defining the thematic 'axes' and, at least in 2001, selecting conference panellists. The lack of transparency and participation in decision-making on these issues prompted criticism in 2001. Klein reports that 'fierce NGO brand wars were waged behind the scenes...and frustrated delegates began to do what they do best: protest' (Klein, 2001: 5). There was, for instance, a protest march of the youth against the OC. In the 2002 forum, the organizers largely managed to avoid such disharmony. Not only has the charter of principles (drafted after the first WSF) made the rules more transparent, but the OC also created a more representative international body, thereby reducing its own autonomy. Surprised by the response to the first WSF, and recognizing the need to 'globalize' the forum in order to give it continuity, it set up an international council (IC) in June 2001. It also introduced some procedural changes, including 'huge attempts to integrate the youth much better' (interview: Codas).

The IC currently comprises the eight OC members, about 70 big regional and global CSO 'networks' (mostly federations or umbrellas) invited by the OC, and other groups who organize international events (for example, the protests against the Free Trade Area of the Americas – FTAA – in Montreal, the Genoa Social Forum and the Rio+10 Parallel Conference in Johannesburg). National-level organizations are excluded in order to avoid 'the logic of nation states' that is seen as potentially harmful to an essentially global process. The IC's composition is left open and fluid so that it can redress remaining regional and sectoral imbalances. Critics suggest that such openness is potentially undemocratic: 'There participates who comes, and there comes who has the money.'

Initially proposed as just a consultative organ, the IC quickly asserted its role as a 'protagonist in orienting the political guidelines, and in defining the strategic directions of the WSF' (WSF/OC, 2001), reducing – in principle – the OC to issues of organization. However, the IC is a large international body whose meetings are costly (and, hence, rare), the discussions are time consuming, and the participation of its members often fluctuates. So far, the IC has held four meetings in June 2001 (in São Paulo), October 2001 (in Dakar), January 2002 (in Porto Alegre) and April 2002 (in Barcelona). The IC also works by consensus, but representation carries real influence: 'Either your opinion is legitimized by a network, a campaign or an organization, or [it] doesn't have any weight... What you represent gives force to what you say' (interview: Codas). The absence of an elected leadership clearly limits the protagonist role of the IC, and keeps the OC de facto in charge. Some OC members have expressed reluctance to transfer this role to the IC 'as long as [it] doesn't construct within itself a core team...[committed to] these values, methodology and principles' (interview: Oliveira).

The election of an executive committee is widely seen as a necessary step in making the IC operational and in shifting power to it from the OC, hence democratizing the forum. However, some resisted this, fearing that the IC would become an arena for power disputes (interview: Whitaker). This tension divided both the OC and the IC. At the Barcelona IC meeting, the two camps reached a preliminary compromise by creating three temporary working groups on methodology and themes, communications, and internal regulation. The latter will outline 'mechanisms to extend participation in the IC' and propose internal rules for the functioning of the IC and its meetings (WSF/OC, 2002).

Legitimizing the structure demands the transfer of the political functions from the OC – a self-selected club of Brazilian CSOs – to an international body that is more representative of the movement that the WSF aims to serve. Yet, the IC's size necessitates delegation, which may trigger power disputes that the smaller OC managed to avoid. Hence, many IC members preferred to maintain the Brazilian OC, even when the WSF is organized outside of Brazil, redefining it as an 'organic and political secretariat' (interview: Oliveira) – of, and legitimized by, the IC (interview: Mendonça). Mendonça reports that: 'we [the OC] have the support of the large majority in the IC... Many ask us not to give up this responsibility. Otherwise it won't work'. Thus, the Barcelona meeting reconfigured the OC but did not resolve questions about the IC's legitimacy; it remains an unelected body whose representivity is questioned. The IC member Nicola Bullard (Focus on the Global South) stresses:

> *We need to establish some criteria for who is on the IC... We need some discussion about representivity, about ensuring that we have a regional balance...that we are genuinely representative (Bullard, 2002).*

Not surprisingly, in this debate there has been a split between social movements, with grassroots constituencies, and NGOs. The legitimacy of the NGOs on both the OC and the IC has been questioned. A group of union leaders with the

Brazilian Union Federation (CUT) union leaders issued an open letter in which they 'deny any legitimacy or authority to the NGOs to speak in the name of the exploited and oppressed'. Sader considers NGOs as part of the process, but stresses that the protagonist role lies: 'much more with social and civic movements'. He perceives some NGOs to be less democratic than traditional right-wing parties, who at least hold elections. He asks: 'How can we wish to govern the world more democratically, when we put [such NGOs] into directing positions? When they question us about our legitimacy they are right' (interview: Sader). Donor–recipient relations compound the problematic cohabitation of NGOs and social movements in the IC. Bullard points out that some organizations 'have an ambiguous role; they are perhaps NGOs but they are also funders. What's the role of organizations like Focus, which is not a mass organization or a social movement' (Bullard, 2002)?

A further question of representivity concerns the IC's relation to the wider anti-globalization movement. Whitaker stresses that the IC does not represent the whole movement; therefore, improving representivity (such as by electing an executive committee within the IC) is the wrong approach. 'We don't intend to represent anybody. We don't want to build up any power as a forum' (interview: Whitaker). Yet, if the raison d'être of the IC is *not* representation, one might wonder why it exists at all. Not to represent means that either all decide or no one decides. If some decide for all without representation, this is autocracy. Indeed, some OC members appear to favour autocracy in order to shelter a horizontal process from the power dynamics of representative democracy. 'This type of management should not be directly influenced by eventual political or ideological divergences among the actors, because the methodology itself presupposes the maintenance of diversity' (interview: Oliveira).

Others, however, prefer the road of representation. Sader asserts: 'We have to have more democracy. The forum is not consulted on anything.' This camp argues for new mechanisms of consultation, consensus-building and even voting. 'We want to introduce internal referenda, consultations by computer, everybody voting' (interview: Sader). Certainly, this demands the formalization of the WSF as a democratic body; however, this would create problems. Firstly, there have to be clear boundaries between those who are in and out, those who have a right to vote and those who haven't. This would make it less of an 'open meeting place'. Secondly, the voting mechanism would have to cope with the enormous diversity of organizations. As Codas points out, there is a 'union federation with millions of members, and a group of five environmentalists in the Atlantic forest. Would it make sense [if] the votes of both are equal' (interview: Codas)? Thirdly, it would drive at least some minority positions out of the WSF. As Patty Barrera of Common Frontiers Canada points out, 'it ends up closing off discussions – it creates a situation where you either fit in or you don't' (cited in Block, 2002).

The 'institution-building' of the WSF is work in progress and will have important implications for the forum's legitimacy and accountability. Both issues have been barely discussed so far within the WSF for three main reasons. Firstly, the organizers take the rising participant numbers and the increasing international media interest as confirmation of their legitimacy. Secondly, the WSF is increasingly recognized by politicians and international officials, such as the then UN High Commissioner for Human Rights (UNHCHR) Mary Robinson, who assured the second WSF that 'the world is listening to the forum' (cited in Block, 2002). And thirdly, the issues of accountability and legitimacy are, in effect, delegated to the participating CSOs and movements, since the WSF itself doesn't officially issue statements or act on anybody's behalf: 'Our legitimacy comes from the organizations... Our function is to facilitate this space, not try to change the dynamic of the movements' (interview: Mendonça). And yet, the WSF does intend to exert influence. Oded Grajew of CIVES, the Brazilian Association of Entrepreneurs for Citizenship, emphasizes: 'we expect to influence the world agenda' (cited in Block, 2002). Thus, to the extent that the WSF does gain influence and impact upon issues of global governance, questions about legitimacy are bound to arise.

As Clark points out, NGO legitimacy can rest on various foundations, such as positive achievements, expertise, representivity, partnerships and values (in Edwards and Gaventa, 2001: 26). Yet, for a forum that promotes a broad-based global process to make 'another world possible', representivity is key to its legitimacy. This is exactly why the legitimacy of NGOs on the OC and the IC is being questioned. Heinrich of CIVICUS (World Alliance for Citizen Participation) perceives a 'rather profound basis of legitimacy' deriving from the diversity of CSOs, mass-based movements and the large number of people participating in the WSF, as well as the expertise many of them bring (interview: Heinrich). This is true; but whether the quantity and diversity of participants confers legitimacy on the WSF depends upon the extent to which it can show that it is in line with the collective will of these actors (that is, its degree of accountability). What are these mechanisms of accountability?

Formal voice mechanisms are restricted to the relatively few organizations who are on the OC and the IC. As a result, some participants have resorted to informal means, such as the protests at the first WSF. Dissatisfied participants can also exit. Yet, in some respect the WSF is a provider of 'unique' services, which means that those who exit would have to create another forum in order to obtain these services. This is a major barrier to exit from the WSF that may explain why protests and rising numbers of participants co-exist. Dissatisfied groups may choose to exit *within* the forum by holding their own extra-official events:

> *If they are not satisfied with any space of discussion and deliberation, they have the right to create their own event within the forum... It's up to you to mobilize the forces around the world...and realize a big seminar or conference, even bigger than the events prioritized by the OC. Yet, if one wants to change the big discussion 'axes', you can propose that, but...within the existing channels that are the council and the committee' (interview: Oliveira).*

Such forms of 'internal' exit keep these actors within the forum. It is in the forum's interest to minimize exit because its relevance depends upon broad-based adherence: 'The forum legitimizes itself by its capacity to express...movements that are external to it and, simultaneously, internal' (interview: Codas) – hence, the 'permanent and systematic efforts' (interview: Codas) to globalize the WSF, and to attract the maximum part of the anti-globalization movement. The WSF – like the WEF – has, in essence, adopted a *market* approach, rather than embrace representative democracy. The political entrepreneurs on the OC and the IC create a 'space' and offer services that they subject to the 'market test' of whether their targeted clientele participates. Nevertheless, to the extent that the WSF is not just about providing services and attracting participants, but about formulating and advancing an inherently political project, demands arise for legitimizing it democratically. This is why the IC was created. The dilemma facing the WSF is that the voice exercised by many leads to the exit of some. A majority voting for reformism would drive the radicals out of the forum. Thus, there is a trade-off between the goals of strengthening 'voice' and minimizing 'exit'. This derives from the heterogeneity of actors, as well as an underlying contradiction concerning the mandate of the forum.

DRAWING THE BOUNDARIES

This heterogeneity has important implications for the way in which the WSF operates, and for arising tensions. In order to understand these better, we need to identify the boundaries. Who participates and who doesn't? How do the main actors relate to each other? And how are internal divisions and tensions addressed? The WSF, by its charter, is a civil society forum; but it does not represent all civil society, globally. Firstly, it excludes CSOs who are not opposed to neo-liberal globalization, as well as those who are opposed to globalization but belong to the political right (for example, nationalists). The WSF is clearly a forum of the left. In 2001, 8 per cent of the WSF participants said that they belong to the extreme left; 60 per cent to the left; 13 to the centre left; and 7 per cent to the centre. Only 1 per cent said that they belong to the centre right; 2 per cent to the right; and 1 per cent to the extreme right (NOP-FPA/FSM, 2001).

Secondly, the WSF clearly excludes armed forces, terrorist networks and civil society segments who oppose globalization by violent means. However, the organizers find it hard to control access to such large events and fear the unauthorized entry of such groups, as well as infiltration by opponents who may try to discredit the forum by provoking violence (interview: Mendonça). Fortunately, both forums in Porto Alegre were, generally, very peaceful events. In some cases, the organizers apparently found it difficult to bar armed groups, such as Mexico's Zapatistas National Liberation Army (EZLN); but, in the end, they maintained their principle:

> *[We rejected] cases like ETA [the Basque separatist movement], [the] IRA [Irish Republican Army], of course. But what about the EZLN? They call themselves an army. We said no, not as an army, because this opts for armed struggle. We were also thinking of FARC [Fuerzas Armadas Revolucionárias de Colombia – a Colombian guerrilla movement], some Arab groups... So it is quite tense to control that, because they seek ways of entering (interview: Grzybowski).*

In fact, FARC did manage to participate in a seminar on peace in Colombia, invited by the Teachers' Association of the Federal University of Rio Grande do Sul (UFRGS), although the OC published a note distancing itself from this invitation. While some delegates defended violent means in order to 'counter the violence of neo-liberal policies', the large majority agreed with Vittorio Agnelotto of the Genoa Social Forum, who considered the violence in Genoa 'counter-productive and harmful to the entire movement' (Sivaraman, 2002b).

Thirdly, the WSF has not been globally representative due to wide regional imbalances. The study by NOP-FPA (2001) on the first WSF shows the regional distribution of delegates in 2001, as presented in Table 7.2. The 2002 figures are from the WSF secretariat.

Table 7.2 *Regional distribution of participation in World Social Forums*

WSF	South America	Western Europe	Central America	North America	Africa	Asia	Not identified
2001	60.70%	12.40%	0.40%	2.50%	1.90%	1.80%	20.20%
2002	70.05%	18.80%	2.48%	4.39%	1.97%	1.95%	0.34%.

Source: adapted from NOP-FPA (2001)

Despite efforts to attract delegates from more countries, the WSF in 2002 maintained its Latin American predominance. More than half of the delegates (55 per cent) came from Brazil alone.

Fourthly, the WSF – unlike the WEF – excludes those who pursue or command state power (that is, political parties and governments). This has caused tensions and inconsistencies. Including 'civil' society and excluding 'political' society cuts across the very movement that the WSF intends to serve. The tensions arise not only because some perceive the ban on governments and parties to be a self-inflicted weakening that the movement can ill afford. There are also fundamental divisions concerning the nature of the WSF project. Some see it as a unique global meeting place of civil society without control by governments, parties and political movements. To them, political action is incompatible with the WSF's horizontal, pluralist, non-hierarchical paradigm of political transformation (Whitaker, 2002). Others resent the liberal concept of a civil society who polarizes itself against the state, rather than aiming to transform it; for them, global transformation entails seeking and gaining state power, rather than just strengthening civil society. A group of Brazilian union leaders made this split explicit, boycotting the official conferences and workshops of the WSF, and denouncing the 'trap of civil society' since this concept 'erases the borders between social classes' and between 'the exploited and the exploiters'. By playing down conflicts and contradictions, they argue, this approach ends up with the inverse of democracy, which recognizes contradictory interests within society. The friction line between the two camps is probably close to the NGO–social movements divide.

This demarcation has also led to inconsistencies. Porto Alegre was chosen to host the WSF not due to its local civil society, but because of pioneering government policies, such as participatory budgeting (interview: Sader). Moreover, the left-wing Partido dos Trabalhadores (PT), the Brazilian Workers' Party, who was then running both the city and the state, granted considerable infrastructure and logistical support. In 2002 they spent Reais (R$)2.3 million, or about US$1 million on the forum, a sum they claim to recover through increased tax revenues. Both PT governments set up a joint executive committee (EC) that, together with the OC and the WSF secretariat, organized the logistics locally. Although the governments did not interfere with substantive planning, they did ensure that the state government's logo appeared on all of the posters and materials. This caused disgruntlement with the organizers and confusion with participants regarding the WSF's non-governmental character (interview: Lyra). The parallel forums of local authorities and parliamentarians – and the participation in the WSF of the state governor, Olívio Dutra, and PT's presidential candidate, Luís Inácio Lula da Silva – reinforced this ambiguity. The latter spoke at the forum to thousands of participants, invited by his NGO, who had organized four workshops. On the other hand, the OC barred the participation of Belgian Prime Minister Guy Verhofstadt and the vice-president of the World Bank, Mats Karlsson. Grzybowski's phone call with the former is illustrative. The prime minister asked:

> '*Don't you speak for the forum?*' *I said, 'No, but I am on the OC.' 'But can't you make a decision?' 'No, there is a pact among us. I can tell you what the criteria are. If I look at these, you aren't invited.'... I told him that he could come as an observer... He said, 'As an observer, I don't want to.' I said, 'Then don't come.'... 'Well, then I want to participate as a delegate.' 'Do you have a CSO?' 'No.' 'Then you can't.' 'Then I will create one.' 'Do you sign the charter of principles?'... It was a crazy discussion. I wasn't taking any decision, I just informed him about the rules. He didn't understand that; he understood it as a veto (interview: Grzybowski).*

Who actually *does* participate in the WSF? Unfortunately, there are no statistics yet available for the WSF in 2002. The Fundação Perseu Abramo (FPA) study on the first WSF showed that 51 per cent of the participants in 2001 were aged 35 to 59, and 22 per cent were 25 to 35 years old. In addition, 50 per cent were white and 38 per cent were coloured; 53 per cent were male and 47 per cent were female; 73 per cent had begun or finished university education; and 75 per cent were trained in social sciences. Table 7.3 shows the categories of CSOs to which the *participants* (that is, the delegates and listeners) said they belonged.

Table 7.3 *Types of participant organizations in WSF 2001*

WSF 2001: Types of participant organizations	Percentage
Non-governmental organizations (NGOs)	25%
Trade unions / professional associations	22%
Social movements	13%
Educational institutes	10%
Political parties	10%
Governmental agencies	4%
Foundations	4%
Entrepreneurial associations	2%
Religious organizations	1%
Others	8%

Source: adapted from NOP-FPA/FSM (2001)

Within and across these categories there is a huge diversity of actors and viewpoints that eventually generate tensions and contradictions. As Grzybowski points out, there are movements that are 'global by origin', based on inherently global problems or values, such as the feminist, environmental and human rights movements, and other more recent 'anti-globalization' movements. He believes that the 'fusion' of both strands explains the power of Seattle, Genoa and the WSF (interview: Grzybowski).[4] However, the relationship between these camps is more likely to be a fragile alliance than a fusion, one in which the members agree on some points but disagree on others. There are those, such as Susan George of ATTAC, who want another globalization, which – according to Grzybowski – is the dominant view within the forum. And there are those who want de-globalization, such as Walden Bello of Focus on the Global South, or the Third World Network.

There are anti-capitalists and reform capitalists. The former, for instance, oppose ATTAC's campaign for the Tobin tax because it 'doesn't interfere in any way with the logic of capitalism' (interview: Marques). Sharp differences also arise concerning questions of whether to reform or abolish the International Monetary Fund (IMF), the World Bank and the World Trade Organization (WTO), and the desirability of a world government (Sivaraman, 2002a). The anti-capitalist camp partly overlaps with the alternative camp, as espoused by its luminaries such as Naomi Klein. Proposals from this strand include a 'gift economy' (Genevieve Vaughan), webs of local initiatives (David Korten) or replacing the 'pyramids of power' by 'concentric circles of compassion' (Vandana Shiva) (all cited in Gillbank, 2002). Moreover, there are inter-sectoral tensions across categories of CSOs. There was a widely felt tension between the union movements and other civil society groups. The unions feel a strong need for cross-sector networking and 'going international', in response to the structural changes provoked by neo-liberalism (interview: Codas). But their relationship with the NGO camp is far from easy:

> *What did the unionists do? A union forum within the WSF! They dis-*
> *cussed four days among themselves. It was...politically a very big*
> *error... So, you see the internal problems of the forum (interview:*
> *Grzybowski).*

Some tensions derive from divergent values or interests, such as those between religious groups fighting against abortion and feminists defending it (interview: Codas). In addition, there are intra-sectoral tensions (for example, between Greenpeace and Friends of the Earth) that are partly rooted in ideological, political or strategic divergences, and partly because they compete for funds, publicity and supporters in limited 'markets'. Finally, there are intra-movement tensions, such as the split within the developing world debt campaign between Jubilee 2000 and Jubilee South (see Chapter 5).

The WSF has responded to these tensions by embracing plurality at the expense of unity. It has adopted a 'laissez-faire' approach, allowing the diverse actors to stage their own seminars, extra-official events and parallel programmes (for instance, a march against FTAA, a manifestation on Argentina or the debt tribunal), even if the WSF hasn't reached a consensus on these issues. As Grzybowski (in interview) puts it:

> *Plurality is sine qua non. If the WSF tries to unify, and give direction to*
> *the anti-globalization movement, it will be reduced. If it loses the char-*
> *acteristic of a forum, it dies. It will only persist if it maintains plurality,*
> *and an almost anarchic space of dialogue between the diverse actors.*

DESIGNING ACTIVITIES

How does the WSF balance the contradiction between maintaining plurality and fostering convergence around coherent alternatives? What are the mechanisms through which the WSF, as Chomsky (2000) puts it, 'offers opportunities of unparalleled importance to bring together popular forces from many and varied constituencies from the richer and poor countries alike, to develop constructive alternatives'? The WSF aims at promoting political alternatives along four broad thematic 'axes':

- the production of wealth and social reproduction;
- access to wealth and sustainability;
- civil society and the public arena; and
- political power and ethics in the new society.

The WSF's usefulness and success depend upon whether it affords opportunities for doing what can't be done better otherwise – for example, via the internet or through existing civil society channels. There are four core functions of the forum: linkage, exchange, education, and planning/coordination.

The linking function of the WSF

The WSF brings together people and groups who rarely meet otherwise due to geographical, sectoral, cultural, ideological and other barriers. It facilitates international cooperation among CSOs, and the creation or expansion of global networks and alliances. Although dialogue and information exchange take place through the internet, the construction of effective cross-sectoral and transnational networks and alliances requires the building of mutual trust, cooperation, common ground and rapport through face-to-face contacts – hence the importance of the forum as a morale booster. Delcio Rodrigues, a former director of Greenpeace in Latin America, affirms that the WSF 'was also a party and we really needed a party' (Block, 2002). Of course, one should not overestimate the possibilities of a five-day annual event to create trust. As Powell (1990: 305) points out: 'each point of contact in a network can be a source of conflict as well as harmony'. Moreover, the forum's diversity potentially erodes trust:

> *The more homogenous the group, the greater the trust; hence, the easier it is to sustain network-like arrangements. When the diversity of participants increases, trust recedes, and so does the willingness to enter into long-term collaborations (Powell, 1990: 326).*

As some OC members have come to realize, it is not easy to encourage the creation of heterogeneous networks. They point out that, although some actors may feel the need for articulating with others, 'many come to the forum to hold their own international meetings' (interview: Mendonça) and end up speaking mostly to themselves. This happened, for instance, with the trade union movement, ATTAC, Via Campesina, Jubilee South and the feminist movement. In 2002, the OC and the IC tried to curb this by introducing changes in the process for conferences and seminars. Unlike the first WSF, the second forum concentrated all conferences and workshops of a thematic 'axis' within a single day in order to encourage the activists of a specific sector to attend events on other topics during the rest of the forum. The second forum also limited the duration of sector-specific seminars to two days in order to encourage people to mix up with participants from different groups.

The exchange function of the WSF

The WSF is, effectively, a market-place for (sometimes competing) causes and an 'ideas fair' for exchanging information, ideas and experiences horizontally. This operates through the workshops that any accredited organization can offer (in 2002 there were 621 such workshops). The workshops allow for 'idea shopping' in 'niche markets', such as very specific questions, localized topics, international 'local–local' exchange, and links to global campaigns. The workshops attract many people because there is an event for everyone. For some individuals, 'the core of the forum isn't the conferences, but the workshops' (interview: Whitaker). Those more concerned with results, however, worry about the fragmenting effect of the workshops that 'disperse the view of the whole' (interview: Oliveira).

The educational function of the WSF

A core objective of the WSF has been to promote a global view. Some define the forum as a sort of 'open university' that attempts to bring together issue-specific, global civil-society actors – working, for example, on financial transactions, taxation, debt, food sovereignty, land reform and sustainability – in order 'to think more broadly, and to construct together a more ample perspective' (interview: Grzybowski). The forum promotes a broader view, demonstrating 'how from a perspective of the whole, the women can assume the campaign of Jubilee, or Jubilee the campaign of Via Campesina...strengthening every specific campaign' (interview: Grzybowski). In addition, it also encourages debates across disciplinary boundaries (for example, between ecology and economics). As Grzybowski stresses, environmentalists tell us that global capitalism is not sustainable; but finding solutions implies rethinking economics (interview: Grzybowski).

The main tools of this 'open university' are the conferences, 27 of which took place in 2002. In 2001, the panel speakers for each conference were experts invited by the OC. This changed in 2002 because of criticisms concerning transparency and consistency; more importantly, the organizers felt that the 'networks' themselves had to speak. In 2002, the IC delegated the organization of each conference to a member organization working on the respective topic. These 'pushing networks' presented their proposals, which were then discussed by debaters. Moderators coordinated the debates and produced syntheses. At the end of each thematic day there were press conferences where the theme syntheses were presented. In this 'open university' approach, concrete and common proposals are intended to emerge. The linking, exchange and educational functions of the forum are assumed to eventually create the basis for integration and the emergence of a coherent alternative. Grzybowski, who analysed and synthesized the results of all 'axes' for the IC, asserts:

> As a whole, we are on a good way; but there are weaknesses… We have to reinforce peace a little. On environment, we are very divided; we have to seek convergence… On the debt issue, we made some progress. But maybe we have to organize a specific forum about debt trying to achieve more convergence… It's easier if you can say, there are some proposals that seem to be consensual… But how can I speak of the Tobin tax as a proposal of the WSF? It was presented, it's legitimate; but it's one among various proposals (interview: Grzybowski).

The WSF's planning and action-coordination function

During the forum, the WSF hosts a world 'summit' of the anti-globalization movement and serves as its headquarters. The broad movement is, of course, fragmented and heterogeneous; as a result, coordination and action planning occur largely at a sub-forum level. The 96 issue-specific seminars partly facilitate this – some of them follow up prior events, such as the Durban conference on racism, or prepare future events, such as the Rio+10 Conference (interview: Mendonça). The forum also fosters new networks and joint initiatives. The 2002 WSF, for instance, saw the launch of Media Watch International, a 'referendum' on FTAA, and a joint campaign of environmentalists and peasant organizations (Via Campesina) to have seeds and water declared a 'human heritage' (interview: Mendonça). The coordination function was evident in the agenda of events and campaigns that occurred throughout the year and 'that was agreed upon between the diverse movements that participated in the WSF, and that was publicly pronounced at the end of the forum' (interview: Oliveira).

Thus, there is some methodological guidance towards convergence – although, on the whole, the forum celebrates plurality and does not take decisions or adopt proposals that are binding for all. Otherwise, the slender consensus, limited to opposing neo-liberal globalization, would break down as various internal groups seek to push their particular concerns onto a common agenda. The WSF has built on a 'pluralist-anarchic' approach, emphasizing autonomy and diversity, and seeking to inter-link, strengthen and empower global civil society through a long-term and unguided, but ever growing (and not necessarily converging), pedagogic process of consciousness-building and mobilization that ultimately transforms national and global governance. The WSF has, therefore, avoided the agony of negotiating over words and phrases of final declarations, and allowed the various factions of the movement to get along with each other by putting common views above divergence. Yet, its weakness is that it cannot convincingly articulate an alternative to neo-liberalism:

> We are well behind in the formulation of this alternative. And one of the reasons is that the structure of the forum itself is fragmented... There is a proposal on trade, another on debt or the financial system. But the sum of that does not add up to an economic project for the world. This has to be a global project, from which you will deduce what to do with trade, etc. So the format itself was bad. It repeated this segmentation of themes (interview: Sader).

The WSF encourages both homogenous and heterogeneous cooperation and networking. Thus, it is designed to produce 'bonding', as well as 'bridging', social capital amongst global civil society. This may facilitate, but does not itself generate, substantive convergence. The problem is how to resolve incompatible interests and values. As a mere 'catalyst', the forum risks reproducing existing divisions, contradictions and conflicts within civil society globally, retaining an emphasis on specific, parochial and often contradictory proposals without ever integrating the fragments into an overarching and plausible alternative. This limitation reduces the WSF's potential as an interlocutor on the global stage, possibly restricting it to what Sader (in interview) calls an 'eternal accumulation of forces within civil society without ever fighting for a political alternative'.

'Pluralist anarchists' question the very desirability of convergence: 'We want to rebuild the world from its diversity' (interview: Whitaker). Yet, the shortcomings of their approach have caused proponents of a 'strategic political' strand to envisage a more representative structure in which the IC would more actively facilitate the development of alternatives. Sader suggests that the IC should nominate commissions for drafting initial proposals and for developing them through regional and thematic forums (interview: Sader). This view also perceives the WSF as a platform for collective political action. Klein, for instance, warned about turning 'the WSF into yet another big meeting bereft of any impact on the real world', asserting that the 'alternative is not civil society but civil disobedience' (Sivaraman, 2002b). For this strand, the forum is an embryonic global interlocutor. It points to its growing recognition (for example, by the UN secretary general) as a 'legitimate space of dialogue about world problems'. Proponents also see the emergence of a new power that is still diffuse and lacks adequate organs. For them, the WSF offers a 'real possibility for the self-organization of civil society, and for using its weight globally and nationally' (interview: Oliveira).

Remodelling the WSF as a platform for collective action rather than reflection implies the need for a representative decision-making structure and formalized leadership. Who would talk to UN or government officials, in whose name and with whose mandate? Thus, there is a 'schism' of two conflicting views. For the first, the essence of the WSF is to provide a space for free horizontal interaction of civil society actors without exerting authority, representing or committing the participants. The second view seeks to link 'civil' and 'political' society and aims to legitimize the forum through representative democratic structures so that it becomes an effective interlocutor and emerging counter-power on the global stage.

TURNING AN EVENT INTO A PROCESS

The first WSF was celebrated as an event that 'symbolically broke the idea that neo-liberal policies are a product of an almost natural and unquestionable force to which all would have to surrender' (interview: Oliveira). Yet, it barely started to construct the aimed-for alternative. This would require a sustained process far exceeding an annual global event. In the IC, there has been much discussion on how to design events that facilitate a process of movement-building from the bottom up (Bullard, 2002). As Sader (in interview) points out, the WSF project cannot merely be an intellectual exercise. It must combine theory with concrete social movements. This link has been a traditional function of parties; but their potential is limited on the international level. Thus, the challenge for the WSF has been to create organizational structures capable of accommodating and facilitating a dynamic process of movement-building on a global scale.

As a result, it has faced a basic tension. If the forum were to build strong ties to the grassroots level, mobilizing local activists and social movements to participate more intensively, it would have to decentralize itself to the regional level, at least. On the other hand, regional decentralization could risk the forum's essentially global characteristic. This tension divided the WSF. The OC opted for decentralization and was against holding another forum in Porto Alegre. The IC, on the other hand, emphasized that a global process required a centralized forum every year:

> *They [the OC] desperately tried not to hold it in Porto Alegre. They went to India...[but] it didn't work. So they changed position saying that...there will be multipolar forums in various continents (interview: Sader).*

At its meetings in Dakar and Porto Alegre, the IC agreed by consensus to combine an annual global forum and a series of decentralized forums preceding it. Thus, prior to the third WSF, there will be regional and thematic forums, probably in Florence, Hyderabad, the Mediterranean, the Amazon, and Oceania, each carrying the name 'World Social Forum of Porto Alegre, held in *X'*. Each will also focus on specific or regional topics, while contributing also to common WSF themes (interview: Whitaker). All those using this brand must observe uniform rules defined by the IC. However, it is not yet clear how they will link to the global forum – the source of another schism. Is the global–regional split about 'maximizing the synergies between the different levels of action, different sectors and different regional groups' (Bullard, 2002) and about fostering convergence within the global forum? Or will 'every regional forum be an event in itself' and the WSF '*not* a final convergence of regional forums' (interview: Whitaker)? The IC's work group on methodology and themes is charged with proposing ways of how the continental, thematic and global forums are to inter-relate.

Some experiences with decentralized forums have already highlighted the risks that the regional and global forums face. The African Social Forum in Bamako, Mali, was stimulated by the OC to boost African participation in the WSF process. It was organized autonomously and led to a substantial increase in the African delegation at the second WSF. However, the Africans ignored the OC's methodology, producing a final declaration. The Amazonian Social Forum in Belém, Brazil, suffered considerable interference by the state government of Pará (interview: Mendonça). The Genoa Social Forum was a 'product' of the first WSF (interview: Codas), but was organized without Brazilian participation (interview: Mendonça) and is 'closely linked to the communist movement which wants to monopolize it. This is unacceptable' (interview: Grzybowski). The risks of being controlled by governments and/or captured by factions within the movement also haunt discussions about moving the global forum to India in 2004.

As the OC was 'persuaded' by the IC to give continuity to a centralized annual forum, it tried to maximize international mobilization by siting WSF 2003 in India and WSF 2004, perhaps, in Africa. The OC sent a delegation to India to discuss the viability of this with the Indian committee, which felt that 2003 was too early. Therefore, WSF 2003 will again be held in Porto Alegre; but the intent is to hold WSF 2004 in India, probably in Kerala or Bangalore. Nevertheless, according to Grzybowski, the problem is that the Indian committee wants:

> *...an autonomy we can't give, because that would mean that it falls into the hand of regional governments... They say, either we control it, or we won't hold the forum. So we won't hold it there, from my point of view. We can't accept government control (interview: Grzybowski).*

Another problem refers to India's civil society, which is diversified but, perhaps, too fragmented to construct a coalition strong enough to host the WSF: 'If one joins in, the other won't' (interview: Grzybowski). This suggests some basic conditions for future forum locations: a tolerant or supportive, but not politically interfering, government; a democratic environment with a free press; and a developed civil society capable of building a common platform broad enough 'to make sure that no one ends up owning the forum' (Bullard, 2002).

Both the decentralization of the WSF to the regional level and the migration of the annual global forum to different continents, are – essentially – mobilization strategies to globalize the WSF process. Yet, there are some voices who suggest that the IC should take on more responsibility for mobilization. Some think it should more forcefully encourage the creation of mobilization committees around the world. Others think that the IC should stimulate participation directly by deepening contacts, and should encourage cross-sponsorship schemes for funding the participation of, for example, Eastern Europeans by Western Europeans (interviews: Grzybowski and Mendonça). Yet, such deliberate strategies accentuate the need for 'guardians of the process' (Bullard, 2002) who 'guarantee the methodology, values, charter of principles and political culture [that the forum] is beginning to develop' (interview: Oliveira).

As Oliveira emphazises, the WSF will need 'a centre that systematizes, synthesizes, and accumulates the experiences... [It] must not be diluted along 70 networks, or by constantly migrating. It would lose its meaning.' Thus, the IC is likely to opt for maintaining the WSF secretariat in São Paulo, as well as the periodical return of the forum to Brazil every two or three years. But, most importantly, the decentralization and globalization of the WSF is bound to recast even more clearly and urgently the need for addressing the central institutional questions concerning the role, legitimacy and representivity of the OC and IC, as well as the nature and mandate of the WSF process.

REFLECTIONS ON ORGANIZATIONAL FORM

Considerable confusion surrounds the WSF's definition. The charter calls it an 'open meeting place'. Various proponents label it a 'movement', a 'movement of movements', a 'network' or even a 'parallel summit' since it is a 'stage on which emerging global social movements are struggling to organize, confront global powers and develop their own political project' (Pianta 2001: 189).

While notions of *space* or *stage* are too static for the forum's dynamic substantive process, the concept of a transnational social movement (TSM) captures its dynamism and goal-orientation. The definition by Smith et al (cited in Cohen and Rai, 2000: 8) seems to depict the WSF well: TSMs 'involve conscious efforts to build transnational cooperation around shared goals that include social change'. However, social movements generally form around shared grievances and convictions in the context of perceived opportunities. Therefore, doesn't the diversity and heterogeneity of the forum – from gay rights to fighting dams – make it meaningless to describe it as a social movement? The only common denominator is a dislike of how the world is run. Tarrow's (2001) definition (see Chapter 5) fits better by focusing on political contention rather than goals. But even this doesn't apply to WSF since its contentious interaction isn't sustained through collective claim-making and political leadership (Tarrow, 2001:10). Though the WSF stands in opposition to the WEF, international financial institutions (IFIs) and the WTO, it has no dialogue with them or authors any policy papers or political actions. Some regret this, though recognizing its inevitability:

> *Many people are against discussing with the WEF, the World Bank, the IMF or the WTO. I am in favour. We have to discuss. But if you take this to the forum, there is either an impasse or you vote, and those who are against don't come to the forum any more. Hence, there is no solution. What is the solution we have adopted? The forum is not an organization... I don't express the opinion of the forum but my own as director of IBASE [the Brazilian Institute of Social and Economic Analysis] (interview: Grzybowski).*

To some extent, this is just a question of formal versus informal leadership: 'There are people who talk and get attention, and others who don't. Of course, there are leaders. The press highlights them. But it's not formalized' (interview: Sader). These informal leadership positions are constructed within the specific movements, campaigns and activities that populate the forum:

> *Walden Bello is a leader; who will dispute that? Bernard Cassen is a leader. João Pedro Stédile is a leader, clearly. Bové is a leader. They assert themselves in the movement through their capacity of proposing, negotiating, disputing and directing movements (interview: Sader).*

Clearly, these leaders do influence and direct the destiny of the WSF – for example, on the IC. But none of them has, so far, asserted leadership over the forum as a whole. Contentious interaction with its logical targets does happen for issue-specific movements and the broader movement against neo-liberal globalization. These overlap with, and are part of, the forum, but are not identical with it.

Even the strategic political strand perceives the WSF more as serving the movement than directing it; but this strand would like to see the forum engage in contention:

> *There has to be something more active and offensive, not just reaction and response, not just criticism... We have to take the initiative to change the agenda. And we need the organs that put this agenda forward (interview: Sader).*

Thus, the WSF may seek to become a movement itself, or maintain a service function for the separate anti-globalization movement. The viability of the first option depends upon the degree of substantive convergence and acceptance by the actors involved. These are political decisions to be taken by the OC, the IC and the participants, in general. Whitaker alerts: 'Neither the IC nor the OC command. If they want to command, I am off and, like me, thousands will leave' (interview: Whitaker).

Many see the WSF more as a network than a movement: it provides social coordination, distinct from both hierarchies and markets, and horizontal links between actors based on reciprocal exchange, collaboration and trust. Networks typically form to allow a variety of actors, possessing complementary resources or capabilities, to realize gains by pooling them (Powell, 1990: 303). Networks are informal and 'lighter' than organizations, and meet the need for fast access to, and dissemination of, reliable information and know-how, flexibility, rapid adaptation to change and trust (Powell, 1990). They are 'open structures, able to expand without limits' (Castells, 1996: 470). Thus, some characteristics of networks seem to suit the WSF well. Networks have little hierarchy (hence, they accommodate diversity); are open and dynamic structures (as a result, they readily accommodate transnational social movements; these often go together, as Tarrow (2001: 12) points out); and have rapid growth potential, suitable for the process of 'globalizing' the WSF.

The forum bears some similarity to transnational *advocacy* networks (TNANs), defined by Keck and Sikkink (1998) as 'those relevant actors working internationally on an issue, who are bound together by shared values, a common discourse and dense exchanges of information and services'. For them, the 'core of the relationship is information exchange', whereby non-traditional actors 'mobilize information strategically' in order to 'transform the terms and nature of the debate' and to influence policies that seek to 'persuade, pressure and gain leverage over much more powerful organizations and governments' (Keck and Sikkink, 1998: 2). Thus, like TSMs, TNANs involve political contention, but not necessarily through mass mobilization. And the concept of TNANs also implies 'shared values' and common issues on which activists campaign.

The WSF is too heterogeneous in values and issues to be a TNAN, and doesn't engage directly in advocacy; but it does share certain features, as it emphasizes the horizontal exchange of information or ideas. Yet, the WSF is also a *service provider*. Its mass events require centralized coordination, mobilization, rule setting, conference organization, planning, facilitation, systematization and control. This demands more central-level institutionalization – akin to an INGO – than we would expect with a network.

'Rethinking the world' from the perspective of heterogeneous civil society actors requires something like a 'world parliamentary process' if it is to generate coherence. In an embryonic form, the WSF is precisely performing such a role. Yet, in this sense, it is no longer a network but a deliberative political arena. Networks often comprise diverse actors 'working on an issue from a variety of institutional and value perspectives' (Keck and Sikkink, 1998: 3). Nevertheless, there must be a shared understanding of what the common enterprise is. This is likely to require a more clearly defined positive cause, rather than just a negative one of opposing neo-liberal globalization.

Diversity and substantive convergence remain conflicting principles, which is why the pluralist-anarchic strand questions the desirability of convergence and, implicitly, rejects the objective of generating coherent alternative policies – a founding rationale for the WSF. Thus, the present tension within the WSF concerning its organization and governance is essentially a question of mandate.

The WSF currently combines elements of three organizational forms. It shares with INGOs a defined institutional structure that governs the formal process; it shares with TSMs the mass mobilization (hence, an undefined membership); and it shares with networks the horizontal interaction, consensual decision-making and informal leadership. The resulting tensions can only be resolved by addressing the underlying question of mandate. If the WSF opts for a 'civic' mandate, it may evolve into an INGO or into a core network of political entrepreneurs, offering facilitation services for the 'anarchic' horizontal interaction of a broad range of global civil-society networks and movements. This would be a 'market' process without aiming at a coherent project and political contention. If the WSF opts for a 'political' mandate, it is likely to develop more defined modes of representation and political leadership, integrating an *advocacy* role and evolving towards a TSM, becoming – perhaps – as Chomsky hopes, 'a new international of global social justice movements' (cited in Ker, 2002). In this case, it would certainly become less diverse, but blur the boundaries between civil and political society.

CONCLUSIONS

The World Social Forum is affected by three basic internal tensions:

- the contradiction between 'market-based' political entrepreneurism versus democratic representation;
- a civic versus a political project; and
- diversity versus convergence (which derives from the second tension).

Is it essential to resolve these tensions? Could the current structure progress indefinitely? After all, the WSF has organized two successful forums with global impact. Yet, the very dynamics of the forum make continuity in its current structure unlikely.

WSF's objectives are global; hence, it must achieve true global participation in order to have legitimacy as a world project. This 'globalization' will further increase its diversity, reducing the likelihood of convergence. This puts the WSF at a crossroads. It can either abandon the objective of developing coherent alternatives or the goal of maximizing diversity. Secondly, the decentralization of the forum is likely to require – paradoxically – a stronger global centre if it is to remain a global process rather than a series of regional processes. Such a centre will probably need clearer legitimization than currently exists – where the OC selects the IC and this, in turn, legitimizes the OC. Thirdly, the WSF has defined itself in dialectic opposition to the WEF, and has raised expectations accordingly.

If it restricts its mission to being purely a meeting place of civil society, it may risk losing momentum and constraining its impact. After all, the anti-globalization movement that the WSF seeks to serve is, essentially, a political movement.

Fourthly, as the WSF gets better known, and opportunities for participation in global governance arise, it will have to rethink how long it can afford to remain silent. The more credible the opportunities, the more acute will become the internal divergences regarding the nature of the project. Fifthly, the WSF is under a self-inflicted pressure to deliver an alternative project for the world. As Immanuel Wallerstein (2002) puts it: 'People want to know where to move. We must begin to think of offensive action. That requires deciding things that have not been decided in Porto Alegre up to now. What is our programme?' Thus, the tensions discussed above are likely to deepen. Their resolution depends both on the relation of internal forces (for example, NGOs versus social movements) and the opportunity structure that a rapidly changing world provides for considering alternatives.

NOTES

1 The institutionalization of the forum is an ongoing process. This chapter was written in March 2002. Some of the questions it addresses might have been resolved or recast at the IC meetings in Barcelona in April 2002; in Bangkok in August 2002; and in Florence in November 2002. The chapter is based on interviews with key representatives of the WSF's organizing committee (OC) and the international council (IC), complemented with media reports, official documents, a quantitative research on the first WSF, the author's participation in the second WSF and a literature review. Interviews, conducted in Portuguese or German, were translated by the author.

2 This figure is an estimate by the WSF secretariat because the number of organizations registered in 2001 is unreliable due to multiple entries.

3 These comprise the Brazilian Association of Non-Governmental Organizations (ABONG); the Association for the Taxation of Financial Transactions for the Aid of Citizens-Brazil (ATTAC-Brazil); the Brazilian Commission for Justice and Peace (CBJP); the Brazilian Association of Entrepreneurs for Citizenship (CIVES); the Centre for Global Justice (CJG); the Central Única dos Trabalhadores (CUT: a Brazilian Union Federation); the Brazilian Institute of Social and Economic Analysis (IBASE); and the Brazilian Landless Peasants Movement (MST).

4 Reference to Seattle and Genoa relates to the protests that took place during the World Trade Organization ministerial negotiations in those cities.

Chapter 8

Campaign for a 'Robin Hood Tax' for Foreign Exchange Markets

Diego Muro

> *My proposal is to throw some sand in the wheels of our excessively efficient*
> *international money markets (James Tobin, 1918-2002).[1]*

Traditionally, the introduction of any new tax produces strong public resistance. Yet, the 21st century's birth is witnessing a hitherto unknown phenomenon: a popular clamour for the introduction of a new tax – one applying to money markets. James Tobin, US Nobel laureate in economics, originally proposed the tax in 1978, arguing that a small levy on short-term international money transfers would substantially reduce financial speculation and instability. Currency trade today amounts to US$1.2 trillion a day, and a very small tax on this could also raise vast sums that could be used to finance development projects in the poorest countries of the world. Tobin's idea, mostly forgotten for 30 years, was resurrected during the late 1990s and has become a totem of the anti-globalization movement.

The organization that has been most effective in campaigning for the Tobin tax has been a French-based non-governmental organization (NGO), the Association for the Taxation of Financial Transactions for the Aid of Citizens (ATTAC) and the international movement that it has spawned. Born in France in 1998, ATTAC has grown to become a transnational network present in almost 40 countries, with an estimated global membership of 100,000 people.[2] Although ATTAC exists in other continents, it has a strong European character. Since its first international meeting in Porto Alegre in 2002, for example, the international movement has decided to focus on a European campaign (where the implementation of the tax seems more likely). In this campaign, ATTAC France holds a hegemonic position and acts as the movement's leader due to the pioneering role of the French association in providing an ideological foundation for the whole movement and some of its most prominent figures.

ATTAC is an interesting case study for a number of reasons. It has grown enormously while maintaining a flexible and horizontal network structure; it has demonstrated the power of clear proposals and prominent spokespeople with good media access; and, as a social movement, it has managed to attract wide support for its powerful views about globalization and how a Robin Hood tax could curb its excesses.

The chapter is divided into five sections. The first describes the birth of ATTAC France and its ideology. Secondly, it describes how ATTAC became a transnational network. Thirdly, it explores its global actions and the debates arising from organizing at the international level. Fourthly, it analyses the tensions that ATTAC faces as a network and discusses some of the organizational debates within it. Finally, the conclusion summarizes the chapter's findings.

THE GENESIS OF ATTAC FRANCE: 'DISARMING THE MARKETS'

The concept of ATTAC came from a 1997 newspaper editorial entitled 'Disarming the Markets', written by the director of *Le Monde Diplomatique*, Ignacio Ramonet. His inspiration was the East Asian financial crisis of the late 1990s that produced the depreciation of the bhat and the collapse of the stock market in Thailand and other countries in the region. The social impact of the financial crisis was harshly felt in these societies through unemployment, wage cuts, debt, reduced government spending, falling living standards and increased poverty (Hayward, 1999: 2). Regardless of the real causes of crisis, says Heikki Patomäki, (2001: 25) the irony is that the so-called 'Asian tigers' had been praised during 1994–1996 by the International Monetary Fund (IMF) and World Bank for their 'sound macro-economic fundamentals' and, yet, now stood accused of practising 'crony capitalism' (Patomäki, 2001: 25). Thus, with the Asian crises in mind, Ramonet's editorial analysed the 'absolute freedom of movement of capital' and the negative consequences this has for democracy. As he pointed out:

> ...*hundreds of billions of dollars are stashed away out of reach of the tax authorities for the benefit of powerful individuals and financial institutions. All the major banks in the world have branches in tax havens and make a tidy profit of their activities (Ramonet, 1997).*

The damage caused by these flows of capital could be remedied, said Ramonet, by the introduction of:

> ...*a new worldwide non-governmental organization, Action for a Tobin Tax to Assist the Citizen (ATTAC) [which] could exert formidable pressure on governments to introduce the tax at last, in the name of universal solidarity (Ramonet, 1997).*

Shortly after the publication of Ramonet's editorial, *Le Monde Diplomatique* received hundreds of letters, indicating the interest that it had provoked. In the following months, the newspaper's staff engaged in a wide-ranging debate and came to play a prominent role in the founding of ATTAC France.[3] Hence, on the 16 March 1998, *Le Monde Diplomatique* invited various associations, trade unions and journalists to discuss the setting up of ATTAC. Participants shared in drafting the statute, and ATTAC France was officially born on 3 June 1998 as the Association Pour une Taxation sur les Transactions Financiers Pour l'Aide aux Citoyens. The organization was initially an aggregation of 10 individuals and representatives of 47 organizations, such as NGOs, trade unions and newspapers, and envisaged a complex structure comprising a general assembly, administrative council, a bureau and a college of founding members, and a scientific council.[4] The organization was soon opened to individual subscription and members. Today, ATTAC France is organized in 250 local communities and claims 35,000 members. It has seven permanent members of staff in Paris and the decision-making is highly decentralized. Through the use of e-mail and the internet, the central office often engages in debate with local communities. As an organization, ATTAC combines a top-down approach, by which its members are informed of activities through a bulletin and e-mail list, and a bottom-up decision-making process, as the local communities propose ideas and engage in national debate about the future of the organization. ATTAC, says Vice-President Susan George, 'is organized like a fractal'.[5]

The rapid success and establishment of ATTAC France owes much to the role played by *Le Monde Diplomatique*. The newspaper was instrumental in creating the organization and, more importantly, provided ATTAC with a cohesive ideology, some of its leaders and an excellent platform to disseminate its proposals. It is a widely respected monthly journal on political and current affairs, with editions in 20 countries. It is for the international left what *The Economist* is for free-market adherents. Although the newspaper does not explicitly support ATTAC in its pages, the links between the two are strong. Bernard Cassen, director-general of *Le Monde Diplomatique* is, at the same time, president of ATTAC France. The newspaper has also urged its readers to join ATTAC. In terms of ideology, it has provided the NGO with a rich body of ideas. It argues that our increasingly interconnected world is a stage in which democracy is losing the battle with capitalism. According to *Le Monde Diplomatique,* the main enemy of the Tobin tax is the consensus of neo-liberals and the political elite, or *pensée unique,* who have a blind faith in the 'invisible hand of the market' and the virtues of free trade. As Bernard Cassen has explained, ATTAC's objective is 'to extirpate the virus of economic liberalism from the brains of the people, and [to] counter the position maintained by politicians that there is only the neo-liberal way to manage the economy' (cited in Wainwright and Juniper, 2002).

The tension Cassen describes is not new and has been identified by other authors, including the scholar from Princeton Richard Falk, who has referred to the dichotomy between global market forces and oppositional responses as 'globalization from above' versus 'globalization from below' (Falk, 1998: 100). Falk sees the organizations promoting 'globalization from below' as counteracting the pressures to privatize and 'marketize' the production of public goods. ATTAC would be, in his view, an organization that tries to 'reinstrumentalize the state to the extent that it redefines its role as mediating between the logic of capital and the priorities of the peoples' (Falk, 1998: 109). According to Desai and Said (2001: 65), the perception civil society has of global finance has led some organizations to think, firstly, that liberal democracy is lagging behind neo-liberal economics, or even being threatened by it; and, secondly, that the abandonment of nation state-based answers to the contradictions of capitalism – be they the welfare state in the North or state-sponsored development or superpower patronage in the South – is generating pockets of extreme poverty in both rich and poor countries.

Following from this analysis, ATTAC would like states to introduce a tax on the most favoured sector of economic globalization – the financial markets. The rationale for such a measure, says ATTAC, is that since the early 1970s the levels of financial transactions have massively increased and often dwarf those in the so-called 'real economy'. In the foreign exchange market, often more than US$1500 billion in different currencies are traded in a day, thanks to the security and speed of fibre optics and modern computers. 'With telephones and computer links, foreign-exchange trading today occurs through a round-the-clock market that connects dealing rooms in London, New York, Tokyo, Zürich, Frankfurt, Hong Kong, Singapore, Paris and Sydney' (Scholte, 2002: 6). Much of this foreign-exchange trade relates purely to speculation and hedging, rather than to international trade. While international trade has always been the reference and key source of demand for foreign exchange, speculation has grown from over 10 times world trade flows in 1979 to over 50 times today (Held and McGrew 2000: 209). This has led some scholars to talk about 'the global casino of high finance', where actors gamble day and night, sometimes with disastrous consequences (Strange, 1986: 2). These new 'gamblers' observe the flaws of foreign-exchange markets and use that information (or its inefficiency) to speculate against currencies.[6]

London School of Economics and Political Science (LSE) scholars describe those pushing 'globalization from below' as comprising four groups: supporters, isolationists, alternatives and reformists (Desai and Said, 2001: 64–75). The supporters consist of businesses and their associations, media outlets, rightist think tanks and others who believe that there is no alternative to market-driven capitalism (such as the Chamber of British Industry, the *Wall Street Journal* and Thomas Friedman). The isolationists are the so-called anti-globalization campaigners who consider globalization and capitalism as synonymous and promote instead deglobalization or localization (such as Friends of the Earth (FOE), the Landless Peasants Movement in Brazil (MST) and Noam Chomsky). The alternatives are concerned with the political and cultural consequences of capitalism and do not defend a particular agenda but a 'way of life' (such as the Zapatistas of Mexico (EZLN) or the UK-based Reclaim the Streets group). Finally, the reformists, who account for the majority of movements and organizations, are made up of groups who do not want radical change but a 'social democratic' agenda. Desai and Said (2001) include in this group organizations such as Oxfam (OI), Jubilee 2000 and ATTAC.

The latter group of organizations has singled out the finance industry for moral condemnation and attempts to promote a creative and positive counter-proposal, framed 'into a broader ethical context' (Clark, 2001: 25). In the case of ATTAC, its reformist proposal is the introduction of an international tax on foreign currency transactions. The tax would charge all foreign transactions a flat rate of between 0.05 and 0.5 per cent. The tax is aimed at hitting speculative transactions, while leaving long-term foreign-exchange transactions virtually unaffected. The revenues obtained from the tax could be phenomenal (up to US$100 billion a year) and could be used to fund sustainable development. The idea has, until recently, been largely ignored or accused of being unrealistic. However, the scientific committee of ATTAC, as well as many independent economists, have argued determinedly that the tax is feasible and could be practically implemented. They have developed an impressive body of evidence to defend their thesis.[7] The symbolic importance of the Tobin tax is clear: a tax on money markets would transfer the money raised from bankers and traders, mainly in the North, to developing countries. Seen in the context of civil society against global capitalism, the measure has been described as a 'Robin Hood tax' that would take the money from the 'bad guys' and give it to the 'poor guys'.[8]

THE ESTABLISHMENT OF ATTAC-INTERNATIONAL

In December 1998, at the invitation of ATTAC France, the platform International Movement ATTAC (henceforth, ATTAC-International or ATTAC-I) was created.[9] The idea was to promote a 'democratic control of financial markets and their institutions' at the international level by linking existing national ATTACs. During the previous months, ATTACs had been created in countries where *Le Monde Diplomatique* was published (and Ramonet's 1997 article had been read). The founding goals of ATTAC were 'to reconquer the space lost by democracy to the sphere of finance, oppose any new abandonment of national sovereignty and create a democratic space at the global level... It is simply a question of taking back, together, the future of our world'.[10] ATTAC-I took the form of 'a network, with neither hierarchical structures nor a geographical centre'.[11] Being a network, says ATTAC's founding charter, allows a flexible structure with no 'central secretariat (which would require heavy financial resources and would also be opposed to the organization's democratic ethos) or usual communication means (which required too much time and cost too much)'.[12]

According to the literature on organizational practices, networks have 'horizontal patterns of exchange, interdependent flows of resources and reciprocal lines of communication' (Powell, 1990: 296). They provide an informal structure, an absence of hierarchy and flexibility that other organizational models don't; they are 'flat' organizations, in contrast to vertically organized hierarchical forms. Network members come together because they are all working towards a common goal. The horizontal character of networks also allows flexible participation from the 'nodes' that might be at very different stages in their campaigns. ATTAC-International is a forum in which ATTACs – at different levels of development –

can learn from one another, share information, exchange speakers, coordinate joint activities and prepare international action. Members of ATTAC-I have common values, worldviews and a shared single goal, but no commitment to collective action or joint decisions.

The initiative to create ATTAC was enthusiastically welcomed, partly because it came at a time when financial markets were being scrutinized by the public and the media, following crises in East Asia and elsewhere, as well as public protests in Seattle and Washington, DC. Public opprobrium, amongst other targets, castigated currency speculation for its role in these crises. Furthermore, ATTACs in other countries (or their equivalent – not all used the same name) were beginning to chart up successes. This was the case, for instance, with the Canadian group who managed to take the issue to a debate in parliament. In the words of Maude Barlow, chairwoman of the Council of Canadians, a currency tax 'presents a critical opportunity…to reclaim some of the sovereignty we've lost as a result of economic globalization' (cited in Stecher and Bailey, 1999). There were parallels with the successful NGO network against the multilateral agreement on investment.

Although these examples indicated that change was, indeed, possible, ATTAC could not find role models for large-scale international events. The coordination of the network via informal means, a loose structure and a large number of social actors would be a disadvantage (Thompson et al, 1998: 15). The use of new information and communications technology (ICT), however, certainly helped the work of ATTAC; its web page (www.ATTAC.org) was its centrepiece in the gathering and exchange of information. However, ICT did not allow for all members to participate equally, and the organizational work had to be done by the leadership of each national ATTAC. The network relies on 'representatives' or 'electronic ambassadors' for the dissemination of information down to the supporters.

Language was another basic problem relating to international meetings. ATTAC-I comprises people from more than 20 linguistic groups; this makes decision-making processes very cumbersome. The preferred languages are English, French and Spanish (Spanish and Portuguese were dominant in ATTAC's first international meeting, which took place at the World Social Forum (WSF) in Porto Alegre). Although English is slowly taking hold as a lingua franca in many social movements and civil society networks, the charismatic leadership of ATTAC France has been able to deter this process within ATTAC. However, the lack of a common language clearly impedes rapid and effective decision-making. According to Laurent Jessover of ATTAC France, it depends on 'armies of translators' to make itself understood.[13] In France alone there are 650 translators who occasionally help ATTAC in its day-to-day work.

Although the network comprises horizontal structures and no hierarchy, the reality is that ATTAC France is the reference point for all ATTACs and the acknowledged authority on the technical issues. ATTAC-I is clearly, in effect, a French-led network. ATTAC France also leads for the network in issues of name or 'branding'. When a country, region or city wants to start its own ATTAC, it is ATTAC France that gives the approval due to its founding authority. It permits the new organization to use the name and add it to the French web page (ATTAC.org), hence linking it to all the other national organizations. Updating the ATTAC-I web page is compiled in France (although each national organization is expected to update the information about itself), as is the e-mail newsletter that goes to all members, *Sand in the Wheels*. ATTAC France also plays a prominent role in coordinating international activities. Thus, although ATTAC-I is a network comprising about 40 countries from Africa, Latin America, Asia and Europe, it has a de facto central secretariat – ATTAC France.[14] This leadership is also partly due to the fact that France and Germany are the only ATTACs with permanent members of staff (France has seven; Germany has four); but, more significantly, the true celebrities of the movement are French-based. People such as Susan George, Bernard Cassen and Ignacio Ramonet have managed to bring ATTAC's concerns to the attention of the media and are respected for having done so.

However, not everyone is pleased with the way in which ATTAC has presented its 'pedagogical and informative movement'. James Tobin himself accused the campaign of having 'abused' his 30-year-old idea of a tax on currency exchange. Although the proposal takes Tobin's work almost in its entirety, ATTAC's views on issues of global financial architecture could hardly differ more from Tobin's views (Lichfield, 2001). He was a great supporter of the IMF and the World Bank, even though he himself never envisaged a single global entity collecting the tax and deciding where and how to spend it. Furthermore, to a large extent he accepted capitalism as the system that offers welfare to a majority of people; in his last year of life, he wrote avidly to distance himself from the movement that uses his name:

> *I support free trade... I support the World Bank and the IMF and the World Trade Organization (WTO) that these movements hate (cited in Lichfield, 2001).*

Today, leaders of ATTAC talk about a 'Tobin-type tax' and continue to lambaste the World Bank and the IMF. ATTAC promotes not only a currency exchange tax but also other 'democratic issues', such as the reform of 'unregulated institutions' of global governance, ecological issues and faults with 'the hegemonic economic model of neo-liberalism'.

To sum up, since 1998, ATTAC has expanded both its geographical focus and its mandate. A large number of countries have founded their own chapters, primarily in Europe but also in South America, Africa and Asia. At the same time, the organization has expanded to other issues beyond the taxation of money markets. It has also made considerable headway in persuading significant political leaders and opinion-makers to look carefully at the case they advance, especially as popular indignation about corporate sleaze and speculation is mounting globally. Its biggest triumph, to date, was gaining the support of the former prime minister of France, Lionel Jospin. In the UK, Labour Chancellor Gordon Brown has stated publicly that it is time to think again about whether the Tobin tax or something like it might be a feasible proposition. ATTAC-I has secured influential parliamentary debates and motions in Argentina, Belgium, Chile, France, India, Ireland, Spain, Uruguay and the European parliament.[15]

GLOBAL COLLECTIVE ACTION: THINK GLOBAL, ACT GLOBAL; THINK LOCAL, ACT LOCAL

ATTAC describes itself as a 'movement for popular education turned towards action' and a campaign for international democracy.[16] Its campaign focus has broadened from the Tobin tax to other issues, such as closing down tax havens, cancelling developing world debt and the reform of international institutions. This expansion of mandate has enabled ATTAC to benefit from the momentum of the anti-globalization movement. As two leaders in the UK newspaper the *Guardian* noted, ATTAC has 'snowballed rapidly into a more general movement for global social justice', providing 'the nearest thing to continental coordination' (Wainwright and Juniper, 2002).

One of the events that boosted the media profile of ATTAC was the World Social Forum (WSF) held in Porto Alegre, Brazil. ATTAC was one of the main organizers, promoters and active participants of this forum (see Chapter 7) and convened its very first international meeting in the second WSF in February 2002. Until that point, ATTAC had been concentrated in Europe and mainly focused on public education, regarding issues of finance, and the promotion of the Tobin tax as a measure to curb the excesses of currency speculation. However, due to the increasing number of national ATTACs, it was felt that more international coordination was needed. In Porto Alegre, the focus was a European campaign to implement the Tobin tax. Basing its decision on the work of the scientific committee of ATTAC, as well as the work of economists such as Rodney Schmidt and Paul Bernard Spahn, ATTAC decided that a Tobin tax at a European level was feasible and that the European Union (EU) should be pressed to initiate the tax. Since then, the European ATTACs – to date the most numerous and better organized – have cooperated closely. Shortly after WSF 2002, ATTAC held its first European meeting in Barcelona in March 2002, coinciding with the EU summit. Although there is, as yet, no single, definitive European campaign, the synergies and level of interaction between national ATTACs have increased greatly, partly due to the relatively short distances and widespread use of ICT throughout Europe. In other parts of the world, such as Africa, Latin America or Asia, coordination has not reached the same levels.

One of the problems facing the international campaign is the very different starting points of ATTACs in different countries. They have different preferences for issues, working methods and structures that must be constantly adapted to the local culture. According to Patomaki (2001: 180):

> *There is no point in speculating on the possible emergence of a universal consent for the Tobin tax... Any significant grouping of countries can proceed quickly, despite the resistance of some of the major centres.*

Maximizing flexibility allows each national centre to decide what issues they think are important and want to work on, how best to build up the image domestically, and how much attention to give to the international arena. Activists do not necessarily see the resulting lack of coherence or unified strategy as a bad thing. The fact that the international campaign is 'a network, with neither hierarchical structures nor a geographical centre' seems to suit the different concepts of ATTAC across the European countries.[17] In the words of Christophe Ventura, spokesperson for ATTAC:[18]

> *We are a network without any bureau or control centre. The only thing we ask people, if they want to build an ATTAC, is to do it on the platform, nothing else... Concretely, our coordination is a political one. It means that we work together on concrete campaigns and themes. For example, each ATTAC mobilizes in its country on the GATT [General Agreement on Tariffs and Trade] issue. All of us are autonomous and there is absolutely no vote in our meeting. We are working by discussion and consensus on proposals. There is no obligation for nothing; but, honestly, for the moment, we have never seen an ATTAC who didn't want to campaign on one of our goals.*

However, many suspect that it is just a matter of time before ATTAC seeks to galvanize effort around a single strategic campaign. To date, ATTAC France actively defends the 'loose network' model; but it is not clear how much other countries agree with this. During the ATTAC Europe meeting in Barcelona, grassroots members of ATTAC Spain actively accused the organizers from both Madrid and Barcelona of ineffectiveness. It was notable, for instance, that national ATTACs from some of the very active countries were absent (such as Germany, Sweden and Finland). It transpired that they had only been informed of the meeting some days before hand. Complaints about the organization of the event continued throughout the meeting and illustrated the frustration felt by many about the absence of any central or global direction.

It is unclear how long ATTAC France can continue to be the de facto leader when it has not been formally given this responsibility and when there are no governance procedures in place to do so. This debate brings other governance questions to the fore, such as who is accountable for the actions of ATTAC France? Susan George replies that: 'ATTAC France is only accountable to its members, to nobody else'.[19] But what about its accountability for matters concerning the international movement? Through this it influences far more than its own membership. Should only the national membership have a say when the affairs of one national ATTAC has implications for groups in other countries?

Governance and leadership issues are particularly vexed regarding questions of international action, such as ATTAC's role in the creation of the WSF in Porto Alegre. ATTAC-I now plans to hold an international meeting annually, initially coinciding with the WSF, while European and other regional meetings might occur more often. The host country designs the agenda and plans the meeting. However, as could be seen in the first ATTAC Europe meeting in Barcelona, the preparatory committees barely knew about the proposals from different countries, the circulation of documents was poor and the attendance was low. Although the internet could have been widely used to circulate documents, this had not been done because no group had truly assumed responsibility. In the event, whoever made most noise had their motions approved – though the fact that 70 per cent of the attendance was Spanish called into question the legitimacy of this as an international decision-making forum. While other networks may have too much procedure, the opposite is the case with ATTAC. It may be bound by a common goal, but its real nature is displayed in the variety and peculiarity of each national structure.

On the other hand, its loose structure allows the movement to emphasize a campaign based on changing attitudes and practices, rather than on fixed norms. Dialogue with opponents is seen as unproductive and ATTAC generally favours more direct confrontation activities. From this perspective, many in the movement see the Tobin tax as a symbol of totemic value, a measure of whether authority takes seriously or rejects a popularly demanded reform. Thus, ATTAC members fear that, through the negotiations they have precipitated, their proposals might become watered down. As Claudio Jampaglia from ATTAC Italy has pointed out:[20]

> *One of the interesting things [about] ATTAC is that it is not interested in power. So, we don't need to be elected, and so on. We are not 'lobbying' in the traditional way. We want a conflict/discussion with institutions. We can demonstrate that their policies are unreasonable…but we are not interested in dealing with them.*

The wariness of meeting with politicians was exemplified by Bernard Cassen. When Jacques Chirac, the French president, invited Cassen to dine before the 2002 presidential elections, although he thought 'maybe we are about to change the direction of the debate in France the way we want it to be', he avoided the meeting, arguing that Chirac's personal agenda was too charged (Godoy, 2000). Because of President Chirac's support for neo-liberal economic and social programmes, meeting him would not have influenced policy and could have embarrassed ATTAC's left-wing membership. As Florini has pointed out, networks remain powerful as long as they maintain their credibility (Florini, 2000: 214). In this case, Cassen preferred to make sure that the Tobin tax was not associated with a particular politician and, therefore, passed over the chance to gain a powerful ally. In Germany a similar episode illustrated ATTAC's reluctance to work with politicians. In August 2001, Daniel Cohn-Bendit, MEP and co-founder of the Green party, criticized his own party for ignoring the anti-globalization movement, thereby estranging young voters. The party, at the time in the ruling coalition government, invited ATTAC Deutschland to assist its policy development; but ATTAC refused on the grounds that the party still supported 'neo-liberal economic policy'.[21] ATTAC has taken an all-or-nothing approach to political parties; it will only support those that subscribe to the Tobin tax campaign. For others, ATTAC prefers to 'make their lives as impossible as we can', says Susan George.[22]

Many in the wider anti-globalization movement accuse ATTAC of not challenging capitalism, just 'smoothening it', thereby possibly even helping to spread global capitalism. However, in an era in which there is little global public space for transnational movements to operate, the possibilities for 'emancipation' are seriously weakened (Cohen and Shirin, 2000: 16). Revolutionary politics has declined and alternative and reformist visions have risen – or, as Susan George put it, 'caviar is not on the menu, only noodles'. Meanwhile, ATTAC's membership and support continue to grow (though global membership data are unreliable). Sociologically speaking, ATTAC members come from the middle-class left and (particularly in the Parisian suburbs) the working class; but the movement remains quite bourgeois.[23] Distinctions between anti-globalization activists in Europe have been pointed out by Daniel Cohn-Bendit, *enfant terrible* of May 1968, who divides them into the 'old, ultra-left ideologies that are hiding inside the movement and young people who are in favour of democratization of the market'.[24] Cohn-Bendit, himself a member of ATTAC, would include ATTAC in the second group.

ATTAC: NETWORK OR MOVEMENT?

In 2001, the German weekly *Der Spiegel* pointed out that 'for the first time, a truly international generation of protestors is turning the heat on politicians and the heads of multinational corporations – and justly so. The global economy, powerful and at the same time prone to crisis, needs new rules'.[25] Such media see the emergence of transnational civil-society advocacy as a potential international actor to counterbalance the global economy and, perhaps, make political change happen. But will this new, amorphous actor become institutionalized? In the view of Cohn-Bendit, 'if the globalization movement became more clearly a political vehicle, and less obviously a transmission belt for international public opinion, its implosion would become a risk' (cited in Vinocur, 2001). ATTAC, like other organizations born during the 1990s, faces the challenge of globalizing its proposals, language, ways of communicating and decision-making.

As it stands, ATTAC-International is a platform where ATTACs from different countries meet and decide international action. But this international network arises from nationally based constituencies where the social movement is the real attraction, not the international network. In order to survive and become more effective, ATTAC will have to deal with at least three tensions. The first relates to decision-making processes and the style of leadership; the second to ATTAC's structure, particularly in relation to accountability and transparency issues; and the third to the character of the membership.

Regarding leadership and decision-making, ATTAC-I both benefits and suffers from the network's informality, making the coordination of international activities a difficult task. In an international meeting, decisions must be reached by consensus, and no one can impose decisions on other members. Yet, in this apparently leaderless system, clear leaders emerge, in practice. This is what Claudio Jampaglia, from ATTAC Italy, refers to as 'the French spirit'. Figures such as

Susan George, Ignacio Ramonet, Bernard Cassen or Manu Chao (lead singer of Mano Negra) are de facto, if not formally, appointed leaders. They are the faces of the movement for the media, and they are as necessary for ATTAC as pedalling is for a bike. Hence, ATTAC France's leadership is, in effect, the leadership of ATTAC-International as a whole.

The second tension concerns the debate about structure. The bigger ATTAC becomes, the more problems it has regarding governance and accountability. Such problems imply the need for clearer institutionalization; but the leaders of ATTAC France are very cautious about creating permanent structures. The trade-offs are obvious, says Christophe Ventura: 'Although this would entail more coordination between all the nodes, just one single strategy would be imposed by the top, and this might not be able to be followed by the peripheries'.[26] Whether this resistance to institutionalization is partly due to the fear that ATTAC France might either lose or formalize its leadership of the network is a matter of speculation. For the present, it leaves the national ATTACs working independently from each other, without a central secretariat imposing any strategy, discourse or organization. They all share core values and follow what is seen as the 'natural leadership' of ATTAC France. Similarly, every national ATTAC is organized differently and varies enormously in membership. However, the low level of institutionalization negatively affects ATTAC's prospects for promoting an effective international campaign.

The third tension concerns the nature of membership. People join groups such as ATTAC because they like its goals and identify with its ethos. Susan George suggests that the Tobin tax campaign is successful because 'who likes bankers anyway?' People join ATTAC 'because the bastards have gone too far. The bastards will take us back to the 19th century. Nowadays, more and more people are realizing about world injustice.' From this perspective, ATTAC's single-issue campaign is not the main goal, but the means to revealing the deeper systemic injustices. According to Bernard Cassen, the campaign for the Tobin tax should not be seen:

> ...as a panacea, but [as] a practical and symbolic means of taking back the initiative from pure market forces and asserting the values of solidarity. ATTAC is a movement of popular education, more a process than a specific goal (cited in Gillespie, 2000).

CONCLUSION

Transnational social movements tend to be headless organizations that come together, transforming themselves into 'a community' (Anheier, Glasius and Kaldor, 2001). ATTAC has many characteristics of a transnational movement and aspires to be one. It has certainly managed to arouse the imagination of many people; but it has not managed to become a single transnational community. It remains unclear whether this transformation would be possible within such an informal network.

Since 1998, ATTAC has grown and evolved rapidly from being a French organization to an international platform. The growing public awareness in many countries of the problems of global capital and contemporary finance owes much to its effectiveness. However, ATTAC faces many dilemmas due to the changing nature of its transnational network. Among the most important are challenges to establish clearer leadership, a clearer mandate, a common campaign platform and a more strongly developed network structure. Finally, ATTAC will have to debate whether it wants to promote a new sort of internationalism that concerns broad issues of global economic justice, or whether it is going to concentrate on being an NGO who works for the implementation of a 'Robin Hood tax'.

NOTES

1   James Tobin (1978) 'A Proposal for Monetary Reform'; also reproduced as an appendix in Patomäki (2001).
2   The data was provided by ATTAC Germany.
3   Interview with Christophe Ventura.
4   The 10 citizens were Manu Chao, René Dumont, Viviane Forrester, Gisèle Halimi, Bernard Langlois, Daniel Mermet, René Passet, Ignacio Ramonet, Jacques Robin and Philippe Val. For the list of organizations and other founding information see ATTAC France's web page: www.ATTAC.org/france/index.html.
5   Interview with Susan George.
6   Surajaras and Sweeney have showed how outdated the efficient markets hypothesis (EMH) is – the dominant paradigm in financial economics since the mid-1960s. The EMH argues that speculators cannot make consistent profits using simple, mechanical buy-and-sell rules because the market is efficient. However, they have shown how financial markets can be inefficient and differences in access to information may be used by speculators to anticipate, detect and/or provoke trends in prices (Surajaras and Sweeney, 1992: 3, 255–256).
7   See the work by Rodney Schmidt (1999) and Paul Bernard Spahn (1996).
8   See War on Want and the New Economics Foundation (2001) 'The Robin Hood Tax', London (www.waronwant.org).
9   See www.ATTAC.org/fra/inte/doc/naissanceen.
10   See www.ATTAC.org/fra/inte/doc/plateformeen.
11   From 'An International Movement for Democratic Control of Financial Markets and Their Institutions', www.ATTAC.org/fra/inte/doc/naissanceen.
12   From 'An International Movement for Democratic Control of Financial Markets and Their Institutions', www.ATTAC.org/fra/inte/doc/naissanceen.
13   Interview with Laurent Jessover.
14   The list as of 2002 comprised Andorra, Algeria, Argentina, Austria, Belgium, Bolivia, Brazil, Burkina Faso, Cameroon, Chile, Colombia, Denmark, Finland, France, Hungary, Germany, Greece, Ireland, Italy, Japan, Luxemburg, Mali, Morocco, The Netherlands, Norway, Paraguay, Portugal, Quebec, Russia, Senegal, Spain, Sweden, Switzerland, Tunisia and Uruguay.
15   See Merino (2001) and Gillespie (2001) 'Tobin Tax on Capital Movements Attracting Growing Support'. *The Irish Times,* 1 September. For an updated list of countries who support the Tobin tax, see www.waronwant.org.

16 See *New Scientist* (2002) 'Globally Local', 27 April.

17 From 'An international Movement for Democratic Control of Financial Markets and Their Institutions', www.ATTAC.org/fra/inte/doc/naissanceen.

18 Interview with Christophe Ventura.

19 Interview with Susan George.

20 Interview with Claudio Jampaglia.

21 *Suddeutsche Zeitung* (2001) 'ATTAC Rejects Co-operation with Green Party, 23 August.

22 Interview with Susan George.

23 Interview with Susan George.

24 Vinocur (2001) 'War Transforms the Anti-Globalization Crowd', *International Herald Tribune*, 2 November.

25 *Der Spiegel* (2001) no 30.

26 Interview with Christophe Ventura.

Chapter 9

Conclusions:
Globalizing Civic Engagement

John Clark

Various forms of global civic action are emerging in response to both the opportunities and threats posed by global change. These are the new and fast-moving tectonic plates of associational activity. They present great challenges to civil society and policy-makers alike. This book has explored many examples of this phenomenon in order to assess the effectiveness of these experiences, the organizational and governance challenges experienced and what general lessons can be deduced. It is hoped that these findings are of use to civil society leaders, to policy-makers who have to respond to civil society pressure and to academics studying civil society.

One of the clearest, but not very helpful, conclusions from our case studies is that the sheer diversity of civil society actions makes generalization dangerous. While civil society organizations (CSOs) in very different sectors face similar challenges as they prioritize transnational ways of working, they respond to them in diverse ways. No grand unified model can be sketched; no dogmatic lessons can be drawn. Perhaps this is to be expected. Our starting point was to study a wide range of case studies – from established charities pressing for better access to life-saving drugs and century-old international trade union structures, to web-based campaigns ('dot causes'), the modern protest movement and the World Social Forum (WSF; see Chapter 7). But such diversity is a hallmark of civil society.

Accepting this caveat, the common challenges experienced present civil society leaders and policy-makers with a set of choices, conundrums and dilemmas. This chapter summarizes these as a set of critical questions to be wrestled with. Finally, it hazards some suggestions as to its future course.

DOES TRANSNATIONAL CIVIL SOCIETY OFFER A CHALLENGE TO GLOBAL GOVERNANCE?

The imperative for transnational action is felt strongest by CSOs who seek to influence policy and public opinion, since policy is increasingly formed in international forums or set by internationally determined norms. This was the starting premise of Chapter 1 and is well illustrated by our case studies.

Policy-makers should offer a more credible and open-minded response than they have hitherto done. Governments, inter-governmental organizations and transnational corporations (TNCs) will find that the gulf between them and popular opinion (including much of the media) will widen and become more conflicting unless they make determined effort to engage critics in serious and genuine debate. They must respond to the mounting concern that today's democracy doesn't reach into forums where important decisions are increasingly made (as described in Chapter 1) – the 'democracy deficit' in global governance. National parliaments, political parties, media and watchdogs have little sway over international decisions – hence, the growing public view that critical decisions driving globalization are made by unaccountable bureaucrats or corporate chiefs, in shadowy global institutions, who are unresponsive to citizens. And campaigning CSOs, who are aware that the international institutions are governed by governments, argue that G7 governments (answerable to Northern publics) dominate these institutions, while the impact of their actions is most acutely felt in poor countries.

All traditional concepts of democracy are based on nation states. Yet, there is a burgeoning civil society agitation for modulating global governance by some equivalent *international* democracy, however difficult this will be to achieve. In its absence, many civil society activities, not least the environment movement, demonstrate the importance of international pressure. How to respond to the protest movement is a particular challenge for governments. Holding international meetings that are protected by ever stronger policing will erode public credibility, as will retreating to undemocratic or difficult-to-reach venues.

WHAT ARE THE BENEFITS AND COSTS OF WORKING TRANSNATIONALLY?

The CSOs and networks we explored confirm that working internationally enhances their civic effectiveness and is of increasing importance – although this is hardly surprising since we selected transnational actors for our study. However, the rationales for working transnationally vary. Some – such as Consumers International (CI), most trade union networks and specific social justice campaigns – primarily seek to influence TNCs. For this to occur, it is necessary to build coalitions with activists in the parent country, in countries where there are important markets, and in countries that best demonstrate the issue at hand. Similarly, networks such as Jubilee 2000, as well as environmental or human rights groups, seek to influence governments (and, perhaps, inter-governmental organizations);

they also need coalitions that embrace countries where the impact is most evident and where most influence is curried. For all of these groups, a conscious decision is necessary to invest in transnational action. With dot causes, however, this is not the case because of the universality of the web. Apart from language barriers, there is no cost difference between working nationally and internationally. The Association for the Taxation of Financial Transactions for the Aid of Citizens (ATTAC) is a hybrid. It is both a web-mediated international campaign and also a powerful social movement in France, organizing national or local events (with smaller social movements in other countries).

The benefits of working transnationally are well illustrated by the campaign to reduce the prices of drugs for HIV/AIDS (see Chapter 4). It would have been unlikely to succeed as a purely national venture of AIDS patients in South Africa, echoed in a few other developing countries. Trade and patent policies are largely determined by governments in the US and the European Union (EU), where the big pharmaceutical companies are based; Southern voices are weak. Northern decision-makers are only sensitive to public opinion on their home turf or in very big markets. Furthermore, many of the issues are highly technical. The campaign succeeded because grassroots CSOs in many Southern countries joined with influential Northern counterparts, and were supported by internationally renowned scientists and the leading health professionals' associations. Together, they comprised an irresistible movement for change since they combined grassroots testimonials and top-quality science, the perspectives of professionals as well as victims, the moral imperative and international credibility.

However, it is not a one-way street. Working transnationally has major costs and requires discipline. Unless the structures are in place and the governance processes are modified for this new way of working, it is likely to be fraught with frustrations for all parties. The culture and practices of CSOs who set out on this course will probably change – not just the targets of the international engagement.

TRANS-SECTOR MAY BE AS IMPORTANT AS TRANSNATIONAL – BUT IS IT WORTH IT?

Our studies suggest that, though it is less immediately obvious, forging non-traditional alliances and broad-based coalitions is just as important as working internationally. Though CSOs find it easiest to work with like-minded counterparts at home or abroad, in order to maximize impact they are seeing a need to climb out of their institutional silos and form cross-sectoral partnerships. Different CSO sectors contribute different skills and political strengths to advocacy. However, while broadening the base adds clout and injects energy, it also heightens difficulties in achieving convergence around coherent policy proposals. The more genuinely global and multi-stakeholder the network, the more difficult it becomes to achieve convergence. The World Social Forum (WSF) illustrates this. Some supporters see it as the first global political platform; it has developed campaign slogans that are powerful and forward-looking ('another world is possible'; movement 'for global economic justice and peace'). However, in practice, the WSF has not managed to construct a holistic, alternative political vision.

Cross-sector partnerships can create other problems, such as differing levels of political responsibility. For established CSOs (for example, unions or mass-membership non-governmental organizations – NGOs), their international credibility is as important as their membership, while dot causes and new campaigns can gamble their reputation on an adventurous publicity bid. Therefore, partnerships between the two are risky for both sides. The former may emerge with a dented reputation; the latter may be frustrated by lost opportunities or cautious strategies. This is particularly evident in the approaches of unions, NGOs (including J2000) and churches to the global protest movement (see Chapter 6). Some openly give support and help to mobilize protesters (greatly adding to its credibility and to the size of the protests), while others who pursue similar campaigns are at pains to avoid being associated and may speak out *against* the global protest movement. They are particularly keen to distance themselves from the tactics of disruption and violence. These issues have become more vexed since 11 September. Mass-membership CSOs (especially US CSOs) feel a strong need to condemn violence of all kinds, and even to moderate their criticism of governments.

Cultural clashes frequently result as partnerships diversify a network's base. There have been angry exchanges between trade unions and NGOs, for example, and the WSF has seen major differences between constituents, angry walkouts and even protests staged against organizers. Non-traditional partnerships are not always very deep; they may be formed for mutual legitimization rather than true cooperation. In the second WSF, many participants spent most of their time clustered into interest groups rather than talking cross-sectorally, to the disappointment of the organizers. WSF and many elements of the global protest movement are beset by clashes over focus (whether to tackle specific issues such as debt or the whole system), strategy (whether to articulate a political platform or simply oppose the system) and tactics (whether to use direct action, what forms of media to use, and whether to engage in dialogue with officials).

When networks diversify geographically, culture clashes can also arise. However, if a core concern unites the network, different global perspectives can strengthen it – though they may be difficult to reconcile, at first. For example, CI moved from an emphasis on product-testing to being a political voice for consumers worldwide as a result of expanding from a Northern clique to a global umbrella (see Chapter 2). Similarly, Friends of the Earth shifted focus from environmentalism to sustainable development; and the Global Union Federations (GUFs) – whose culture and strategy derive greatly from their origins within Western European trade unionist traditions – now tackle issues that they previously ignored, such as casual work and the informal sector (see Chapter 3).

Traditional civil society needs to construct both international strategies and effective partnerships with CSOs in other sectors in order to achieve optimal impact. This entails trade unions and environment groups in the North appreciating, for example, why Southern NGOs resent the inclusion of social and environmental conditions in trade deals. It also entails traditional CSOs carefully deciding how to relate to the protest movement. Identifying too closely might lead to loss of membership and credibility; too great a distance might alienate them from potential supporters.

HOW TO TACKLE THE HORIZONTAL–VERTICAL CONUNDRUM?

The previous two dilemmas reflect the same core challenge: how do CSOs – particularly long-established ones – move into the 'network age'? To date, where CSOs have grown in size and power, it is usually because (as in the business world) they have been models of *'vertical* integration' – keeping to their areas of expertise and growing through evolving hierarchical structures. However, the imperative in our globalizing world is *horizontal* integration – working in a diversity of disciplines, as well as countries. How CSOs are run domestically influences their success in responding to this challenge. Those who are unswervingly vertical in structure find it most difficult to form horizontal partnerships.

The larger and longer-established CSOs find this transition most difficult. Their leaders have probably been trained in management skills for growth and for running hierarchies. Their institutional cultures and norms, and what their supporters or members expect of them, have been moulded by their history; these things are difficult to change quickly. Hence, it is often easier for new entries to work in these new ways. They may be smaller, at least initially, and they don't have the institutional baggage of the traditional CSOs. Groups such as ATTAC (see Chapter 8) are therefore able to capture the imagination and support of idealistic students, leftist intellectuals, the development lobby, radical churchgoers and rank-and-file workers. Its membership is increasing rapidly while traditional mass-membership CSOs often face decline.

IS THERE A DEMOCRACY PARADOX?

Transnational civil society networks (TCSNs) challenge the lack of democracy in international decision-making; but some are starting to ask: 'How democratic are we ourselves?' Democratic CSOs use participatory approaches in their own decision-making, embrace pluralism (not ignoring voices that are different from the leadership's), are clear whom they represent (members or supporters), and can demonstrate the legitimacy of this representation.

As CSOs and networks grow in size and scope, these things become more cumbersome. Some – especially federations such as CI, Amnesty International and the GUFs – evolve their board and management processes accordingly, but inevitably discover a trade-off between member participation and efficiency – particularly where membership is geographically and culturally diverse. Small networks (such as those cooperating for lowering the price of AIDS drugs, or joint union–NGO campaigns against child labour) face less difficulty but are limited to specific and shared purposes. Others, such as J2000 and ATTAC (see

Chapters 5 and 8) are, in effect, founder-led. While trust in the de facto leadership remains strong, their decision-making can be swift and imaginative. However, growth can take them to a point where internal divisions manifest; at this stage, governance becomes contested and competing strategies and leaderships emerge. Unitary or centralized associations (such as Human Rights Watch or Greenpeace) face less difficulty because they have hierarchies and single boards to which national sections are subservient.

There appears to be a democracy paradox. Transnational civil society is a response to the democracy deficit in global governance. In the absence of global parliaments, it fosters public debate, informs the media and alerts politicians throughout the world to its analysis and alternative perspectives. But in this 'CNN age' there is a considerable premium on being the first to stake a position in response to a new situation or on having the simplest, sharpest critique. Carefully qualified remarks or positions that are announced after the press pack has moved on to new issues don't make the headlines. Hence, CSOs who are best equipped to challenge the democracy deficit may often be, ironically, those who are less democratic themselves or who represent few people.

This relates to the controversies about CSOs' legitimacy, representivity and leadership. Specifically, many networks purport to be global. Yet, Southern members see them as largely North-driven; the leadership of CSO networks is often contested; Southern voices at global forums often represent small organizations who are better known to donors and Northern partners than to any domestic constituency (Northern CSOs may also be small cliques); and foundations and bilateral donors have strong influence within TCSNs because they are major providers of funds, obviating the need for large due-paying memberships. Mass-based Southern CSOs are usually primarily concerned with local or national issues; it is generally the more intellectual, capital, city-based, donor-funded CSOs in the South or in transition countries who engage in TCSNs. An alternative perspective is that CSOs who engage in TCSNs find it easier to mobilize external funding, providing they have staff with relevant management and communications skills, and therefore don't need to mobilize large domestic constituencies.

WHOSE VOICE GETS HEARD?

A related dilemma is the vexed question – in transnational, multisectoral alliances – of who speaks for whom. How can claims towards representivity be gauged? This question has three variations. Firstly, which CSOs are most legitimate? Advocacy NGOs often have excellent communications skills and are generally respected by the media and others who shape public opinion; but their legitimacy is challenged from within civil society as well as from outside. Trade unions have charged them with just speaking for themselves and with promoting elite and Northern concerns at the expense of the world's workers. Mass organizations have challenged the prominence of NGOs within the organizing of the WSF (though the initiative largely came from the Brazilian NGO association, who even owns the name 'World Social Forum') – arguing that they are not legitimate spokespeople for the exploited and are undemocratic. In many networks there is a tension between democracy and political entrepreneurship.

Secondly, does the network truly speak for a global constituency? International networks are often represented by Northern spokespeople since they have easier access to international institutions and the world media. But this is increasingly resented in the South (though it should be added that grassroots Southern CSOs often equally resent their policy-oriented, capital city peers, who they think are far removed from ground reality). Many networks that purport to be international (even global) are, in reality, overwhelmingly biased towards the North or to one region. Even Southern-initiated ventures display a regional bias. For example, participants in the WSF are largely from Brazil and its neighbouring countries. Southern trade unions agree with their Northern counterparts that an urgent review is needed of the roles of their international structures; but it appears that they feel rather left out of the Millennium Review currently underway (see Chapter 3) and question its relevance to their needs.

Thirdly, who decides who has a right to speak? It is increasingly common to hear Southern voices in international forums, but they are usually handpicked and financed by Northern partners. Southern consumer groups, for example, usually don't have the mass base of their Northern counterparts but are assisted and financed by Northern partners. Similarly, considerable resentment has been voiced towards the WSF organizers for their subjectivity in choosing who gets to speak in the plenary sessions (including judgements about which politicians are allowed a platform – such as the new president of Brazil – and which are denied – such as the prime minister of Belgium).

HOW BEST TO ENGAGE THE MEDIA?

Websites reach global audiences at negligible cost, short-circuiting the need for mainstream media in many mobilization and dissemination activities. However, they are not a total substitute. The latter usually have more stringent quality control (although, perhaps, with a political bias) and are studied by policy-makers. Hence, CSOs – particularly those seeking to reform policies and engage decision-makers in dialogue –usually thirst for media coverage. But how can they get it?

Protests – particularly large and aggressive ones – are reported; but is it the issues or just the violence that is described? Journalists covering dull inter-governmental meetings may simply be looking for a spicy news story to give variety to their reportage. The liberal media have become increasingly fond of advocacy NGOs and give fuller coverage of their campaigns (often covering the substance), and they generally give greater prominence to NGOs' arguments in disputes with official or corporate targets. But unchallenging reportage may encourage sloppy research on the part of the NGOs. CSO leaders need to focus on the credibility and integrity of their sector, as a whole, and not just on the column inches achieved for the particular issue at hand.

IS A TECHNOLOGY DIVIDE REPLACING
THE GEOGRAPHIC DIVIDE?

The emergence of transnational civil society at the time of a global communications revolution is no coincidence. Cheaper travel and information and communications technology (ICT) are clearly enabling factors, as is the increasingly widespread use of English in international networks (in regional networks, other languages are often more important). But while new communications have opened the door of Northern-led civil society to Southern voices, these voices are mostly of the well educated, the digitally connected and the Western oriented. Others have scarcely noticed the new opportunities or choose to remain with traditional local roles. Moreover, the barriers of geography remain severe, as do issues of class, culture and language. ICT has democratized communications for some, but by no means for all (see, in particular, Chapter 6).

ICT has other limitations. While it permits extremely cheap, instantaneous exchanges of information and is a powerful tool in mass mobilization and research, few CSOs have found ways of using it for building trust within their networks and, therefore, for making key decisions or resolving conflicts. Ensuring the quality of information posted is also problematic. Those networks that rely most on the internet (particularly the dot causes and groups such as ATTAC and WSF) find it difficult to evolve strategy or to clearly define what exactly they stand for. As a result, contemporary campaigns (particularly the components of the global protest movement) find it relatively easy to describe what they are against, but extremely difficult to prescribe viable alternatives. On the other hand, CSOs who make great use of the web (starting with the Free Burma Campaign and the International Campaign to Ban Landmines) can reach out more widely than they previously dreamed of; demystify official processes; organize events swiftly and cheaply; appeal to the younger generation; and present new conduits for challenging or strengthening global governance.

HOW AND WHEN TO ENGAGE THE SYSTEM?

The partnership issue that is most difficult for diverse networks to resolve is how to relate to governments, inter-governmental organizations and TNCs. In general, CSOs with a mass base, particularly those with broad support, and CSOs with a strong research and analysis capacity are most confident at engaging – and, indeed, cannot afford to appear to stand against the system. The Global Union platform, for example, is clear that it is no longer sufficient to organize collective bargaining with individual employers on behalf of its members; it needs to influence the policy environment of the labour market internationally. As a result, it needs to engage with the International Monetary Fund, the World Bank, the World Trade Organization, the International Labour Organization and the Organization for Economic Cooperation and Development, as well as with the major TNCs. Some transnational CSOs, such as the GUFs and CI, are traditional engagers and see negotiation as one of their principal roles. However, they now find that some of their newer Southern members are challenging the apparent cosiness of this relationship and want a much sharper edge.

Tension often arises between TCSNs and Southern governments. This stems from conflicting aspects of solidarity. On the one hand, those campaigning on macro-issues promote global justice and, hence, express solidarity with Southern societies, including governments. On the other hand, those concerned about vulnerable people promote local justice – and the greatest obstacle to this may be the national government.

This ambivalence is reflected in the divided attitude of Southern governments towards civil society. Some (such as in South America, Central and Eastern Europe, or mature democracies) generally welcome civil society in all its diversity, while others deride CSOs as largely Western constructs or resent their power and resources. Much depends upon the cause in question. Until recently, most international CSO campaigns have created resentment (such as human rights campaigns, and opposition to large dams or child labour). Lately, governments have begun to see symbiosis with CSOs in many campaigns. They have, generally, welcomed the role of transnational civil society in seeking debt relief, increased aid and trade/economic justice. They primarily support its effort to lower the price of AIDS drugs (although the South African government resents the pressure that the success of this campaign has put on their health service to provide these drugs) and they support some objectives of international trade union campaigns (though they are keen to avoid being seen as anti-TNCs). On other issues they remain largely silent (such as on the Tobin tax campaign, since most governments are keen to encourage foreign direct investment and worry that currency controls may be a deterrent) or are hostile (such as many environmental or human rights campaigns, as well as the anti-global capitalist movement).

TNC–CSO engagement is also controversial for all parties. Most TNCs keep as far away from advocacy CSOs as possible, and CSOs who engage often find themselves criticized by peers in their networks. However, the experience of the HIV/AIDS campaign and some GUF experience show that critical engagement can help to check the power of a TNC. There is also evidence that TNCs may benefit by being ahead of their rivals in making reforms or engaging with their critics. Hence, many are now engaging with NGOs in exercises of 'corporate social responsibility' or in serious dialogue with their critics.

WHEN DO CAMPAIGNS BECOME MOVEMENTS?

Chapter 1 described three different broad civil society forms found in transnational action – the international CSO, the transnational network and the social movement. Our case studies have shown that these forms may not be rigid. In particular, networks may broaden and evolve into social movements, as was the experience of J2000 and ATTAC. When this happens, the original, clear goal (such as reducing the debts of the poorest countries to affordable levels, and introducing a Tobin tax on currency transactions) becomes blurred and broadened. What becomes more important is the growing community of activists who share a conviction that there is injustice in the current order and who develop a shared language to convey this.

Various social movements and campaigns, whose only common denominator is a link to issues of globalization, have coalesced in today's global protest movement. The flimsiness of this common base yields definitional problems. It isn't a movement in the traditional sense. Its causes are multiple and shifting (for example, in some countries it has morphed into a campaign against a war with Iraq). Indeed, it has been well described as a 'movement of movements'. Likewise, its events are usually called 'protests'; but they also have the characteristics of political conventions, mass lobbies, teach-ins and carnivals. They appear to be global; yet, the different regional constituents may have very different cultures. For example, the Latin Americans celebrate pluralism and want the WSF to simply be a forum in which civil society speaks for itself, while the Africans, at their regional social forum, passed resolutions and agreed a final declaration.

The plethora of dot causes within the protest movement mobilize large numbers for it, but also appear to inject characteristics of uncertainty. It is highly diverse; it isn't clear who is in and who isn't; it has no common focus or strategy; its tactics range from violence to non-violence and from rejection of authority to engagement; it has no recognized leadership; and it provides an infrastructure for protest (rather than direction) through its 'days of action', where anything goes and all groups participating decide for themselves the cause, the argument, the action and the tactics.

THE WAY AHEAD

There has been a strong international dimension to social movements since the campaign against slavery; but the phenomenon we have been exploring – civil society networks working across national boundaries in integrated transnational activities – is a quantum leap from this. It is clearly at an early stage in what will be an influential career. It faces challenges both from within and outside of the establishment. Our review of experience suggests that the degree to which it is able to withstand these challenges and play a decisive role in reshaping the processes of democracy and policy deliberation depends upon how the sector addresses six contradictions inherent in its ascendancy.

Firstly, there are strong advantages to forming cross-sector networks; however, these heighten risks of cultural and tactical clashes. Most CSOs are culturally attuned to their peers (even their rivals) and, hence, usually practice vertical integration. Horizontal integration with other types of CSOs (who have different priorities and 'languages') may be a more important skill in today's world, but one that most CSOs haven't learned. The dialectic is between achieving the energy possible in a broad movement (evidenced, for example, by J2000's growth out of a development NGO and grassroots church network) and maintaining the clear message that is possible in a close partnership.

Secondly, the increased influence of civil society in shaping policy is largely due to a deficit in conventional democracy; yet, the most influential CSOs are often not those who represent large constituencies or who are studiously democratic in their decision-making. As the sector becomes more powerful, and as policy-makers and the media become more sophisticated in responding to civil society, it is likely that the challenge to demonstrate representivity will become stronger. This might elevate the stature of those mass-membership organizations who are also internally democratic (such as the GUFs, CI and Amnesty International), putting a premium on such organizations finding swifter ways of reaching decisions without sacrificing democracy. This needn't mean that smaller or non-membership organizations lose influence. But they might need to demonstrate representivity in other ways, such as through participatory research, widespread consultations or opinion polling. It is particularly important that TCSNs learn ways of ensuring equity for Southern and non-English speaking voices.

Thirdly, new currents in civil society tend to reject leadership, seeing it as antithetical to democracy. However, the CSOs who have achieved most in influencing policy or, indeed, in delivering services demonstrate that effective, democratic decision-making requires leadership – albeit of the right sort. The rejection of leadership in some networks and social movements may stem not so much from an idealistic deference to democracy but from a recognition that there are no governance arrangements in place for authenticating the leadership selection. In this absence, de facto leaders emerge (those individuals who speak on platforms around the world); but because they are not called leaders, there is no pressure to account for why these spokespeople have been selected and by whom.

Fourthly, today's protest movement has mobilized millions because it embraces so many causes that are loosely in opposition to the current economic order. But no movement can make an impact unless it articulates an alternative and convinces public opinion of its case. A critical challenge for TCSNs, generally, is to assert what they stand for, rather than what they are opposed to. The protest movement has no collective manifesto, despite the efforts of some WSF leaders, other than its opposition to neo-liberalism. There are signs that it is starting to reject violent tactics and to engage more in dialogue; but this might alienate much of its support base. Will it lose its sharp edge and become more reformist – will it, perhaps, start looking a bit grey in the temples? Resolving such internal tension is vital if it is to become more than a medley of protests, perhaps growing but defined just by opposing the establishment.

Fifthly, new communications technology can narrow the North–South gulf in transnational civil society; but it may be widening the gulf between capital city-based and grassroots CSOs. ICT offers immense opportunities not only for international networking, but also for mobilizing new constituencies in campaigns and social movements. However, it isn't universally available and very real barriers of geography remain. A sophisticated class of global civil-society activists may be emerging, who is also losing its connection with the grassroots. A digital divide may be reinforcing, not eliminating, the geographic divide.

Sixthly, the resources conundrum: CSOs, particularly mass organizations, are usually self-financed through membership dues; but transnational advocacy networks are largely financed by international NGOs, foundations and bilateral aid agencies. Is the tail wagging the dog? Does the ready availability of funds for international work, and the increasingly frequent international gatherings on global policy issues, distort civil society – especially in the South? This ready funding may distract Southern and transition country CSOs away from national priorities towards topics that are of greater interest in the North. It might make it easier to form a CSO who addresses global rather than national issues, on top of which are seductive travel opportunities. Conversely, working transnationally may help Southern CSOs to enhance their advocacy capacity, achieve greater influence with their national governments and strengthen solidarity links internationally. What is important is that Southern CSOs are in the driving seat and that equal partnerships emerge.

These issues relate to questions of civil society governance. Even at a national level, it is hard for a CSO sector – for example, NGOs – to resolve the governance challenges that it faces. There are few cases of effective self-regulation; increasingly, governments, parliaments and even donors are devising ways of giving seals of approval or disapproval. This trend is dangerous; if official bodies started categorizing firms in this way, it certainly wouldn't be tolerated (other than for branding law-breakers). This indicates that civil society itself needs to give much more attention to effective codes of conduct, certification schemes, internal policing mechanisms and independent watchdogs. With transnational and multisectoral civil society, these issues are even more intractable – but it is critical that TCSNs address them, at least in facing head-on the organizational, governance, strategic and tactical challenges described in this book.

References and Interviews

CHAPTER 1

Amnesty International (2000) 'Changing the Way We Change: Options for Reforming AI's Decision-Making Processes and Structures', Paper submitted to all AI sections and to the 2001 International Council Meeting

Anheier, H (2000) 'Notes on Decision-Making and Accountability in International NGOs', Mimeo, London: London School of Economics

Anheier, H, Glasius, M and Kaldor M (eds) (2001) *Global Civil Society 2001*, Oxford: Oxford University Press

Anheier, H and Themudo, N (2002) 'Organisational Forms of Global Civil Society: Implications of Going Global' in Glasius, M, Kaldor, M and Anheier, H (eds) *Global Civil Society 2002*, Oxford: Oxford University Press

Boehle, J (2001) 'The Growth of International Inter-religious Activity', Note presented at seminar on Transnational Civil Society, London School of Economics, London

Chiriboga, M (2001) 'Constructing a Southern Constituency for Global Advocacy: The Experience of Latin American NGOs and the World Bank' in Edwards, M and Gaventa, J (eds) *Global Citizen Action*, Boulder, Colorado: Lynne Rienner

Clark, J (1991) *Democratizing Development: the Role of Voluntary Agencies,* London: Earthscan, and West Hartford, Connecticut: Kumarian Press

Clark, J (1999) 'Ethical Globalization: the Dilemmas and Challenges of Internationalizing Civil Society', Paper presented at the 1999 International NGO Conference, Birmingham University; published in Edwards, M and Gaventa, J (eds) (2001) *Global Citizen Action*, Boulder, Colorado: Lynne Rienner

Clark, J (2003) *Worlds Apart: Civil Society and the Battle for Ethical Globalization,* London: Earthscan, and Bloomfield, Connecticut: Kumarian Press

Edwards, M (1996) 'International Development NGOs: Legitimacy, Accountability, Regulation and Roles', Discussion paper for British Overseas Aid Group, London

Edwards, M (2000) *NGO Rights and Responsibilities: a New Deal for Global Governance,* London: Foreign Policy Centre

Edwards, M and Hulme, D (eds) (1995) *NGO Performance and Accountability: Beyond the Magic Bullet,* London: Earthscan, and West Hartford, Connecticut: Kumarian Press

Edwards, M and Gaventa, J (eds) (2001) *Global Citizen Action*, Boulder, Colorado: Lynne Rienner

Florini, A (ed) (2000) *The Third Force: the Rise of Transnational Civil Society,* Washington, DC: Carnegie Endowment for International Peace

Fowler, A (1997) *Striking a Balance: a Guide to Enhancing the Effectiveness of NGOs in International Development,* London: Earthscan

Fox, J (2000) 'Assessing Binational Civil Society Coalitions: Lessons from the Mexico-US experience', Mimeo, Paper presented at University of California Santa Cruz Conference on Human Rights and Globalization, December

Hlobil, P (2001) 'East–East Skill-Sharing and East–West Collaboration', Paper presented at Seminar on Transnational Civil Society, London School of Economics, June

ICFTU (2000) 'Millennium Review Process', Executive Board Paper, Brussels, November; also ICFTU website: www.icftu.org

ICFTU (2001) 'Millennium Review: Report of the Progress Group to ICFTU's Executive Board', 117/EB/E/7, November, Brussels

Jordan, L and van Tuijl, P (2000) 'Political Responsibility in Transnational NGO Advocacy', *World Development*, vol 28(12): 2051–2065

Keck, M and Sikkink, K (1998) *Activists Beyond Borders: Advocacy Networks in International Politics,* Ithaca and London: Cornell University Press

Lindenberg, M and Bryant, C (2001) *Going Global: Transforming Relief and Development NGOs,* Bloomfield, Connecticut: Kumarian Press

Oxfam International website: www.oxfaminternational.org

Oxfam International (2000) 'Towards Global Equity: OI's Strategic Plan, 2001–2004', Adopted by OI's board, November, Melbourne

Putnam, R (2000) *Bowling Alone: The Collapse and Revival of American Community,* New York: Simon and Schuster

Rodrigues, M (2000) 'Searching for Common Ground: Transnational Advocacy Networks and Environmentally Sustainable Development in Amazonia', Mimeo, Paper presented at University of California Santa Cruz Conference on Human Rights and Globalization, Santa Cruz

Salomon, L (1994) 'The Rise of the Nonprofit Sector', *Foreign Affairs*, vol 73(2): 109–122

Selverston-Scher, M (2000) 'Building International Civil Society: Lessons from the Amazon Coalition', Mimeo, Paper presented at University of California Santa Cruz conference on Human Rights and Globalization, Santa Cruz

Stark, D (2001) 'NGO Network Development in Eastern Europe', Paper presented at Seminar on Transnational Civil Society, London School of Economics, London

Vianna, A (2000) 'The Work of Brazilian NGOs on the International Level: Discussion Paper', Mimeo, INESC, Brazil

Interviews

Charles Secrett, director, and Tony Juniper, director designate, Friends of the Earth UK (FOE UK)

Marieke Torffs, Friends of the Earth International (FOE-I)

Gordon Shepherd, Jenny Heap and Gonzalo Oviedo, World Wide Fund for Nature International (WWF-I)

Dave Bull, former director, Amnesty International (AI) UK

Roger Clark, former Africa director, Amnesty International (AI)

Patti Whalley, deputy director, Amnesty International (AI)

Robert Archer, International Council for Human Rights Policy

Ernst Ligteringen, former director, Oxfam International (OI)

Justin Forsyth, policy director, Oxfam GB

Ed Schenkenberg, International Council of Voluntary Agencies

Rajesh Tandon, Participatory Research in Asia (PRIA)

Manuel Chiriboga, Latin American Association of Popular Organizations (ALOP)

Ann Pettifor, Kwesi Owuso and Adrian Lovett; Jubilee 2000 UK

Kumi Naidoo, director, CIVICUS (World Alliance for Citizen Participation)

Florian Rochat, Centre Europe–Tiers Monde, Geneva

Peter Prove, Lutheran World Federation
Martin Robra, World Council of Churches (WCC)
Wendy Tyndale, World Faiths Dialogue on Development
Josef Boehle, United Religions Initiative
James Howard, International Confederation of Free Trade Unions (ICFTU)
Alan Leather and Mike Waghorne, assistant general secretaries, Public Service International (PSI)
Phil Boyer, Union Network International (UNI)
Bob Harris, former general secretary, Education International
Tony Hill, United Nations NGO Liaison Service
Peter Utting, UN Research Institute for Social Development

CHAPTER 2

Sim, F G (1991) *IOCU On Record: A Documentary History of the International Organisation of Consumers Unions 1960–1990*, Yonkers, New York: Consumers Union of United States Inc

Interviews

Julian Edwards, director-general, and Jayanti Durai, Consumers International (CI)
Phil Evans and Allan Asher, Consumers Association (CA), UK
Pradeep Mehta, Consumer Unity and Trust Society (CUTS), India
Mohideen Abdul Kader, vice-president, Consumers Association of Penang
Anwar Fazal, former president, International Organization of Consumers Unions (IOCU)

CHAPTER 3

Anheier, H and Themudo, N (2002) 'On Governance and Management of International Membership Organisations', Centre for Civil Society Working Paper, London School of Economics, London
Ashwin, S (2000) 'International Labour Solidarity after the Cold War' in Cohen, R and Rai, S M (eds) *Global Social Movements*, London: Athlone Press
Brook, K (2002) 'Trade Union Membership: an Analysis of Data from the Autumn 2001', *Labour Market Trends*, July, pp343–355
Castells, M (1996) *The Rise of the Network Society*, Oxford: Blackwell Publishers
Davis, R (2002) 'Anti-globalization Activists and Unions Can Still Work Together', *ATTAC Newsletter*, no 121, March
Gordon, M E and Turner, L (2000) *Transnational Cooperation among Labor Unions*, New York: Cornell University Press
Handy, C (1989) *The Age of Paradox*, Boston: Harvard Business School Press
ICFTU (2000a) 'Launching the Millennium Review: The Future of the International Trade Union Movement', Congress Statements, www.icftu.org
ICFTU (2000b) 'The Millennium Debate: The Review for Change', *ICFTU Online Bulletin*, www.icftu.org
ICFTU (2001) Background report to the 117th meeting of the ICFTU executive board, Appendix, 117EB/E/7, Brussels: ICFTU
IFBWW website: www.ifbww.org

ILO Bureau of Statistics (2002) 'Statistics of Trade Union Membership', Mimeo, October, data for 45 countries taken primarily from national statistical publications, Geneva

Jordan, B (2000) Address by ICFTU general secretary to the COSATU 7th National Congress, 20 September

Kidder, T (2002) 'Networks in Transnational Labor Organizing' in Khagram, S, Riker, J and Sikkink, K (eds) *Restructuring World Politics*, London: University of Minnesota Press

Lindenberg, M and Dobel, J P (1999) 'The Challenges of Globalization for Northern International Relief and Development NGOs', *Nonprofit and Voluntary Sector Quarterly*, vol 28(4), Supplement: 2–24

Madisha, W (2000) Address to the ICFTU 17th Congress Debate on the Millennium Review, 6 April, at www.cosatu.org.za/speeches/2000/wm000406

Martin, A and Ross, G (2001) 'Trade Unions Organizing at the European Level: the Dilemma of Borrowed Resources' in Imig, D and Tarrow, S (eds) *Contentious Europeans: Protest and Politics in an Emerging Polity*, Lanham, Maryland: Rowman and Littlefield

Moody, K (1997) *Workers in a Lean World: Unions in the International Economy*, London: Verso

Munck, R (2000) 'Labour in the Global: Challenges and Prospects' in Cohen, R and Rai, S M (eds) *Global Social Movements*, London and New Brunswick, New Jersey: Athlone Press

O'Brien, R, Goetz, A M, Scholte, J A and Williams, M (2000) *Contesting Global Governance: Multilateral Economic Institutions and Global Social Movements*, Cambridge: Cambridge University Press

Ramsay, H (2000) 'Know Thine Enemy: Understanding Multinational Corporations as a Requirement for Strategic International Laborism' in Gordon, M E and Turner, L (eds) *Transnational Cooperation among Labor Unions*, New York: Cornell University Press

Rifkin, J (1995) *The End of Work: The Decline of the Global Force and the Dawn of the Post-market Era*, New York: Putnam's Sons

Ryder, G (2002a) 'From Local to Global Level: Ensuring Continuity in the Unions' Action', Spotlight Interview, *Trade Union World*, at www.icftu.org/displaydocument.asp?Index=991216282&Language=EN

Ryder, G (2002b) 'Coherent Global Governance Geared to Global Improvements in People's Lives', Spotlight Interview, *Trade Union World*, at www.icftu.org/displaydocument.asp?Index=991216279&Language=EN

Tarrow, S (undated) 'Beyond Globalization: Why Creating Trans-national Social Movements is so Hard and When is it Most Likely to Happen' at www.antenna.nl/~waterman/tarrow.html

Tarrow, S (2001) 'Contentious Politics in a Composite Polity' in Imig, D and Tarrow, S (eds) *Contentious Europeans: Protest and Politics in an Emerging Polity*, Lanham, Maryland: Rowman and Littlefield

Tarrow, S (2002) 'Rooted Cosmopolitans: Towards a Sociology of Transnational Contention', Mimeo, 5 January, Cornell University, Cornell

Western, B (1997) *Between Class and Market. Post-war Unionization in the Capitalist Democracies*, Princeton: Princeton University Press

Zinn, K (2000) 'Solidarity across Borders: the UMWA's Corporate Campaign against Peabody and Hanson PLC' in Gordon, M E and Turner, L (eds) *Transnational Cooperation among Labor Unions*, New York: Cornell

Interviews

Giampiero Alhadeff, secretary general, Solidar

Luis Corral, director for political affairs, Trade Union Congress of The Philippines

Alan Leather, deputy general secretary, Public Services International (PSI)

Tim Noonan, director of campaigns, International Confederation of Free Trade Unions (ICFTU)

Annie Watson, director, Commonwealth Trades Union Congress

CHAPTER 4

Heywood, M (2001) 'Debunking 'Conglomo-Talk: A Case study of the Amicus Curiae as an Instrument for Advocacy, Investigation and Mobilization', Paper presented at the conference on Health, Law and Human Rights: Exploring the Connections, An International Cross-Disciplinary Conference Honouring Jonathan M Mann, 29 September to 1 October 2001, Philadelphia, Pennsylvania

International Centre for Trade and Sustainable Development (ICTSD) (2001) 'Drug Companies Drop Case Against South African Government', *BRIDGES Weekly Trade News Digest,* vol 5(15): 3–5

Love, J (1999) 'Notes on the USTR Watch Lists and Reports' at www.cptech.org/ip/health/whatrlists.html

Manoochehri, M (2001) 'Unethical Patent Law: How the United States and the WTO Impact the Health of Brazilian Citizens', 26 April, www.freeipx.org/display.php3?id=46

Oxfam (2001a) 'Dare to Lead: Public Health and Company Wealth', Oxfam Briefing Paper on GlaxoSmithKline, Oxford: Oxfam

Oxfam (2001b) 'Drug Companies versus Brazil: the Threat to Public Health', Oxford: Oxfam

Raghavan, C (2001) 'Doha Public Health Declaration May Help South – But to What Extent?' Reproduced from the *South-North Development Monitor* (SUNS), vol 5009, www.twnside.org.sg

Robins, S (2002) 'Race, Cultural Identity and Aids in South Africa', *The Sunday Independent Newspaper,* South Africa

Soal, J (2001) 'Treatment Action Campaign: an Overview', www.tac.org.za

CHAPTER 5

Barrett, M (ed) (2000) 'The World Will Never Be the Same Again', December, Jubilee 2000 Coalition and World Vision, UK

Bauck, A (2001) 'Oxfam and Debt Relief Advocacy', from the Electronic Hallway, University of Washington, Washington, www.hallway.org

Bunting, M (2000) 'Special Report: Debt Relief – 2000 Deadline Brought Sense of Urgency', *Guardian,* 28 December

Clark, J (2001) 'Ethical Globalization: the Dilemmas and Challenges of Internationalizing Civil Society' in Edwards, M and Gaventa, J (eds) *Global Citizen Action,* Boulder, Colorado: Lynne Rienner

Clarke, M, Vanderslice, M and Joyner, K (2002) 'Determined to Fail: the Heavily Indebted Poor Country Initiative', Report from Jubilee USA Network

Collins, C, Gariyo, Z and Burdon, T (2001) 'Jubilee 2000: Citizen Action across North–South Divide' in Edwards, M and Gaventa, J (eds) *Global Citizen Action*, Boulder, Colorado: Lynne Rienner

Denny, C and Elliott, L (2002) 'Short Wants G7 Top-Up for Poor', *Guardian*, 27 September

Dent, M and Peters, B (1999) *The Crisis of Poverty and Debt in the Third World*, Aldershot: Ashgate

Desai, M and Said, Y (2001) 'The New Anti-capitalist Movement: Money and Global Civil Society' in Anheier, H, Glasius, M and Kaldor, M (eds) *Global Civil Society Yearbook 2001*, Oxford: Oxford University Press

de Senillosa, I (1998) 'A New Age of Social Movements: a Fifth Generation of Non-Governmental Development Organizations in the Making?' *Development in Practice*, vol 8(1): 40–53

Dor, G (2001) 'Discussion paper on strategy, organisation and structure', Jubilee 2000 South Africa; http//aidc.org.za/2nd_conference/discussion_paper

Edwards, M (2001) 'Introduction' in Edwards, M and Gaventa, J (eds) *Global Citizen Action*, Boulder, Colorado: Lynne Rienner

Grint, K (1997) 'Alternative Leadership' in Grint, K (ed) *Leadership: Classical, Contemporary, and Critical Approaches*, Oxford: Oxford University Press

Hanson, I and Travis, A (eds) (1999) *Breaking the Chains: the New Jubilee 2000 Debt Cutter's Handbook*, London: Jubilee 2000 Coalition

Hutton, W (1999) 'The Jubilee Line that Works', *Observer*, 3 October

IMF and World Bank (2002) 'Heavily Indebted Poor Countries Initiative: Status of Implementation', Paper presented by staff members of the IMF and World Bank, 21 September

Jubilee 2000 Coalition (2001) 'Learning Points', 9 March, Report of Jubilee UK core team meeting to 'identify and capture the key learning points from their experience in the coalition', London: Jubilee 2000 Coalition

Kekk, M and Sikkink, K (1998) *Activists Beyond Borders: Advocacy Networks in International Politics*, Ithaca and London: Cornell University Press

Mandlate, Bishop Bernadino (1999) 'The Meaning of Jubilee and Debt', Paper presented at the South–South Summit Johannesburg, 18 November, www.jubileesouth.org/news/EpklpAlplpXSLTNoNP.shtml

Marks, N (2000) 'Jubilee 2000 UK: Report on Assessment of Future Needs Survey', Presented at the September board meeting of Jubilee UK, London: New Economics Foundation

Owuso, K (2002) Speech at the Jubilee Debt Campaign Annual General Meeting, March 2002

Rorty, R (1998) *Achieving Our Country – Leftist Thought in Twentieth Century America*, Cambridge, Massachusetts: Harvard University Press

Scholte, J (2001) 'The IMF and Civil Society: An Interim Progress Report' in Edwards, M and Gaventa, J (eds) *Global Citizen Action*, Boulder, Colorado: Lynne Rienner

Tarrow, S (1998) *Power in Social Movements and Contentious Politics*, second edition, Cambridge: Cambridge University Press

Tarrow, S (2001) 'Transnational Politics: Contention and Institutions in International Politics', *Annual Review of Political Science*, vol 4: 1–20

Verdict on Genoa Summit, (2001) Comments by Adrian Lovett (director, Drop the Debt), Ann Pettifor (director, Jubilee Plus), Ben Niblett (Leeds Jubilee 2000 Network), Chester Jubilee Group, campaigners in Africa, David Malin Roodman (senior researcher, Worldwatch Institute) and Hilary Benn (parliamentary under secretary of state, Department for International Development), and reports from Oxfam, World Development Movement, Jubilee Movement International and Nick Buxton (campaigner with Jubilee 2000); see: www.jubileedebtcampaign.org.uk/news/Commentary.htm

Websites

Jubilee 2000: www.jubilee2000.org.uk
Jubilee 2000 Coalition Petition: www.jubilee2000uk.org/jubilee2000/petition
Jubilee 2000 South Africa: www.aidc.org.za
Jubilee Call, from Jubilee Rome Meeting, 17 November 1998:
Jubilee Debt Campaign: www.jubileedebtcampaign.org.uk
Jubilee Movement International (JMI): www.jubileeplus.org/jmi/main
Jubilee Plus/Jubilee Research: www.jubileeplus.org
Jubilee South: www.jubileesouth.org
Jubilee USA Network: www.j2000usa.org

Interviews

Martin Dent: co-founder, Jubilee 2000; board member of Jubilee Debt Campaign
Adrian Lovett: deputy director, Jubilee UK; director of Drop the Debt
Tim Moulds: board member, Jubilee UK; staff member of Christian Aid
Kwesi Owuso: Africa Desk, Jubilee UK and Jubilee Plus; co-director of Southern Links
Ann Pettifor: director, Jubilee UK; director of Jubilee Research

Questionnaires and meetings

Brief open questionnaires were sent on 26 February 2002 and 1 March 2002 via e-mail
to 67 Jubilee groups listed on the JMI website: www.jubilee2000uk.org/jmi/jmi-
contacts/jmi-contacts. Of these, 35 bounced back, probably due to out-of-date
addresses or groups that no longer existed in that form. It was difficult to judge exactly
how many active Jubilee groups existed at that point. Seven organizations sent back
the questionnaires from: Burundi, Cameroon, Ecuador, Ireland, Japan, Korea and
Zambia. Groups in Austria and France sent reports and other information.

The author is grateful to Jubilee Debt Campaign for allowing her to attend their AGM
on 16 March 2002 at the Trades Union Congress in London.

CHAPTER 6

Adams, J (2002) 'WSF2002: Hopes for a True International' in Znet Visions Strategy
Watch at www.zmag.org/content/VisionStrategy/AdamsWSF.cfm
Boggs, C (2001) 'Economic Globalization and Political Atrophy', *Democracy and
Nature*, vol 7(2): 303–316
Business Week (2001) 'When Demonstrations Turn Violent', 6 August; www.business-
week.com/magazine/content/01_32/c3744018.htm
Canadian Security Intelligence Service (2000) *Anti-Globalization – a Spreading Phenom-
enon*, Report no 2000/08, www.csis-scrs.gc.ca/eng/miscdocs/200008_e
Clark, J (2001) 'Ethical Globalization: the Dilemmas and Challenges of Internationaliz-
ing Civil Society' in Edwards, M and Gaventa, J (eds) *Global Citizen Action*, London:
Earthscan
Cockburn, A and St Clair, J (undated) 'So Who Did Win in Seattle? Liberals Rewrite
History', www.webdsi.com/jbrite/news/so_who_did12-16.htm

De Léon, J P (2001) *Our Word Is Our Weapon: Selected Writings by Subcomandante Marcos*, New York: Seven Stories Press

Desai, M and Said, Y (2001a) 'The New Anti-Capitalist Movement: Money and Global Civil Society' in Anheier, H, Glasius M and Kaldor, M (eds) *Global Civil Society 2001*, Oxford: Oxford University Press

Desai, M and Said, Y (2001b) 'Global Civil Society and Global Finance', Public lecture at the London School of Economics, 28 November, London

Financial Times (1998) 'Network Guerrillas', 30 April

Financial Times (2001) 'UK at Loggerheads with France Over Tax on Speculators', 11 September; www.globalpolicy.org/socecon/glotax/curtax/2001/0913uk.htm

Florini, A (ed) *The Third Force: the Rise of Transnational Civil Society*, Washington, DC: Carnegie Endowment for International Peace

George, S (2002) Presentation during a debate on Globalization and Civil Society, London School of Economics, 14 February, London

Giddens, A (2001) 'The Future of Global Inequality', Public lecture, London School of Economics, 21 November, London

Giuni, M (1999) 'How Social Movements Matter: Past Research, Present Problems, Future Developments' in Giugni, M, McAdam, D and Tilly, C (eds) *How Social Movements Matter*, Minneapolis, Minnesota: University of Minnesota Press

Handy, C (1995) 'Trust and the Virtual Organization', *Harvard Business Review*, vol 73(3): 40–50

Harding, J (2002) Presentation during the public debate Globalization and Civil Society, Organized by ATTAC UK, London School of Economics, 14 February, London

Harris, P, Walsh, N P, Bright, M and Carroll, R (2001) 'You Could Sense the Venom and Hatred', *The Observer*, The Globalisation Debate – Observer Special Report: Globalisation, 29 July; www.observer.co.uk/focus/story/0,6903,529074,00.html

Jordan, L and Van Tuijl, P (2000) 'Political Responsibility in Transnational NGO Advocacy', *World Development*, vol 28(12): 2051–2065

Keck, M and Sikkink, K (1998) *Activists Beyond Borders: Advocacy Networks in International Politics*, Ithaca, New York: Cornell University Press

Khagram, S, Riker, J and Sikkink, K (2002) 'From Santiago to Seattle: Transnational Advocacy Groups Restructuring World Politics' in Khagram et al (eds) *Restructuring World Politics: Transnational Social Movements, Networks and Norms*, Minneapolis, Minnesota: University of Minnesota Press

Klein, N (2000) *No Logo: Taking Aim at the Brand Bullies*, New York: Picador

Klein, N (2001a) 'Signs of the Times: Protests Aimed at Powerful Symbols of Capitalism Find Themselves in a Transformed Landscape', *The Nation*, 22 October

Klein, N (2001b) 'The Unknown Icon', *Guardian*, 3 March

Klein, N (2001c) 'A Fete for the End of the End of History', *The Nation*, 19 March, see www.forumsocialmundial.org.br/eng/bnaomi.asp?l=eng

Kobrin, S (1998) 'The MAI and the Clash of Globalizations' *Foreign Policy*, no112: 97–109

Kriesi, H (1996) 'The Organizational Structure of New Social Movements in Relation to their Political Context' in McAdam, D, McCarthy, J and Zald, M (eds) *Comparative Perspectives on Social Movements: Political Opportunities, Mobilizing Structures and Cultural Framings*, New York: Cambridge University Press

McAdam, D, McCarthy, J and Zald, M (1996) 'Introduction: Opportunities Mobilizing Structures and Framing Processes' in McAdam et al (eds) *Comparative Perspectives on Social Movements: Political Opportunities, Mobilizing Structures, and Cultural Framings*, New York: Cambridge University Press

McCarthy, J (1997) 'The Globalization of Social Movement Theory' in Smith, J, Chatfield, C and Pagnucco, R (eds) *Transnational Social Movements and Global Politics: Solidarity beyond the State*, Syracuse, New York: Syracuse University Press

Mekata, M (2000) 'Building Partnerships toward a Common Goal: Experiences of the International Campaign to Ban Landmines' in Florini, A (ed) *The Third Force: The Rise of Transnational Civil Society*, Washington, DC: Carnegie Endowment for International Peace

Naughton, J (2001) 'Contested Space: the Internet and Global Civil Society' in Anheier, H, Glasius, M and Kaldor, M (eds) *Global Civil Society 2001*, Oxford: Oxford University Press

O'Brien, R, Goetz, A M, Scholte, J A and Williams, M (2000) *Contesting Global Governance: Multilateral Economic Institutions and Global Social Movements*, Cambridge: Cambridge University Press

O'Neill, K (1999) 'Internetworking for Social Change: Keeping the Spotlight on Corporate Responsibility', Discussion Paper No 111, United Nations Research Institute for Social Development, Geneva

Oxfam International (2000) 'Towards Global Equity: Oxfam International's Strategic Plan, 2001–2004', Adopted by the Board of Oxfam International, November 2000, Melbourne

Oxfam (2002) *Rigged Rules and Double Standards*, Oxford: Oxfam

Pettifor, A (2001) 'Post Genoa and Beyond', www.jubileedebtcampaign.org.uk/news/Commentary.htm

Scholte, J A (2001) 'New Citizens Action and Global Finance', Note for seminar on Transnational Civil Society: Issues of Governance and Organization, London School of Economics, 1–2 June, London

Shiva, V (1999) 'This Round to the Citizens', *The Guardian*, 8 December ; www.guardian.co.uk/Print/0,3858,3939018,00.html

Smith, J (1997) 'Characteristics of the Modern Transnational Social Movement Sector', in Smith et al (eds) *Transnational Social Movements and Global Politics: Solidarity beyond the State*, Syracuse: New York: Syracuse University Press

Smith, J, Chatfield, C and Pagnucco R (eds) (1997) *Transnational Social Movements and Global Politics: Solidarity beyond the State*, Syracuse, New York: Syracuse University Press

Stiglitz, J (2002) *Globalization and its Discontents*, London: Allen Lane

Tarrow, S (1996) 'States and Opportunities: the Political Structuring of Social Movements' in McAdam, D, McCarthy, J and Zald, M (eds) *Comparative Perspectives on Social Movements: Political Opportunities, Mobilizing Structures and Cultural Framings*, New York: Cambridge University Press

Tarrow, S (2001) 'Transnational Politics: Contention and Institutions in International Politics' *Annual Review of Political Science*, June, vol 4: 1–20

Tilly, C (1978) *From Mobilization to Revolution*, New York: Random House

The Economist (1999) 'Will NGOs Democratise, or Merely Disrupt, Global Governance?', 11 December

Wade, R (2001) 'Global Inequality: Winners and Losers', *The Economist*, 28 April

Warkentin, C (2001) *Reshaping World Politics: NGOs, the Internet and Global Civil Society*, Lanham, Maryland: Rowman and Littlefield

World Development Movement (WDM) (2001) Report on the G8 summit, Genoa: www.jubileedebtcampaign.org.uk/news/Commentary.htm

Woods, A (2000) 'Global Protest or Political Tourism: After Prague, Where Next?' Mimeo, personal comment, Bretton Woods Project, London

Websites

Zapatistas National Liberation Army, Mexico (EZLN): www.ezln.org
Google: www.google.com
IndyNews: www.indynews.org
Nedstat: www.nedstat.com
Protest: www.protest.net
Subversive Enterprises International: www.geocities.com/Heartland/2484/intro.htm

CHAPTER 7

Anheier, H, Glasius, M and Kaldor, M (2001) 'Introducing Global Civil Society' in Anheier et al (eds) *Global Civil Society 2001*, Oxford: Oxford University Press
Block, J (2002) 'Today, Porto Alegre. Tomorrow…? Can the World Social Forum Have a Meaningful Impact without a More Formal Structure?', 6 February: www.mother-jones.com/web_exclusives/features/news/ world_social_forum
Bullard, N (2002) Interview on the Porto Alegre meeting of the International Council of the WSF, 15 February: www.attac.org
Castells, M (1996) *The Rise of the Network Society*, Oxford: Blackwell Publishers
Chomsky, N (2000) 'Why the World Social Forum?', Text written for the WSF launching in Porto Alegre and reproduced in the newspaper *Folha de Sao Paulo*, 10 September, Library of Alternatives: www.worldsocialforum.org.br
Cohen, R and Rai, S M (eds) (2000) *Global Social Movements*, London: Athlone Press
Edwards, M and Gaventa, J (eds) (2001) *Global Citizen Action*, London: Earthscan
FSM-Comité Mineiro (2002) *Um Outro Mundo é Possível – e Necessário*, Pamphlet
Gillbank, M (2002) 'Other Worlds are Possible: 60.000 Can't be Wrong?' IPS Terraviva: www.ipsnews.net
Grzybowski, C (2002) 'Uma Nova Agenda Global em Construção': www.worldsocialfo-rum.org.br
Keck, M E and Sikkink, K (1998) *Activists Beyond Borders: Advocacy Networks in International Politics*, Ithaca and London: Cornell University Press
Ker, R (2002) 'WSF: Anti-Globalization Movement Comes of Age': www.worldsocialfo-rum.org.br
Klein, N (2001) 'A Fete for the End of the End of History', *The Nation*, 19 March
NOP-FPA/Núcleo de Opinião Pública-Fundação Perseu Abramo (2001) 'Fórum Social Mundial de 2001: Perfil sócio-demográfico dos/as participantes, avaliação da orga-nização e dos conteúdos cobertos, e opinões a respeito de alguns temas discutidos', Relatório de Pesquisa, Fórum Social Mundial, unpublished
Pianta, M (2001) 'Parallel Summits of Global Civil Society' in Anheier et al (eds) *Global Civil Society 2001*, Oxford: Oxford University Press
Powell, W W (1990) 'Neither Market nor Hierarchy: Network Forms of Organization', *Research in Organizational Behaviour*, vol 12: 295–336
Sivaraman, S (2002a) 'Global versus Regional versus Local', IPS Terraviva, 15 February: www.ipsnews.net
Sivaraman, S (2002b) 'The Alternative Is not Civil Society, but Civil Disobedience', *Terraviva*, independent daily of the second World Social Forum, 4 February
Tarrow, S (2001) 'Transnational Politics: Contention and Institutions in International Politics', *Annual Review of Political Science*, vol 4(1): 1–20

Wallerstein, I (2002) Speech at the second World Social Forum, 15 February: www.attac.org

Whitaker, F (2001) 'World Social Forum: Origins and Targets': www.worldsocialforum.org.br

Whitaker, F (2002) 'Lessons from Porto Alegre', Text revised from a communication to the Episcopal Pastoral Commission of CNBB, 19 February, Brasília: www.worldso-cialforum.org.br

WSF/OC (2001) 'Report on the First Meeting of the International Council,' June: www.worldsocialforum.org.br

WSF/OC (2002) 'Report of the World Social Forum International Council Meeting in Barcelona', 28–30 April, WSF secretariat, São Paulo

Interviews

Volkhart Finn Heinrich, CIVICUS (World Alliance for Citizen Participation)

Maria Dirlene Trindade Marques, Federal University of Minas Gerais (UFMG)/Mobilization Committee (MC) – Minas Gerais (MG)

Carlos Tibúrcio de Oliveira, Association for the Taxation of Financial Transactions for the Aid of Citizens (ATTAC)/Organizing Committee (OC)

Emir Sader, University of the State of Rio de Janeiro (UERJ)/International Council (IC)

Cândido Grzybowski, Brazilian Institute of Social and Economic Analysis (IBASE)/ Organizing Committee (OC)

Maria Luiza Mendonça, Centre for Global Justice (CJG)/Organizing Committee (OC)

Gustavo Codas, Brazilian Union Federation (CUT)/International Council (IC)

Pe Luíz Bassegio, Grito dos Excluídos/International Council (IC)

Carla Lyra, World Social Forum (WSF) Secretariat

Francisco Whitaker, Brazilian Commission for Justice and Peace (CBJP), National Conference of the Bishops of Brazil (CNBB)/Organizing Committee (OC)

CHAPTER 8

Anheier, H, Glasius, M and Kaldor, M (eds) (2001) *Global Civil Society 2001*, Oxford: Oxford University Press

Clark, J (2001) 'Ethical Globalization: The Dilemmas and Challenges of Internationalizing Civil Society' in Edwards, M and Gaventa, J (eds) *Global Citizen Action*, Boulder, Colorado: Lynne Rienner

Cohen, R and Rai, S M (eds) (2000) *Global Social Movements*, London: Athlone Press

Desai, M and Said, Y (2001) 'The New Anti-Capitalist Movement: Money and Global Civil Society' in Anheier et al (eds) *Global Civil Society 2001*, Oxford: Oxford University Press

Falk, R (1998) 'Global Civil Society: Perspectives, Initiatives, Movements', *Oxford Development Studies*, vol 26(1): 99–110

Florini, A M (ed) (2000) *The Third Force: the Rise of Transnational Civil Society*, Washington, DC: Carnegie Endowment for International Peace

Gillespie, P (2000) 'Idea of Transnational Tax on Currency Speculation Taking Off', *The Irish Times*, 24 June

Godoy, J (2002) 'France-Politics: French Politicians Flock to Porto Alegre', *Inter Press Service*, 25 January

Hayward, H (1999) *Costing the Casino: the Real Impact of Currency Speculation in the 1990s*, War on Want: www.waronwant.org

Held, D and McGrew, A (2000) *Global Transformations: Politics, Economics and Culture*, Cambridge: Polity Press

Lichfield, J (2001) 'Economic Guru Shuns Anti-Global Movement', *Independent*, 11 September

Merino, S (2001) *La Tasa Tobin: Tres Años de Historia*, Buenos Aires: Ediciones Continente

New Scientist (2002) 'Globally Local', 27 April

Patomäki, H (2001) *Democratising Globalisation: the Leverage of the Tobin Tax*, London: Zed Books

Powell, W W (1990) 'Neither Market nor Hierarchy: Network Forms of Organization', *Research in Organisational Behaviour*, vol 12: 295–336

Ramonet, I (1997) 'Disarming the Markets', *Le Monde Diplomatique*, December: www.en.monde-diplomatique.fr/1997/12/leader

Schmidt, R (1999) 'A Feasible Foreign Exchange Transactions Tax': www.nsi-ins.ca/ensi/publications/messenger/tobin1

Scholte, J A (2002) *Governing Global Finance*, GSGR Working Paper No 88/02, January: www.warwick.ac.uk/fac/soc/CSGR/wpapers/wp8802.pdf

Spahn, P B (1996) 'The Tobin Tax and Exchange Rate Stability', *Finance and Development*, vol 33(2): www.worldbank.org/fandd/english/0696/articles/0130696.htm

Der Spiegel (2001) No 30

Stecher, H and Bailey, M (1999) *Time for a Tobin Tax? Some Practical and Political Arguments*, Oxfam GB Discussion Paper, Oxfam

Strange, S (1986) *Casino Capitalism*, Oxford: Basil Blackwell Ltd

Suddeutsche Zeitung (2001) 'ATTAC Rejects Co-operation with Green Party', 23 August

Surajaras, P and Sweeney, R J (1992) *Profit-Making Speculation in Foreign Exchange Markets*, Oxford: Westview Press

Thompson, G, Frances, J, Levacic, R and Mitchell, J (eds) (1998) *Markets, Hierarchies and Networks*, London: Sage Publications

Tobin, J (1978) 'A Proposal for International Monetary Reform', *Eastern Economic Journal*, vol 4(3–4): 153–159

Vinocur, J (2001) 'War Transforms the Anti-Globalization Crowd', *International Herald Tribune*, 2 November

Wainwright, H and Juniper, T (2002) 'Ante Upped', *Guardian*, 13 February

War on Want and New Economics Foundation (2001) *The Robin Hood Tax*, London: www.waronwant.org

Interviews

Susan George, vice-president, Association for the Taxation of Financial Transactions for the Aid of Citizens (ATTAC) France
Claudio Jampaglia, ATTAC Italy
Bruno Jetin, Scientific Committee of ATTAC France
Laurent Jessover, ATTAC France
Matti Kohonen, ATTAC London
Dr Jonathan I Leape, London School of Economics (LSE)
Steve Tibbet, War on Want
Christophe Ventura, spokesperson for ATTAC

Index